Marc Mimram
Selected Works

Marc Mimram

Structure | Light · Landscapes of Gravity · Selected Works

Through the Lens of Erieta Attali

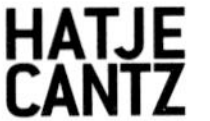

Sharing the Project

Marc Mimram

Representation of the Project

Architecture is often represented as a product, a disembodied object. This mercantile view, frequently extreme, distances and transforms inhabitants into mere spectators of an architecture that is dematerialized, delocalized, dehumanized.

I believe it is important to present our work through the values it brings with it—values that are social and material, geographical and cultural—explaining the rationale for things, the choices involved, and the approach and commitment demanded of us.

What was required here was not a glossy presentation of the project with a series of dazzling blue skies, panoptic angles, and Photoshopped colors, but, rather, a disciplined, clear, and communicable approach.

The eye of the photographer is important. The collaborative project with Erieta Attali has resulted in a joint sharing of her "point of view" and our work. Photography is used here not simply to enhance a public presentation. It seeks instead to raise theoretical and concrete concerns held in common. If photography is an art, it is also technique and determination.

The texture, grain, and contrast of photography chime with the material aspect of our architecture. The framing, horizon, and situation call up the landscape underlying the project.

Erieta Attali's work concentrates on extreme landscapes with an acute, taut, and determined eye. We work to achieve frugality, weight, the expression of mechanical forces in a technical world, always seeking an economy of means and a sobriety, the tenuous nature of which photography is able to capture.

Both for the photographer and for us, the landscape is an essential element in all initial conditions, a way of expressing the local character and the context from which the project will emerge.

It is through this relationship—between the local and the global—that our involvement with the conditions of exploitation of the planet forms the basis of architecture as the art of transformation.

Here and Elsewhere

Here, in the roots of an ancient geology, in the taut line between land and sky formed by the apparent horizon of the place, in the length of the crossing dictated by the required link, in the position of the sun, in the geometric conditions of the extent of usage. Here, and nowhere else.

Elsewhere, because belonging to a place is concomitant with the territorial dimension of the infrastructure, which takes over the large-scale geographical unity, fixing a global unity while the project enters into a dialogue with the place it has constructed.

Local and global: these are the two oxymoronic dimensions brought together by the project.

This is why I felt it important that the representation of our work should express this geographical vision. Photography is able to play a role by taking photographs at different times and in different weather: illuminated, in the mist, in different seasons, or with features appearing flat beneath heaped up clouds or radiant blue skies.

No matter what the season or lighting effects, the projects stand out, and this accentuates the emotion that I hold most dear: the sense of belonging.

Responding to the Surrounding Conditions

The Site

The starting point. The landscape is at the basis of the project, but disrupted, radically and violently transformed by it. Neither a receptacle nor a void to be filled, but a geographical reality informed by history. Here we see the skyline, the tension between sky and land, the confines of the place where the observer stands, the telluric currents of the topography, the anchoring points, the fault, the breach, its opening, the real or supposed extent, the fundamental geological conditions.

The site is an expression of time, season, wind, light . . . lights.

It is here that the scale of the project and its different scales of appearance are defined: a single construction or a group of items; continuity of form or discontinuity of components arranged in a hierarchy, opaque or transparent; unity of material or diversity of the building orders. The project starts here in this contemplation of the landscape, in the dialogue with a horizon stretched almost to breaking point, an equilibrium stabilized by a radical metamorphosis of the world, a reasoned, intense, and delicate morphogenesis.

The Link

Beyond the simple functional—and often trivial—requirements, where the chosen system takes account of the landscape, multiple conditions of use will become apparent: different paths, inhabited voids, anchor points, and boundaries, or designated topographical situations. Alongside the main elements of the structure lie all the possibilities of choice: path, walkway, or stopping place, the continuity or alteration of the structure or the geometric variations allowed by its components. The link then becomes a place. It comes to life, an expression of the sharing offered by public spaces, spaces that belong to everyone and are for everyone, a physical expression of democratic representation.

Gravity

These constructions are not simple static building schemes; they are an interpretation of a revealed gravitational hypothesis—a structure of ground or sky, an expression of apparent mass or extreme fragility. The work is anchored in or freed from the powers of attraction—now a lace-like covering arranged under the lights, now a folded leaf stretched continuously between its supports, now an abstract construction reaching up to the sky, now hugging the ground.
The expressions of gravity are many, reasoned, and deliberately chosen. The work is this expression, the structure its interpretation.

Materiality

An implementation of material that gives meaning, both through the expression of the art of transformation—from its extraction from the ground to the implementation of human craftsmanship or industrial work—and through the way in which the project becomes a visible and readable memory of it, a record of accumulated skills.
The material leads to the conception of the project, incorporating its genesis in the radical transformation of the world it brings about. Uniting thought and action means integrating construction into a project that would otherwise be cut off from reality, indulging in frustrated, paralyzed virtuality; it means marking one's connection with the world in order to oppose a dematerialization of the mind.

Structure

Meditated expression of static and gravitational contingencies, resistance of the material and the resilience of the site—the project is the product of this reasoned choice, the structure of the work ensuring the consistency of the conditions expressed here.
It is obviously not an ideal, perfect, unambiguous solution, for which the rationality of the static scheme would be the guarantee. There is no single, mathematical solution that will provide an abstract and consummate catalogue of referential models. The specific must replace the generic: the place speaks, the project belongs there and nowhere else, it is feeling and reason, it is the delicate shaping of the scholarly understanding of the relationships between the static and geometry, between the pleasures of the landscape and an awareness of the radical nature of the transformation generated, between the universality of constraints and the specific aspects of their implementation. The logic behind it has multiple aspects, but the project will always show a generous contemporaneity, attentive to the world. As it takes shape it seems to leap up with joy.
The infrastructure project then becomes an architectural work of art.

Between Structure and Infrastructure

Our projects generally include aspects of infrastructure. This is obviously the case with bridges and footbridges, but it is equally true of our designs for amenity and other buildings.
I believe that our work is of service to the common good and that it should offer, besides the program required of the project, generous conditions enabling its users to adopt and appropriate it for themselves. The project must go beyond this initial condition of the program so as to allow everyone to live and be represented in the space offered and made available to them.
In this sense, the project is an infrastructure, a network of conditions allowing for an extension of use. A bridge is not a link, or not only. Obviously it makes it possible to pass from one side of the river to the other, but the project can make it into a place. The place is offered to all for them to share. The place becomes established in the landscape it wishes to inhabit. The space thus created legitimizes the radical transformation of a steep valley, a network of roads, a raging river or multiple railway lines, offering something more: a place that is available to everyone, where they can feel welcome.
The deck becomes a balcony over the landscape; the expanded space becomes a space offered to the public. The place takes its place. The pathway is metamorphosed into a device for meeting, thinking, understanding the landscape, the geography, of nature as transformed by man, never virgin and always hostile, most often socially revealing. Infrastructure is usually considered a necessary evil. Let us turn it into a shared benefit. Roads are unpleasant, motorways even more harmful. Railways are useful and respected if kept at a distance. Only rivers seem pleasant, except when they become threatening torrents.
Our work is to cross, cover, and travel through infrastructures, valuing them through their ability to define horizons other than themselves, to consider the geography and social organization of the territory, to create places where people pass one another, where they meet, and where expressions of hospitality and generosity between people take place. Thus, the infrastructure we create and the infrastructure we cross come together in a common project: the public good.

Public Space as the Initial Condition

When society represented itself through the buildings of power, institution, and religion, it invested architecture with a role that was translated into order, composition, its style and even its manner of construction being an expression of it. Public spaces play this role too, taking power in order to offer it to all and give to all the opportunity to take it over: it is the space of democracy.

It is in this hypothesis that our work finds its meaning. It determines our attitude towards the project and leads us to relate it to the collective, to everyday life, and to the exceptional. It is an approach for everyone in the face of the power of certain individuals where an institution is involved in commissioning architectural monuments.

The street, the square, the link created by the crossing are at the center of this approach, one that seeks to pay careful and generous attention to public spaces. Infrastructure is not a functional tool governed by the rationality of constraints, such as speed that cuts itself off from the world in order to focus on saving time in the safest way. This has the effect of separating out dedicated and differentiated spaces according to the different means of transport. On the contrary, we must come together, share, and pool the common benefits of public spaces, so enhancing the way we live together. Infrastructure cuts, separates, and divides one side from another as much as it connects two points at the territorial level. We need to reverse this unacceptable assumption.

We make this a condition of any project.

In Rabat the underside of the access viaduct becomes a roof sheltering a long space that can be used by the public, rather like Borough Market under the railway in London.
By taking account of the geographical conditions, the central meeting point on the Rhine Footbridge highlights not the battles of the past but the coming together of a shared landscape.
With the Roland-Garros Stadium the glass houses enclosing the tennis court bring together sport and botanical garden in a positive project that gives equal pride of place to seemingly antagonistic interests.
In Paris the Airtime Panorama is not only a building but also a bridge, holding up the roof of the railway lines below and installing an open urban continuity on the city's skyline.
These are just some of the projects that show how a positive approach by the infrastructure can add value by making the public space the central element in the design, going beyond the limitations of an often restrictive commission to create a project that can be an invitation to democratic appropriation.

Belonging or Integrating?

We are often asked to ensure that the project is integrated into its host site. What an attitude!
How can we imagine that the Garabit Viaduct in all its redness and riveted lattice structure could ever merge with the Truyère Gorges? This is no more a question of integration into the landscape here than anywhere else. The word suggests some kind of dissolution by symbiosis or even camouflage. This is all wrong.

Whatever its scale, no infrastructure or structure can disappear, and that is how it should be. Our work is based more on reading the landscape and its geography shaped by history so that it can find its proper and informed place.

We need to read the horizon and the topographical or constructed variations that inhabit it; understand the place of the sky, its extent, its installation, its layout; capture the movements of the ground in a nature shaped by human hands; observe the expanses of vegetation in the different seasons; compare the features and contour lines of a changing topography.
The initial conditions of the project are preexistent. The presence of the constructed work will reveal itself in this situation—each time unique—qualifying a visible appearance of belonging, often strong, sometimes brutal, and defining in the change it makes.

The choice of structure in such cases is essential, determining the gravitational scheme by expressing itself as something anchored, raised, embedded, or skimming over the land. To decide to float a giant mass such as the Zhong Sheng Da Dao Bridge in Tianjin, or to throw a crossing of lacy concrete over the Bou Regreg River in Rabat.
Let us follow the example of Louis Harel de la Noë and his Breton railway system or Gustave Eiffel in Saint-André-de-Cubzac; let us follow their variations in scale, their surprising combinations of materials, and their challenge to the landscape.

The gravitational scheme is the tool for this reasoned transformation of the horizon against which the project takes form. The structure can be massive or spider-like, shaped in a continuum of surfaces with form strength or in an assemblage of discontinuous members, given texture by the material, or made to reflect light. It can associate statically components that are articulated or entirely embedded. These reasoned choices always lead to a formal expression, but the multitude of possibilities reveals the determination of the choices. What a pleasure it is to have this dialogue between intuition and reason, between the large scale of the landscape and that of the planned construction, between the strength of the whole and the choice of components, scale and span.
Calculation has been greatly aided by the digital revolution making possible what, yesterday, was limited, reduced to a range of established choices. Tedious calculations have made way for a new freedom underpinned by mathematical accuracy. In construction the material expresses different or opposing ways of building, the ordering of the structure leading to specific resolutions.

The structural system is here at the service of this calm or determined dialogue with the landscape. It is reasoned, but never imposed by an alleged ideal structural solution or suggested according to a catalogue of universal solutions.
Nothing is more terrible than to see the spread from Helsinki to Shanghai of prefabricated elements that arch indiscriminately across a site under the pretext of an indisputable rationality often inviting an ideal of mathematical purity.

All this is simply a complete misappropriation of funds. Let us call up the impure to find again the conditions of resonance with the landscape, to restore dialogue with the site, however radical it may be.

And going beyond the predetermined computational solutions, let us allow the project itself to justify the reasoned choices of its contribution to the site rather than believe in an illusory integration.

A Construction Project Is Not a Work of Art

Another confusion makes the project inoperative: that which seeks to confuse a construction project with a work of art.
The social, cultural, and intellectual position of the artist in society is not the same as that of the architect. Our work is based on the transformation of matter into a project from a particular starting point. The theoretical content that supports it calls for specialist know-how and is part and parcel of the discipline of architecture.
It is not a matter of questioning society through the structure, of taking a critical look, nor of putting something into perspective by offering the tools for a theoretical interrogation, even if this may happen through the physical experience of architecture by the senses.
A project carried out in a landscape is not land art. The realization of structures is not sculpture. To confuse these approaches is to have a reductive view of the structure, often confined to its material or imagined appearance.

While the works in steel by Richard Serra and his experimentation with balance have introduced me to the use of continuous shaping for metal sheets, the Toulouse and the Yangzhou Footbridges should not be seen as sculptures. Dan Graham's work on reflections and the materialization of transparent and two-way glass showed me how space could be refracted, but one should not expect the dematerialization of architecture in the projects I have worked on.
The dialogue between art and architecture can lead to a valuable understanding of our relationship with the world. But the architect is not an artist, any more than a project of civil engineering is a work of art.

Architecture as the Art of Transformation

Architecture can better be viewed as the art of the material transformation of reality.
What is built, as we well know, is shaped from the limited resources of our planet, this unique material supplier to architecture. Our belonging to the world begins here. Nothing is exogenous and the system does not feed on any "extraterrestrial" production.
Thus, architecture has a responsibility in the process of consumption, and this parameter should form the basis of our approach. With the modernist rejection of the vernacular project leading to abstraction, globalized consumption seems to accelerate this lack of awareness of the link between the material world and architecture.

We need therefore to reconnect with this theoretical reason for implementation, this acuity of the senses that distinguishes construction and architecture, but bases the project on a critical materiality.
In the long process of building, from the extraction of materials to the demolition of buildings with the attendant issues of gray energy and requalification, without making extravagant ecological claims or showing off, we must develop an informed, reasoned, and constructive ecology, one that will always accept the hypothesis of progress.
Without agonizing over the matter, it is reasonable that architecture should be part of a responsible approach to the transformation of the world it affects, from the extraction of resources to the building site.
The skill and the refined expression of this attention to the world give architecture its place in the pleasures of "making"—making to stimulate thought; making to lead to experimentation; making and rejecting the specious effects of an excessive formalization in favor of a science of touch, innovative assemblages, accepting aging or the impure.
Let us not forget that the word "poetry" derives etymologically from the Greek verb *poiein* meaning "to make." Let us rediscover the indissoluble link between poetry and making, the poetry of creation, the poetry of construction.

A Memory Project

The built project can be understood as an accumulated memory of absent moments to which architecture is the witness.
Memory of a disrupted situation: that from before, of this landscape without the physical presence of the project. And yet, this encounter with the landscape is indeed the original condition of its creation.
Memory of a transformation of the world: that of resources accumulated worldwide and for which the project is the repository in a revealed or hidden, structural or ornamental way.
Memory of the site: that of work, often hard physical work, and of refinement too. Of the accumulation of hours, skills, and passions that the site disseminates into architecture, as a condition for conceiving the project.
Architectural plans on the drawing board valued as theoretical foundations have too often consigned the project site to an inferior position, viewing it merely as a soulless phase where the work is executed, without being part of the design process. In fact, the reverse is true. The construction site makes it possible to conceive the project. It does not execute, it lays the material and theoretical foundations of the project. Let us not leave architecture out of the realm of progress—progress in working conditions as well as in the digital and robotic revolution, progress in the physical characteristics of materials and methods of implementation, progress in complex geometries and economical and sophisticated structures.

In finding the path to belonging to the world that it transforms, architecture moves into memory and opens itself to the pleasures of sharing knowledge: yesterday's forgotten buildings, those proposed today, those of the workers on the building site, those of the people it welcomes. It thus becomes a generous and non-ideological architecture, capable of authorizing and arousing our responsive feelings and emotions.

Preface
Paul Chemetov

Between 1978 and 1989 I taught architecture at the École nationale des ponts et chaussées (ENPC). At that time it was situated in Rue des Saint-Pères, opposite the Faculty of Medicine and next to the School of Fine Art, between the Seine and Saint-Germain des Prés. And, if you ventured a little further, there were cafés, boutiques, and museums all close by. The city was open to the inquiring mind.

And the classes that we—Bruno Fortier, Jean-Louis Cohen, Yves Lion, Christian Devillers, and I—set out to teach also sought to decipher the urban library that Paris spread out before us. Marc Mimram—as some may know—was one of our first students.

It is fair to say that Marc's contribution to this relationship was his open-minded approach. By this time we no longer thought of engineers as mere calculating machines, but as the inventors that they are and should be. We did not set ourselves up as tasteful designers or arbiters of refined elegance, but rather as architects versed in history, form, and usage, together with a proper understanding of construction methods. In other words, both students and teachers were learning to be *polytechnos* or multi-skilled.

On completing his studies in Paris, Marc spent a year at the University of California, Berkeley, and then went to Brazil to do his national service. While there, he met Oscar Niemeyer. When he came back to France, I first invited him to work with Plan Construction et Architecture (PCA) and then, on a more professional basis, for our projects for Les Halles, the Ministry of Finance, and the National Museum of Natural History.

In 1983, twenty-five years ago, Marc Mimram published his first book, *Structure et Forme: Une étude de l'œuvre de Robert le Ricolais*. He asked if I would write a preface. I would not change a word of what I wrote then in those two pages, setting Marc within the context of his connections and influences, including Camille Polonceau, inventor of roof trusses under tension. This was my conclusion: "The naivety of the Encyclopédistes has been replaced by the certainties of computers. The possibilities they offer in terms of calculations—impossible to do manually—and the almost instantaneous simulation of the consequences of a proposed solution has, at the same time, had the effect of introducing predetermined routines. While computers can speed up tedious tasks, their arrival is a threat to that endless questioning of this or that subtly different constraint, a process that is one of the conditions of invention: the sudden discovery of another way of doing things when the usual way has always seemed the only possible one. This almost mechanical repetition, this constant temptation to make what is unknown obey known rules is necessary, in order that, once in a while, the unknown will forcefully interrupt, dictating a new law!"

These words that I dedicated to him have been repaid in the form of a set of photographs of unusual format with enlarged yet precise images. They are photos of building sites, of frameworks resembling rib cages, embracing not only the air but also particularly capacious volumes.

Leafing through these pages and shuffling them like a deck of cards, we can compare the half-light filtering through the safety nets of the Avenue de France building site with the delicate roofing of the Montpellier Station building, or the series of bridges, pausing at the Passerelle Solférino, the only modern river crossing in Paris that, in my opinion, can match, in terms of form and construction, the long series of Parisian bridges from the Pont Neuf to the Pont de la Concorde—the latter originally designed by Jean-Rodolphe Perronet, founder of the ENPC—or Jean Résal's metal bridges and the stone and steel viaducts of the Paris metro.

Three exotic bridges in China and in Morocco complete the list. The former bounces like a pebble dancing over the water against a backdrop of horrifying and unbridled construction. In the foreground, a leaning form in the reeds arouses feelings of both hope and anxiety, a questioning of the world as it is, between two shores, between two lives.

The bridge passing over the estuary of the Bou Regreg, linking Rabat with Salé, is surprising because it draws on Eugène Freyssinet's ideas, but renders them more daring—the problem that engineers have to battle with is, as always, that of stress—by using concrete connecting with the flanges and webs of the metal beams. Here again, thoughtless building construction looms along the horizon. A small fishing boat, its form equally well adapted to its function, moves upstream. A very beautiful approach viaduct prolongs the bridge: one of the most difficult aspects of bridge design. Something similar can be seen with the Tancarville and Normandie bridges, two magnificent feats of engineering.

Hassan II Bridge | Jin Liu Lu Bridge | Montpellier Railway Station

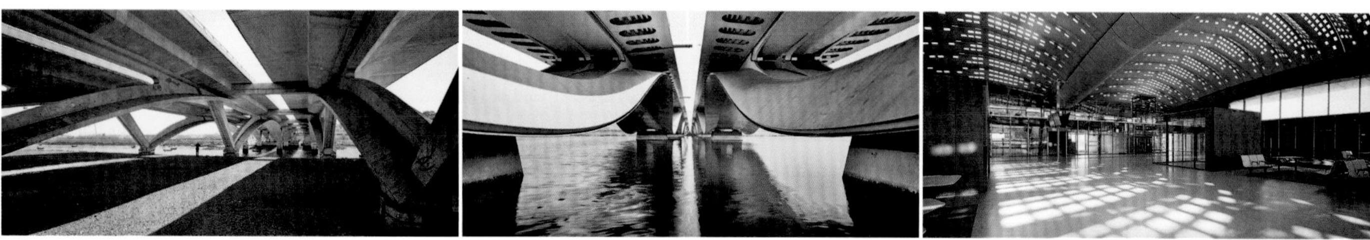

And our attention is caught by other photos: Roland-Garros, or the bridge in Bordeaux, the Batignolles footbridge, or the one of the two sides of the river in Strasbourg, where Marc was responsible for designing the School of Architecture.
I am drawn towards two projects in particular: firstly, because they are the most fully illustrated, and, secondly, because they are both in Paris and therefore close at hand. Work at the Avenue de France site is now complete; the photographs show it exposed like an archaeological dig—something that we shall never see again, and that is a pity. Everything becomes telescoped into our imagination, these images, references, and memories.
They bring to mind New York City and the construction workers with their lunch boxes, sitting on the beams of a half-built skyscraper, or Mark Riboud's photo of a painter working on the Eiffel Tower, part tightrope walker, part clown. We long to preserve these skeletons, like vertical grottoes, the capacity of the air volumes as beautiful as the cranes used to construct them. In one photo, the façade of the Bibliothèque de France seems to be on the verge of rising up from its foundations and crossing the road to enclose this world with triumphant steel.
But I have a particular soft spot for the Solférino footbridge. It picks up and extends the structural idea of pre-stressing anticipated by the Pont des Arts with its trusses supported from below. Some of the photos show the floods in Paris, with the footbridge looking increasingly taut as it apparently rises up out of the water, leaving dry land and becoming the pure expression of crossing, a materialized theorem, like the undulating blades of that other bridge in China.

But let us return to Paris, to the Seine, to our lovers, to the barges or *bateaux mouches*, mobile in the floodwaters. Night is falling, the big wheel lights up, passersby, couples with their picnic baskets, habitués of the Left and the Right Banks, modern tritons and contemporary naiads are there to bear witness to this project. They gaze at it, and so do we.
Even if infinite span-zero weight is nothing more than an asymptomatic metaphor, Marc Mimram's constructions, with their careful inventiveness, transport us not only from one shore to another, from one constructed hypothesis to another, from the darkness to the light, but also from the past to the present, from what came before to what came after.

Crossing the Curves
Erieta Attali

I was born in Tel Aviv, but grew up in Istanbul and Athens, always in the vicinity of the earth-enclosed sea. One of my most vividly impressed memories of childhood in Istanbul was watching the construction, and eventual completion of the Bosporus Bridge, which spans the Bosporus Straight, connecting Europe with Asia. I was seven years old at that time; old enough for such an impressive infrastructure to intrigue my curiosity and get me to start reading geography books, looking for more wonders like the one I was witnessing. This is how I learned about the Panama Canal, the waterway connecting the Atlantic Ocean with the Pacific, and the Straight of Gibraltar, connecting the Mediterranean Sea with the Atlantic. Observing the infrastructure works, the highways, how oceans and seas are connected with each other, the extreme lands among other far away locations, became my pastime and obsession.
Since the age of twenty I was already imagining traveling the world, from one edge to another, photographing oceans, far away territories, bridges, highways, airports; these locations have become my permanent home for the past three decades of photographic practice and research. Between the years 2014 to 2016, when I was photographing contemporary architecture, stranded in extreme landscapes across Australia, I was slowly turning my gaze toward megastructures and expanding cities. This shift brought me to Paris, a city that I had promised to return to in 2003, when I visited it for the first time.

It was around the same time that I found myself in an auditorium full of people at the Victoria and Albert Museum in London, attending a lecture by Marc Mimram. I was astonished. With his award winning bridges in Morocco, China, and Kehl—just to mention a few—here was someone whose mission was to link geographies and connect seas with earth. I saw curves diving into the water, windows opening towards the sky, reflecting, floating, and creating new crossroads. Looking at his bridges in China, I felt as if I were descending into the painting *Humboldt Current* (1951/52) by Max Ernst, while Airtime reminded me of the works of Lyonel Feininger.

The very first photographs that I shared with him were of far-off landscapes; places which I like to call "the edges of the world." There were almost no structures, no human traces in them. I did not care to catch his attention with glossy images of architecture, but rather to challenge him with a new visual language with which to share our practices.

Through my lens I began to follow his lines in space, the curves, touching down softly on the ground only to take off again. I chased the illusory spaces reflected through voids in water, but also the real ones, fueled by a vision of a deeply democratic public life. It is rare to find such a rational expression of beauty; the binary of emotion and logic often gets in the way. Not only undulating in form, but also undulating in expression, from the civic to the poetic, Marc's works invite the passerby to a different experience, a rediscovery of the familiar through the unfamiliar. They also invited me into a journey that still has a long way to go: creating a world that at the same time demands to be experienced, and to be captured.

Solférino Footbridge, Paris, France

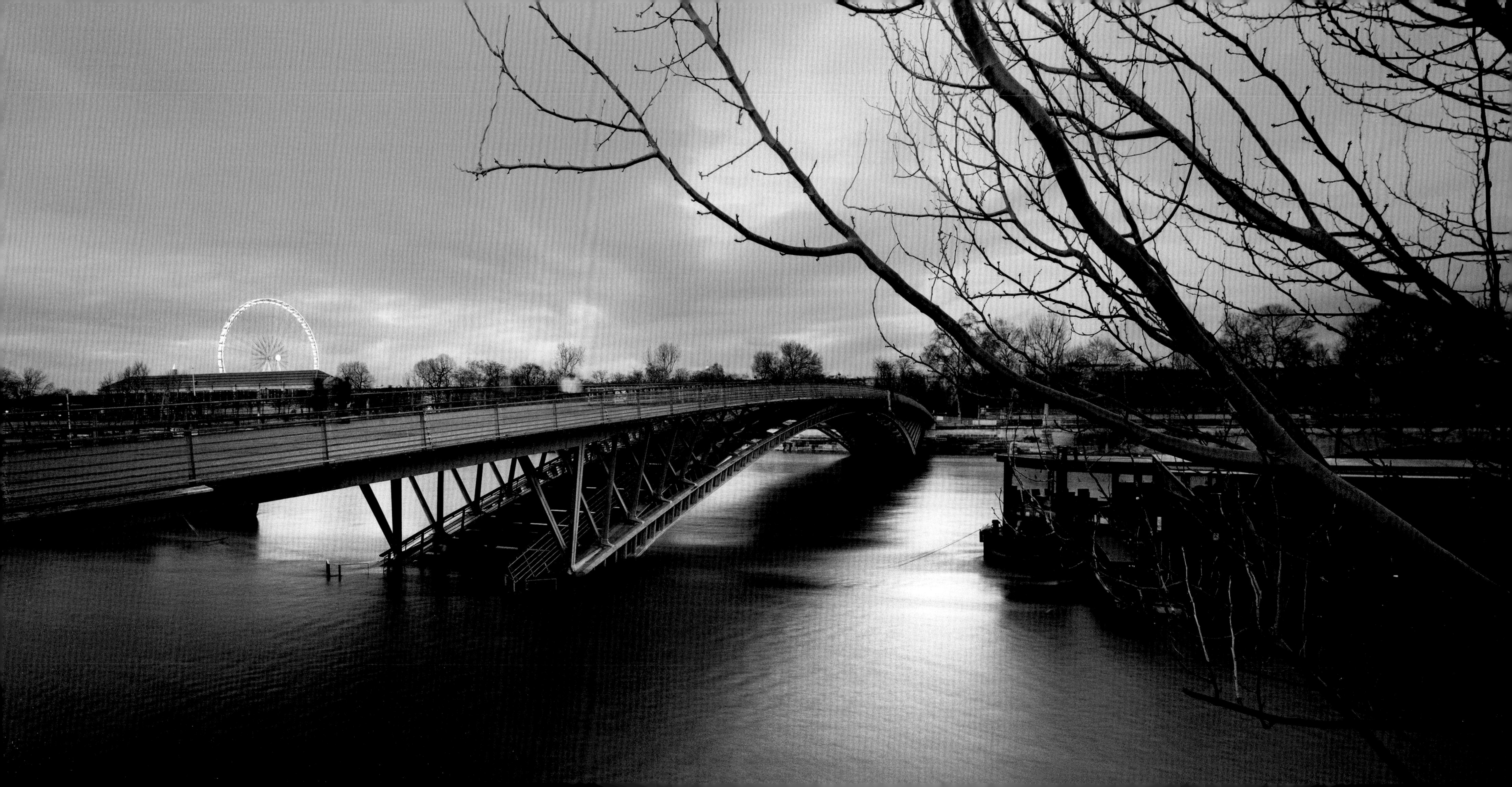

The Passerelle Léopold-Sédar-Senghor,
Formerly Known as Passerelle Solférino
Paris, France

I can still hear my whoop of joy. At the age of thirty-seven I had just won the competition for the new Solférino footbridge in Paris, the thirty-sixth bridge to cross the river Seine. An unbelievable moment! One of total commitment, without critical distance, without fear, almost reckless in the face of the project for a construction in the very heart of Paris's historic center, linking the Tuileries Gardens and the Musée d'Orsay.

The structure is classic in form—an arch with a 106 meter span—but what is new is the way the footbridge can be used, with access to different levels within the structure, linking the upper and lower quays of the Seine and making this piece of engineering a genuine public space, both because of the multiple ways it can be crossed and its spaciousness with a balcony opening on to a panorama of the river and the city.
The structure is a passage. The void between the arch and the deck, a void that is a unique feature of this bridge, is inhabited and recalls the emotions I experienced when I traversed the significant void between the two shells of Brunelleschi's dome in Florence's Cathedral—a void that gives meaning and resistance to the structure.

Here, the direction of forces meets the direction taken by the pedestrian. Opening up between the ground and the deck is a window giving onto the sky.
The structure of the arches embedded in the abutments varies from 55 centimeters at the highest point to 105 centimeters at the bottom and uses Vierendeel trusses. Here the diagonals typical of nineteenth-century riveted metal architecture are replaced by welded supports. The steel plates were cut using oxy-fuel cutting and shaped, and are very thick (120 millimeters / 4.7 inches), with the welding being carried out on site.

This kind of construction would not be possible without modern technology. And yet it is not a radical departure. It still offers the pleasures of place and presence.
A good piece of engineering is a project that is specific to its position, anchored to its site.
For many people it seems as if the footbridge has always been there. It does not flaunt its strength or impose a formal triumphal interruption. It could be seen as a paradigm of sympathetic modernity, of generous contemporaneity.
I have designed many other structures since then. Construction techniques have adapted themselves to different projects, specific requirements, and the characteristics of a particular place or country. But already present at that time were the basic principles of attention to method, expression of technological possibilities, ambition to offer more than a mere connection to transform a link into a place, and, above all, the desire to establish a rapport with the site.

I could have lost my nerve at the thought of filling the "void" between the Pont de la Concorde and the Pont Royal, of laying out my structure within sight of the Tuileries, of creating walkways over this river, the heart of the city. But instead what I learned in the development of this project was the relationship between understanding and responsibility, and the pleasures that arise from this.

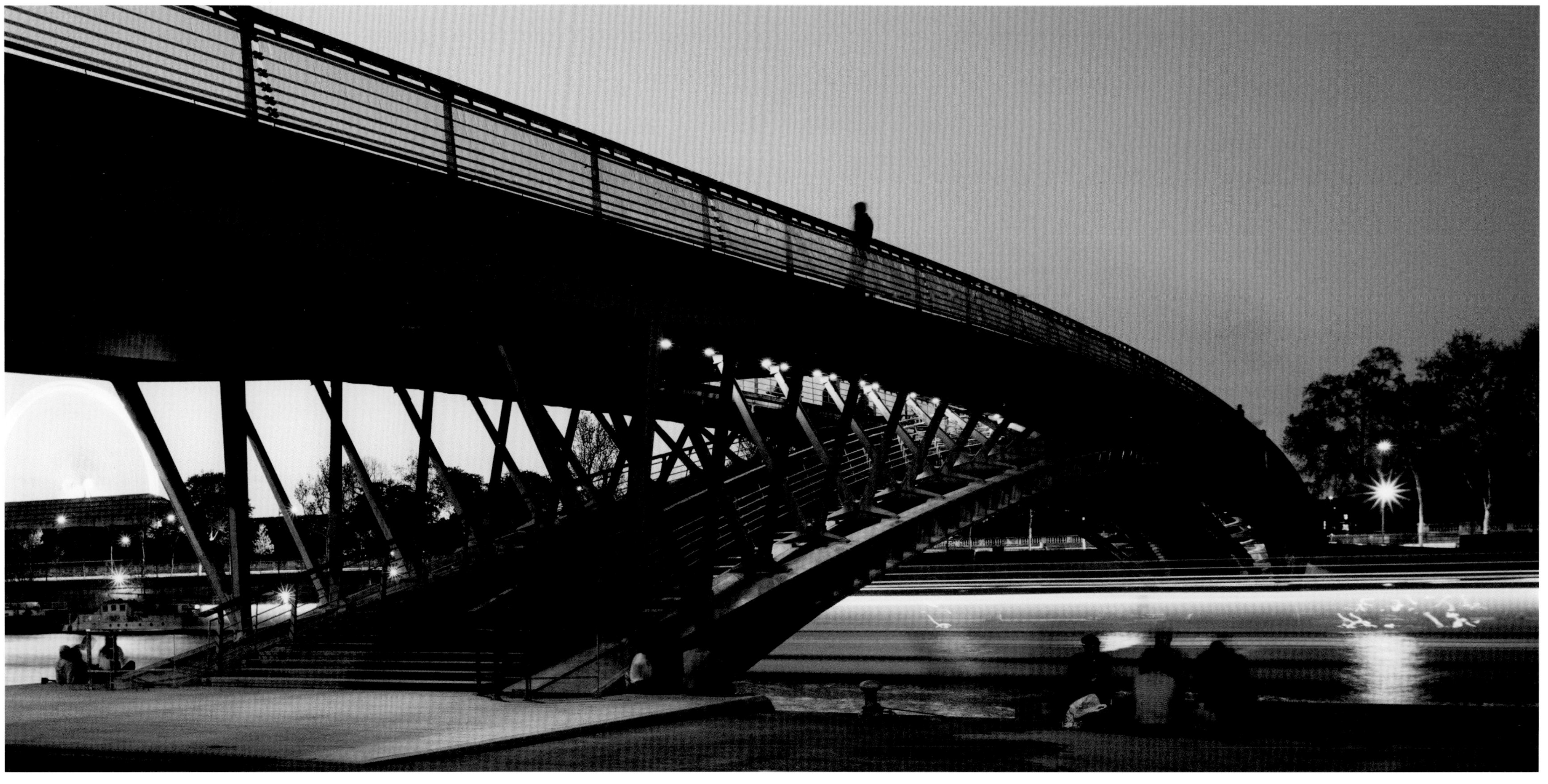

Solférino Footbridge, Paris, France

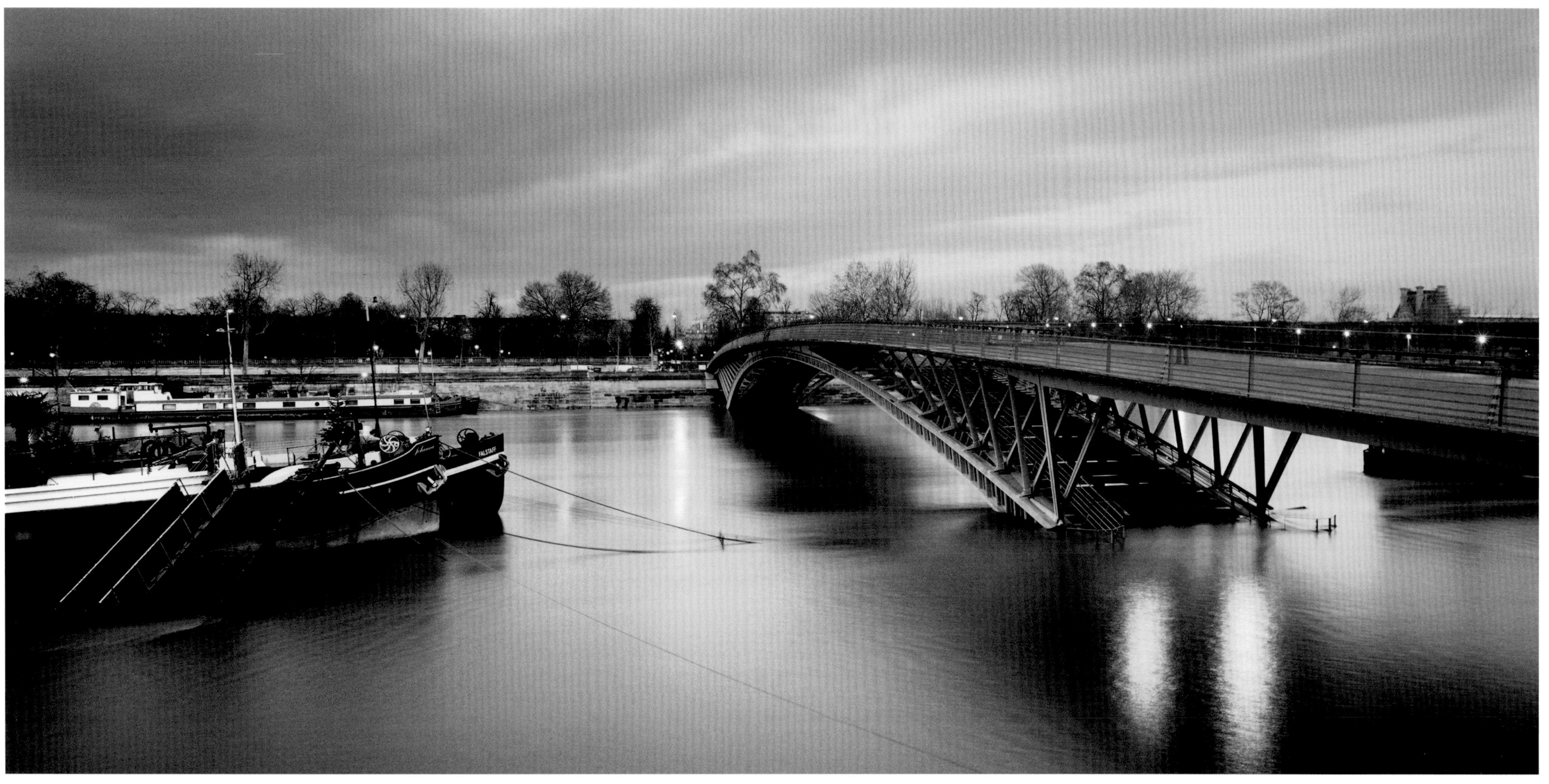

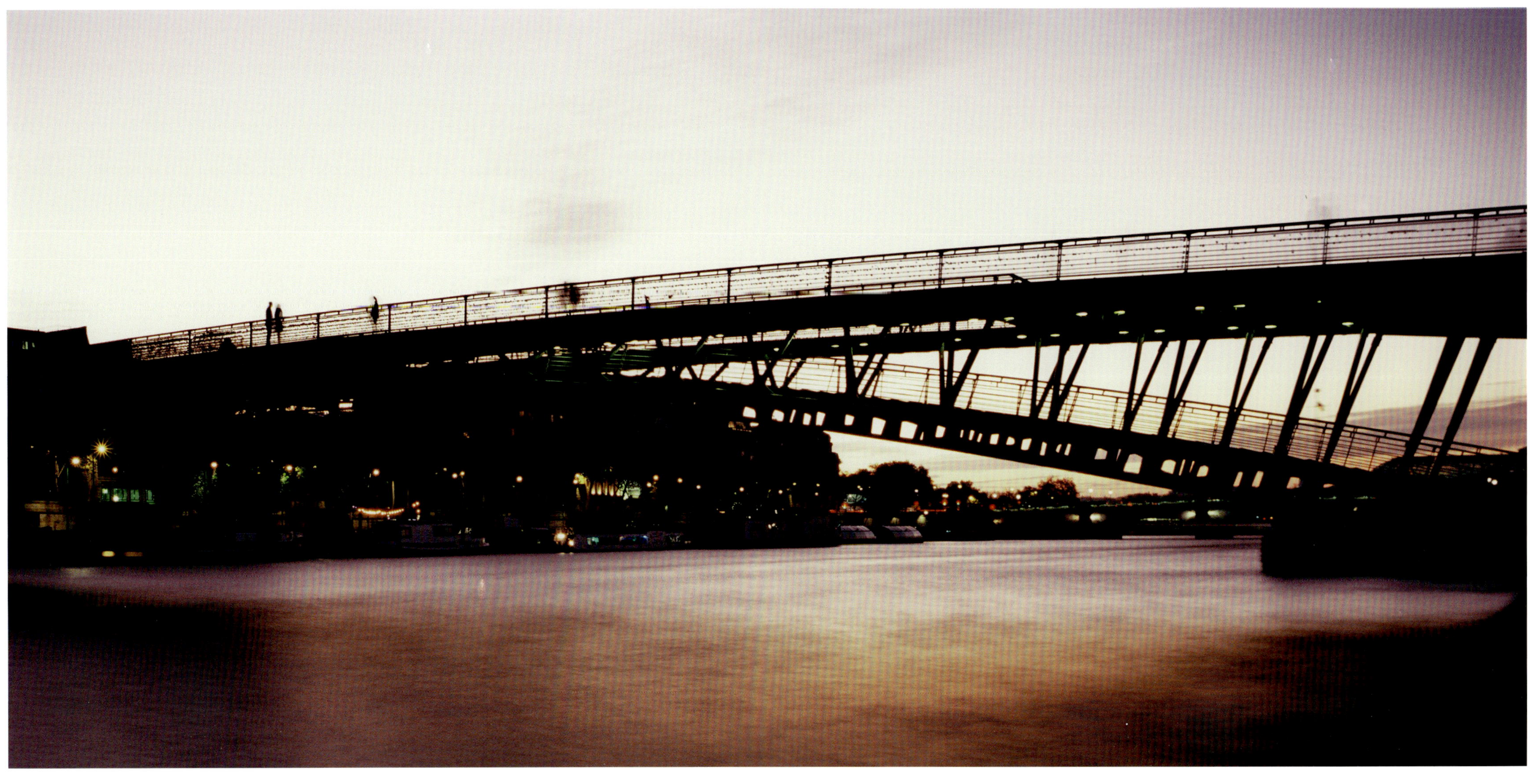

Solférino Footbridge, Paris, France

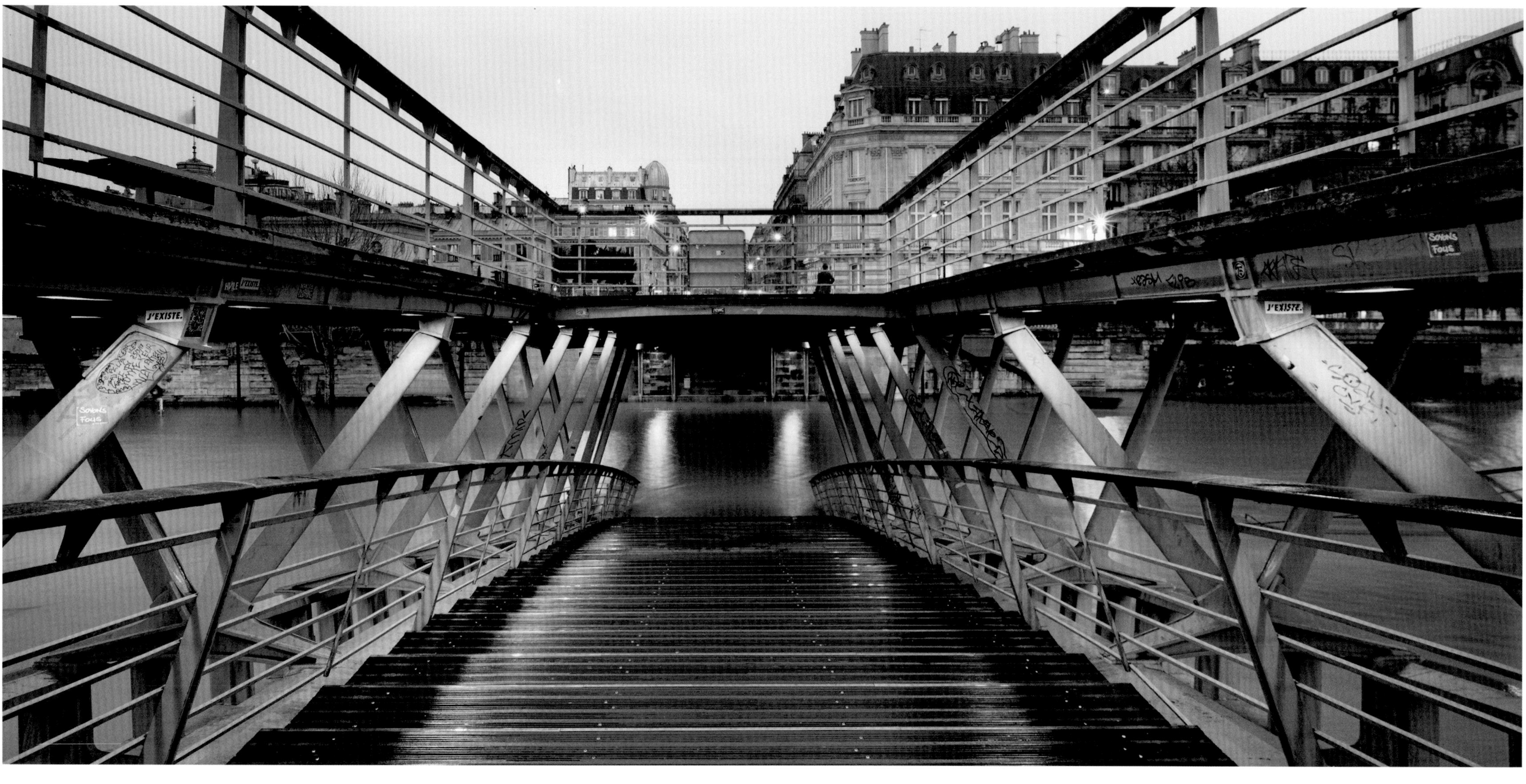

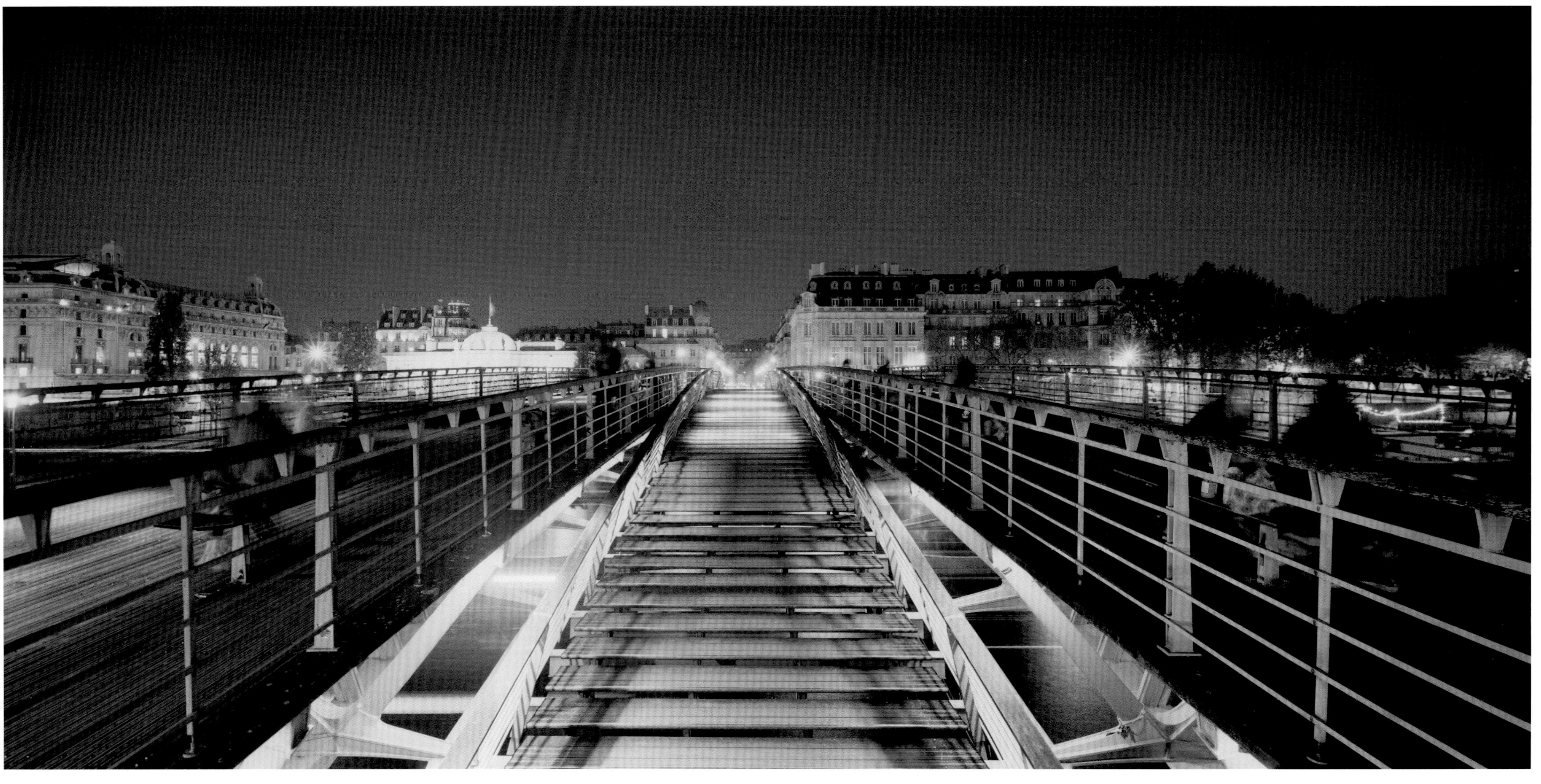

Solférino Footbridge, Paris, France

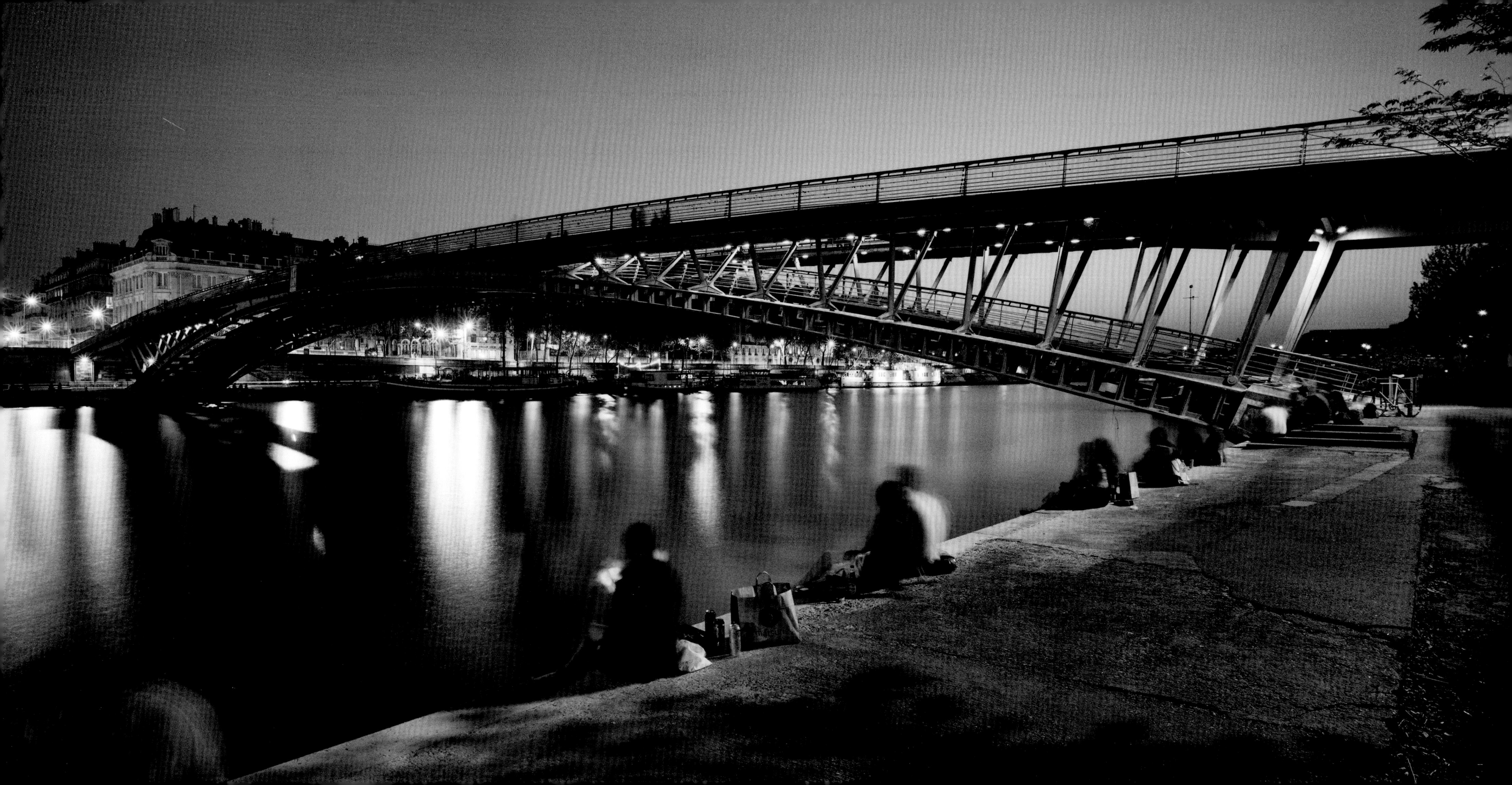

Hassan II Bridge
Rabat—Salé, Morocco

Becoming Part of the Landscape's Horizon

Beautiful and fragile, the city stretches out before us. The esplanade of the Mausoleum of Mohammed V forms a plateau, while, in the distance, the Medina and the Kasbah of the Udayas weave a delicate texture between the sky and the mouth of the river preparing the way for yet another horizon: the sea.

The walled city of Salé has a strong attachment to the soil. The new bridge sought to create a relationship with this built horizontality, preserving the views, offering new panoramas, allowing light to filter through without obstacle, framing openings without concealing them and, most importantly of all, not obscuring the sky. For the only thing to rise up on the horizon from this sculpted material is the Hassan Tower. Our project sought to create a dialogue with this built horizon, not only a bridge—a public space where the river lies at the core of the historical development of the city.

A Structure of Change and Direction

In this case what was needed was not a solitary viaduct but a structure that could form a permanent presence in the urban landscape. The lateral spans are created from L-frames that increase in size as they approach the center of the river from either side, finally shaping the central span. The whole construction forms a long continuous curve, open to the sky, its center over the river.

A Concrete Lace

The succession of arches is based on a single motif gradually increasing in size. The bridge consists of three juxtaposed decks that are separated so as to allow the moving light of the sun to shine through the arches. Its north-south orientation means that the sun travels across it, transforming the structure into a receptacle for the interplay of light and shade, avoiding the deep shadow cast by a single deck. Looking west, pedestrians and users of the tram can enjoy views of the Medina, the Kasbah of the Udayas, the river, and the city horizon. The deck of the access viaduct, 800 meters long and perfectly horizontal, forms a roof over the alluvial plain that slopes gently towards the river. Its structure shelters an attractive public space and promenade and provides a roof for a market or any other kind of temporary public event.

Designed for this spot and nowhere else, this bridge is the result of careful appraisal of a unique landscape carved in white and ocher against the horizon. This link between Rabat and Salé enters into a dialogue with the river, taking from it its rhythm, its geometry, and its structure in the changing reflections of the water.

But this project is also resonant of the human adventure: that of the workers, the builders, and the laborers. Their work is hard but with it comes pride. The project highlights the work involved in both construction and conception. It brings together highly skilled calculation, implementation, and craftsmanship. A successful project must consider both its situation in the landscape and its implementation. A major construction like this creates a generous link embracing the public space it has formed, where its technical brilliance is at the service of a modernity sensitive to the fragile landscape of the Bou Regreg.

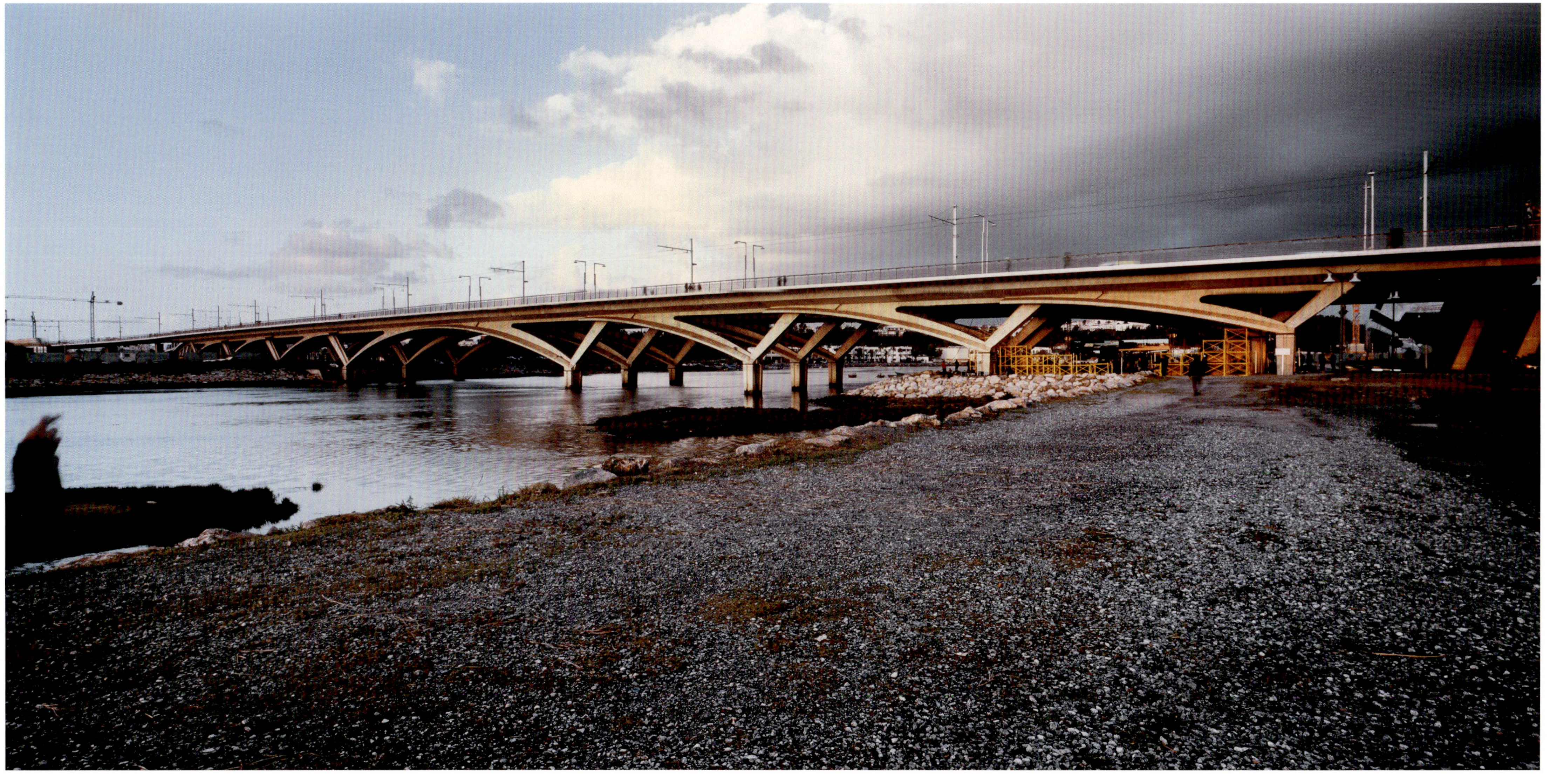

Hassan II Bridge, Rabat—Salé, Morocco

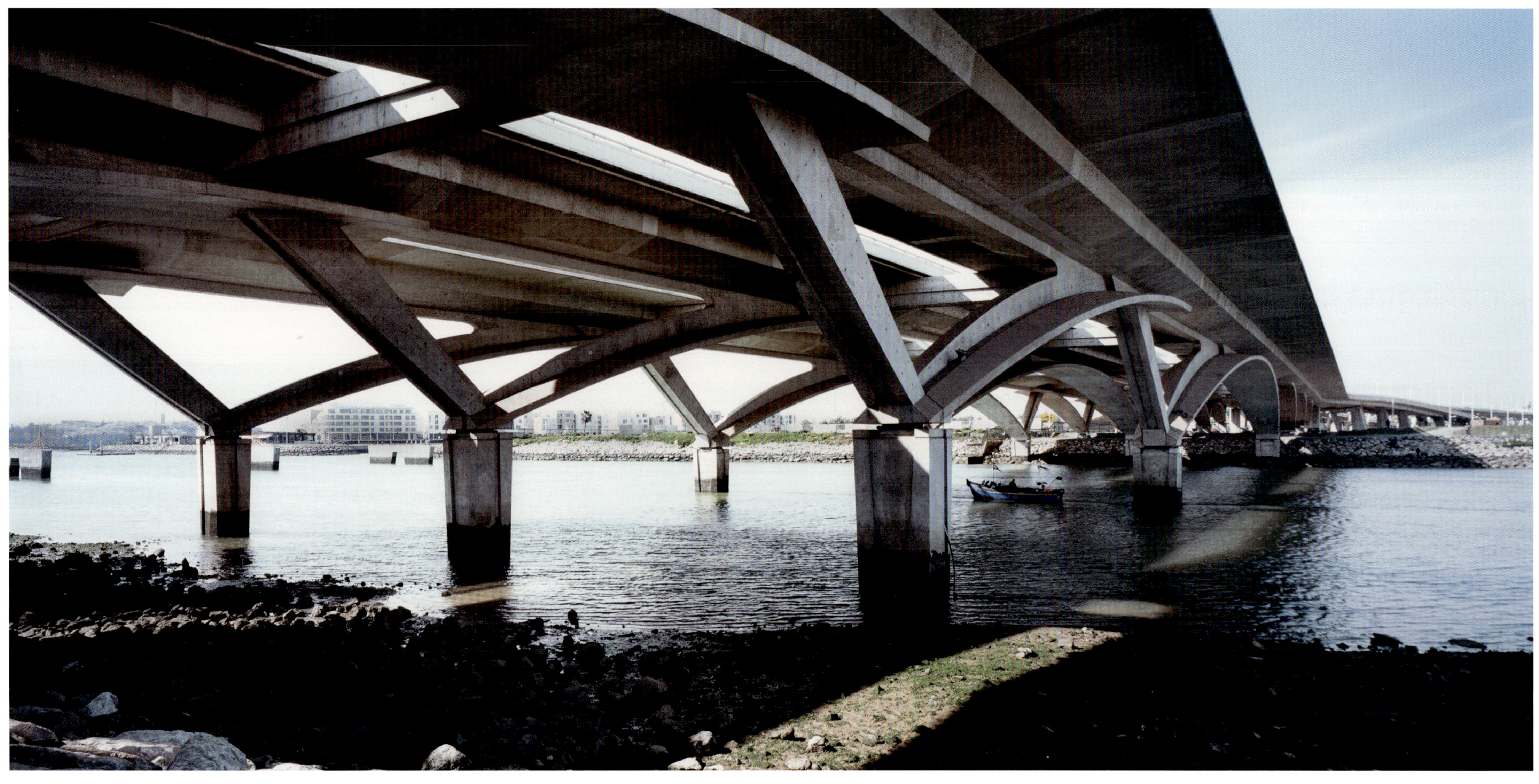

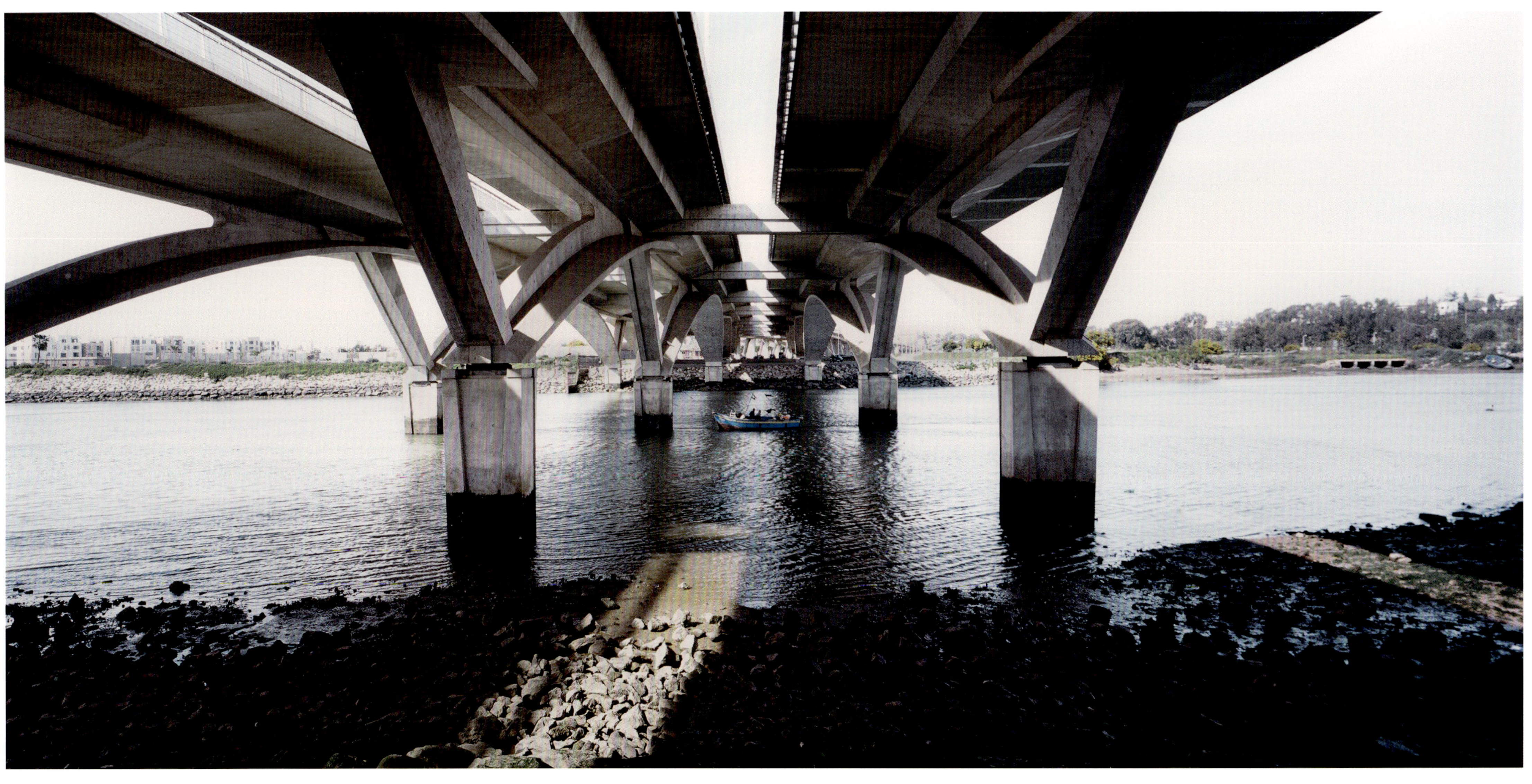

Hassan II Bridge, Rabat—Salé, Morocco

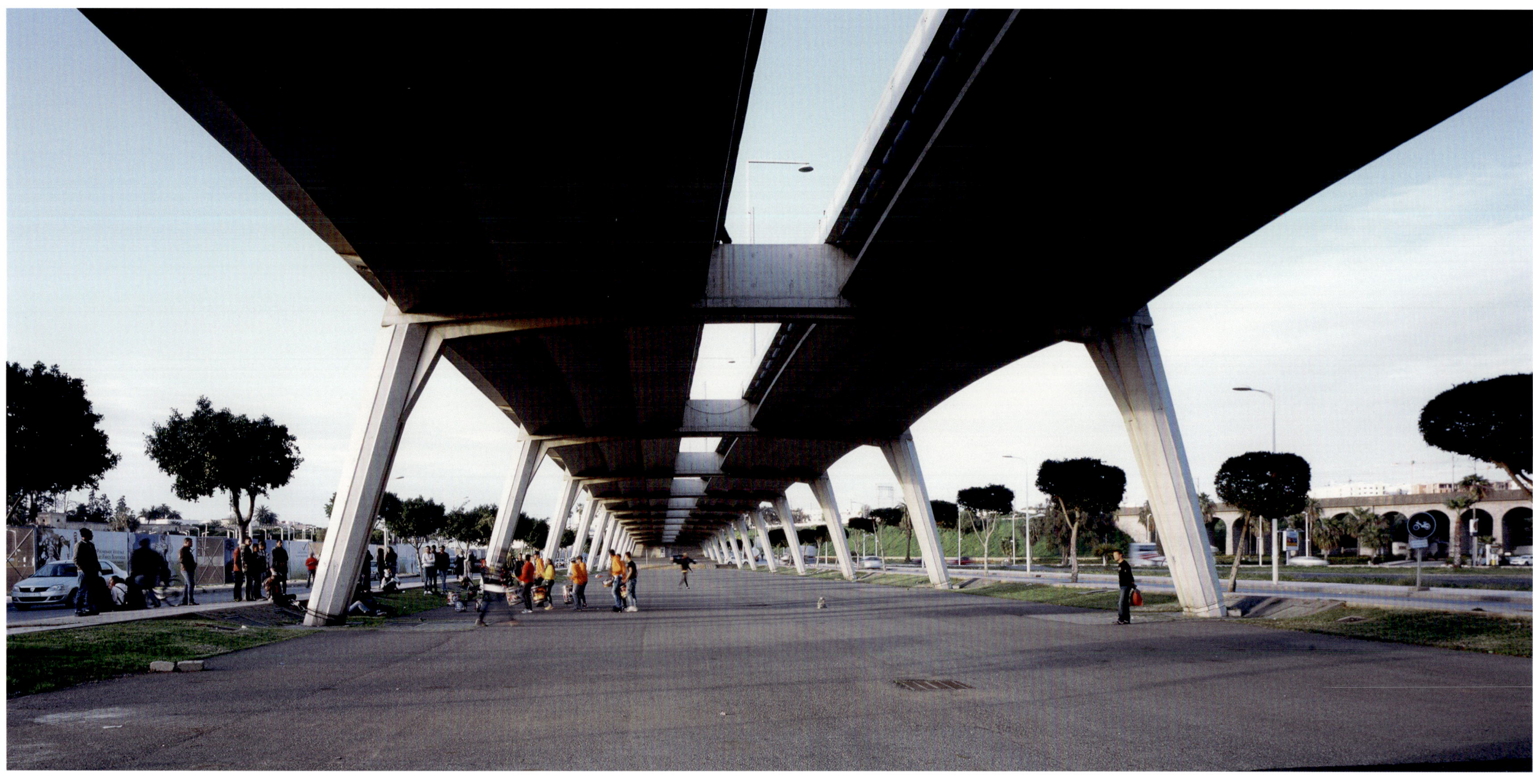

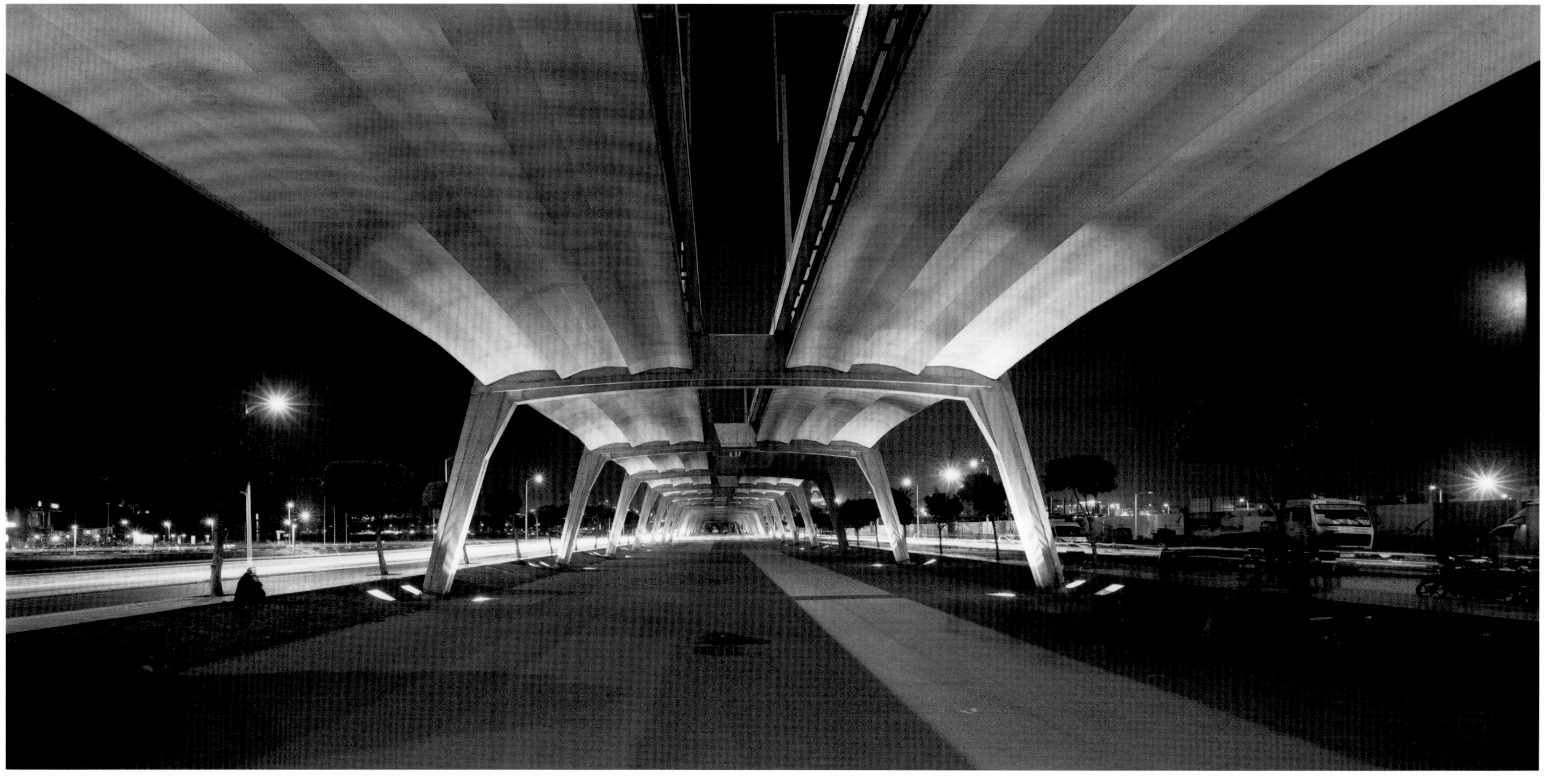

Hassan II Bridge, Rabat—Salé, Morocco

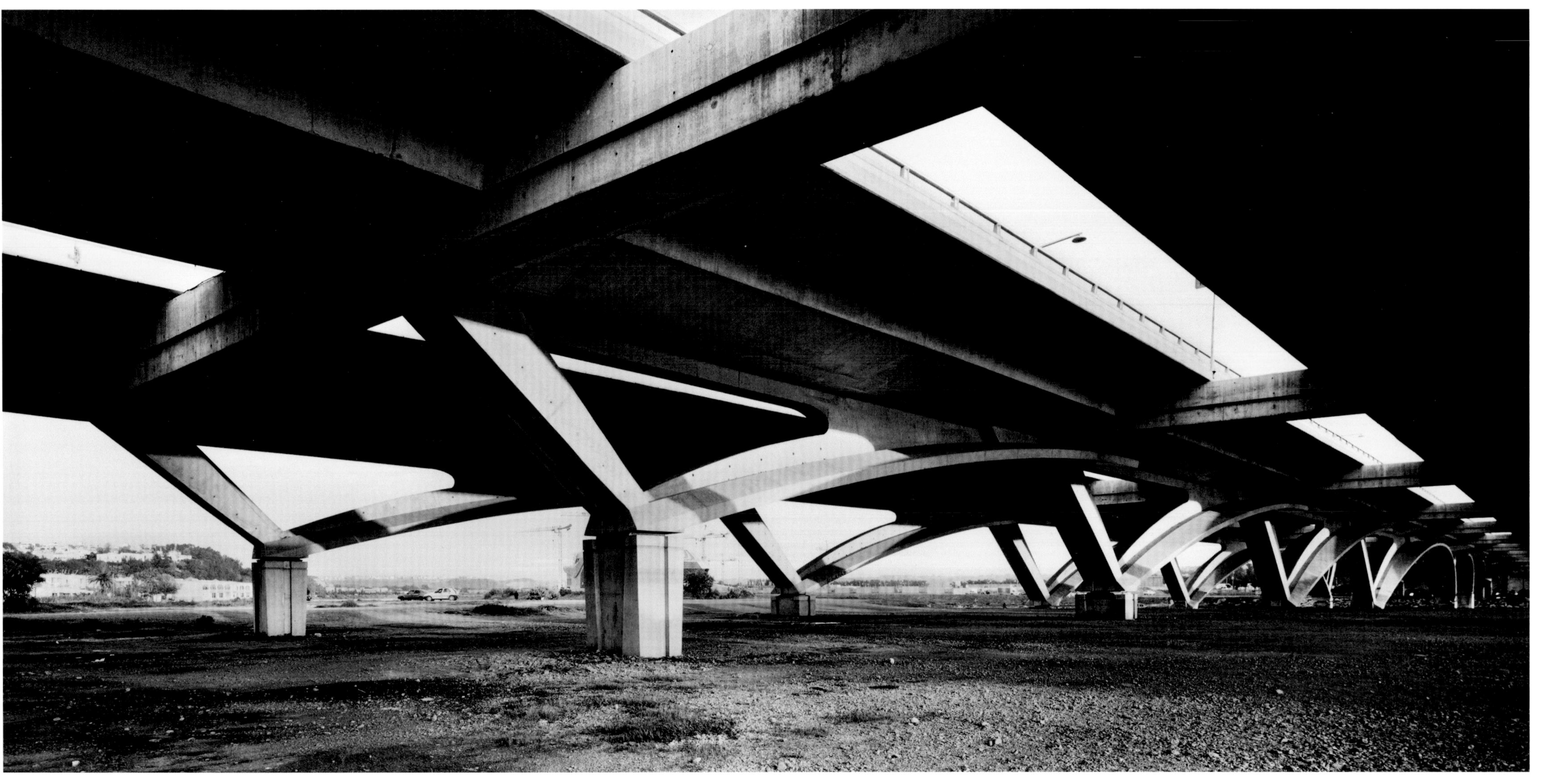

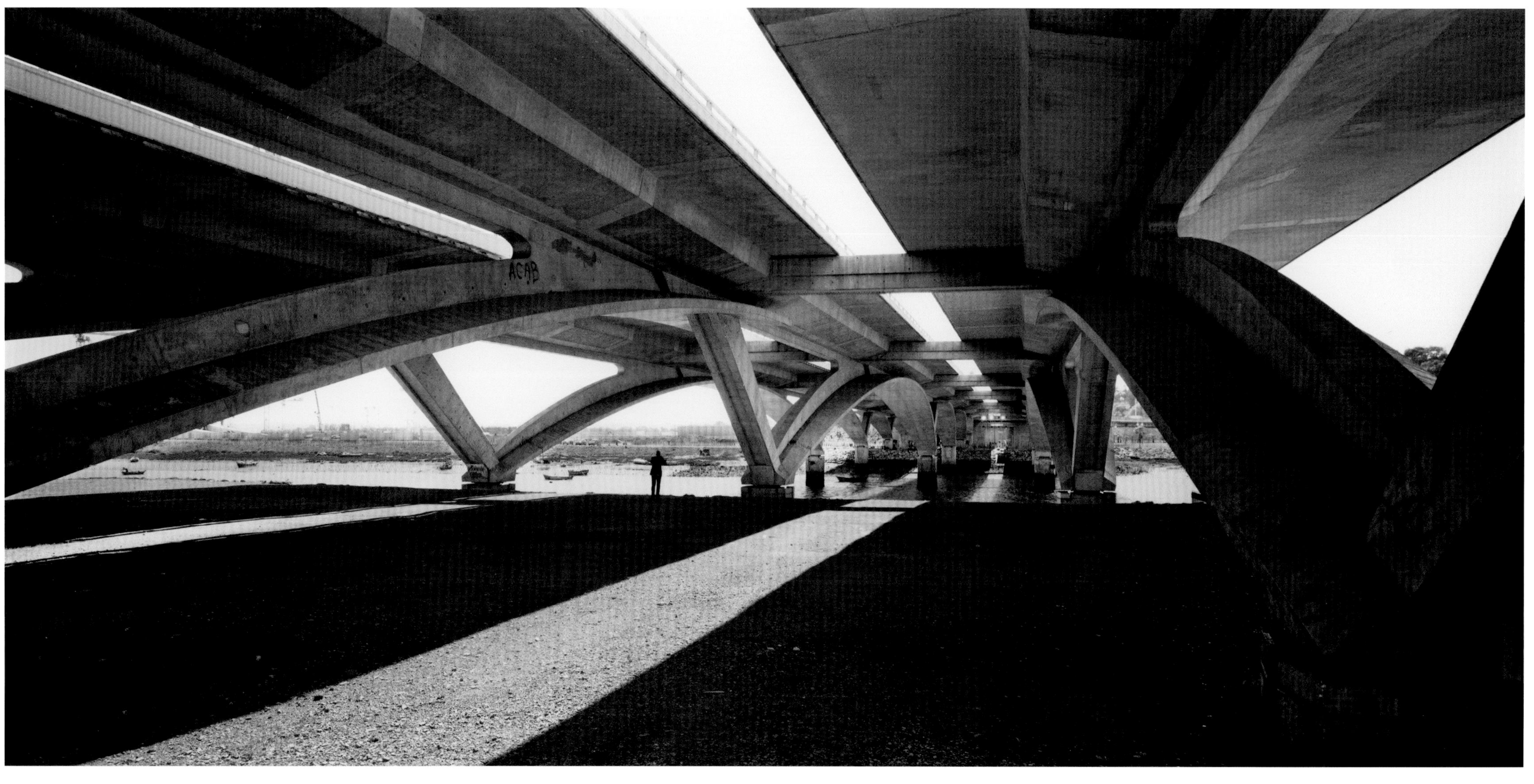
ACAB

Hassan II Bridge, Rabat—Salé, Morocco

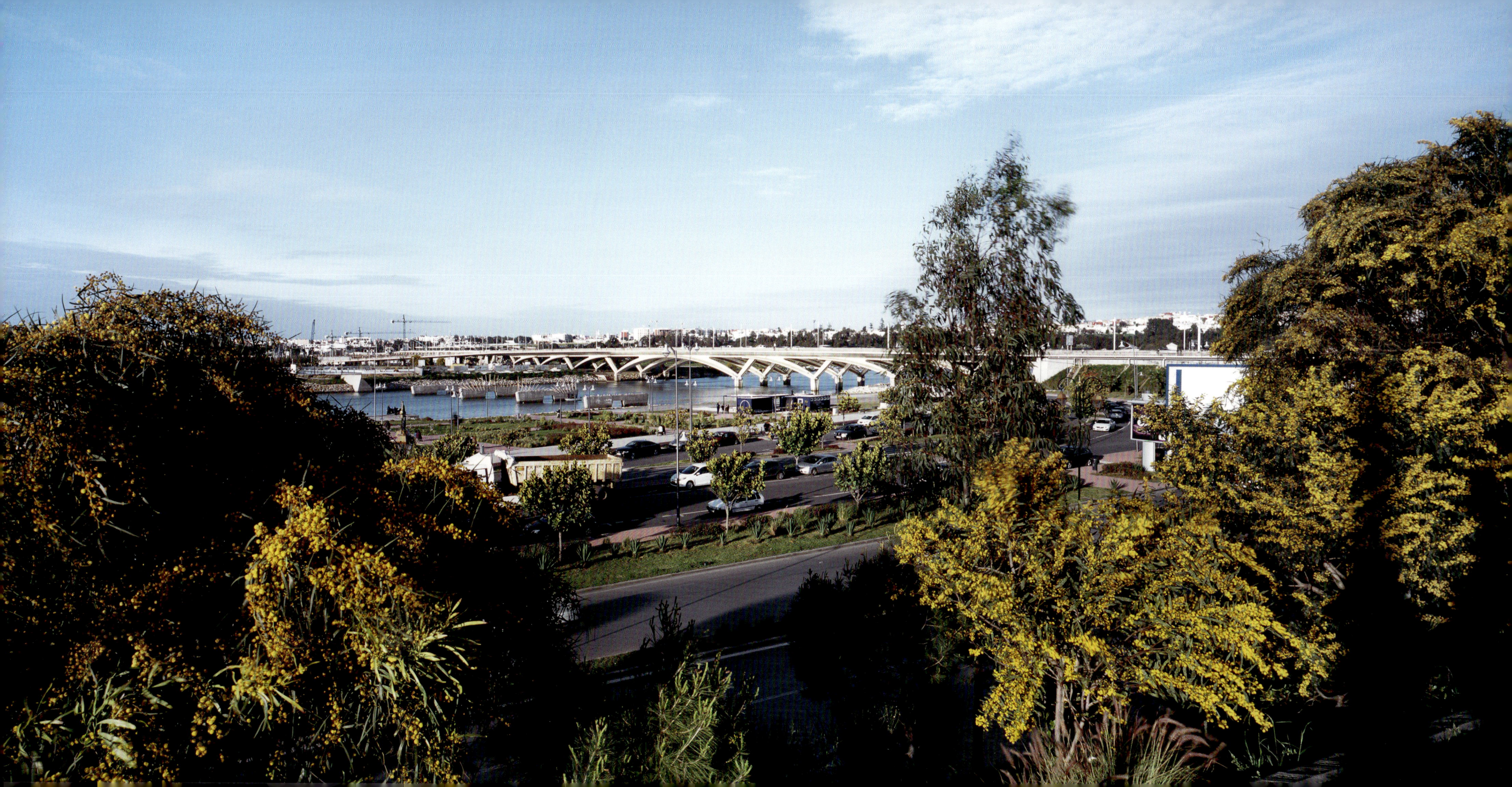

Marcelle Henry Footbridge – ZAC Clichy Batignolles
Paris, France

The Marcelle Henry Footbridge in the Clichy Batignolles ZAC (Development Zone) provides a link to Rue Saussure so as to anchor the urban project in the Clichy Batignolles district within the fabric of the city of Paris, extending over the encircling railway lines spreading out from the Gare Saint-Lazare.
The task was not simple since it had not only to take account of the usage of the public space and the site for anchoring the new urban development, but also had to consider what was near and what was in the distance—the daily usage and the landscape from the stream of railway lines over which the footbridge runs and which it echoes.
Elements taken into account by the project included the need to provide a public space and the different levels and areas still to be developed, bringing together the small square leading into Rue Saussure and the gardens on the other side.

How to Create a Genuine Public Space above the Railway Network

The structure of the span depends not only on the limitations of the site but also on the elements rising up from the railway lines, which we wanted to integrate into the structure of the new bridge. The bridge, composed of double curvature beams, their curves varying from one side to the other, incorporates within itself elements of balance, rest, and contemplation. Here, public space and structure are integrated in the surface geometry of the project.
The sides of the wide walkway, opening up into a series of long curves, form alcoves on either side. These balconies follow the variations in inertia of the structure at right angles to the supports to create a soft, continuous line along the sides of the bridge, both in elevation and plan. In combination with the curved arches, and Vierendeel beams with variable inertia, they give rigidity to the edges.
The two sides of the bridge are asymmetric and interlinking, delicate then open, curved then lightened, demonstrating the careful attention paid to the public space and the siting of the structure.
The link becomes a place.
Delicate and weightless, the bridge is open to the sky, the mesh of its surrounds arching up to allow light to filter through. The play of light passing through the mesh onto the walkway—with its east-west orientation—varies according to the time of day, changing our view of the infrastructure. The economy of materials and the elegant simplicity of design speak to the care and attention devoted to the development of this structure.

Delight from a Delicate and Ageless Structure

Thus from one end to the other of the footbridge, the project gives coherence to the different ways of crossing it and the rational constructed expression of its structure placed at the service of pedestrians and the public space.
The new footbridge belongs to the public space that is formed by creating a highly flexible urban landmark of different scales, respecting the needs of the pedestrians who cross it, who live there and have adopted it, but heedful also of its appearance from further off in the urban landscape that is here being transformed.
With its continuous and slender outline, its feet firmly planted in the universe of the city, the gently curved design of the new footbridge is warm and welcoming.

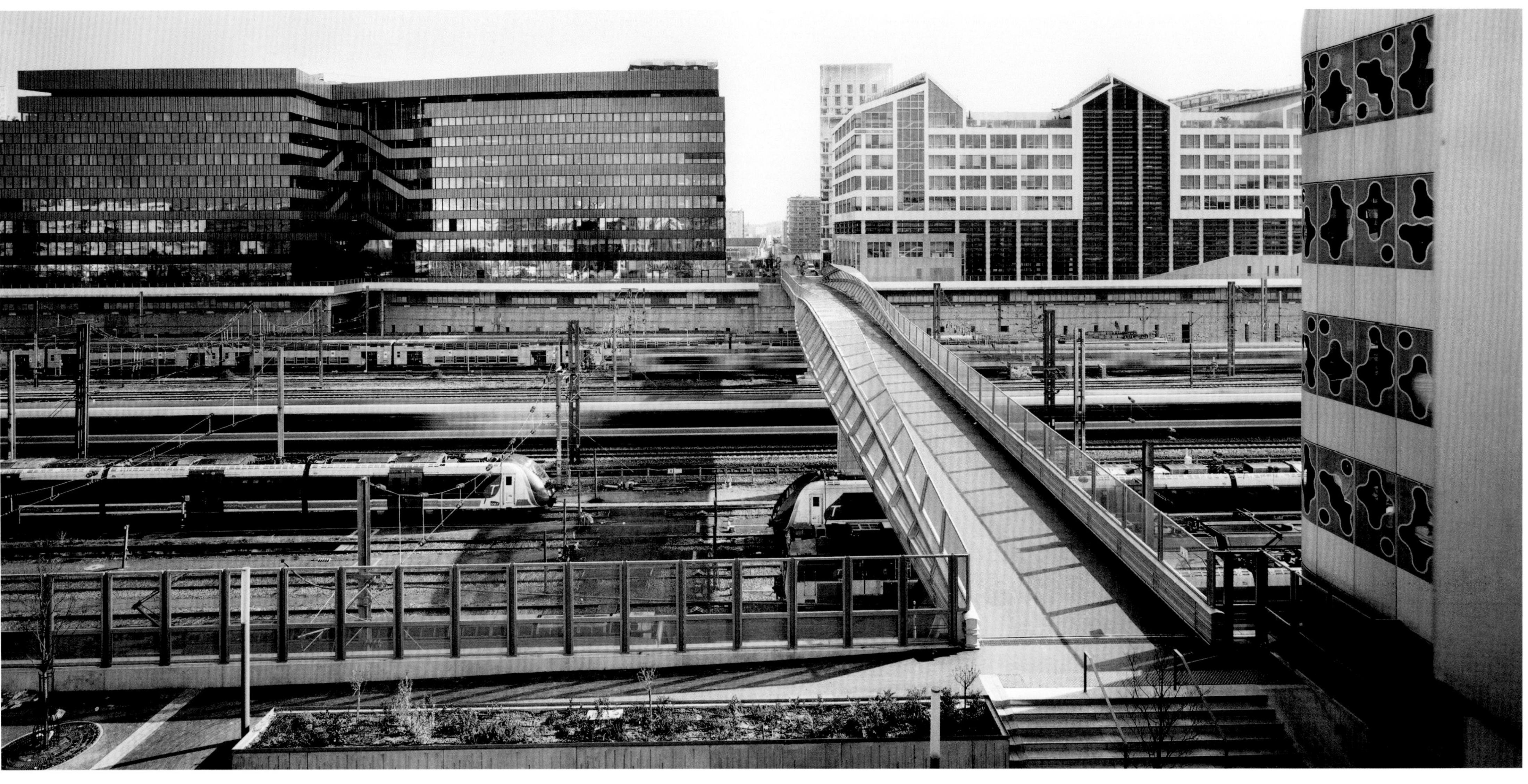

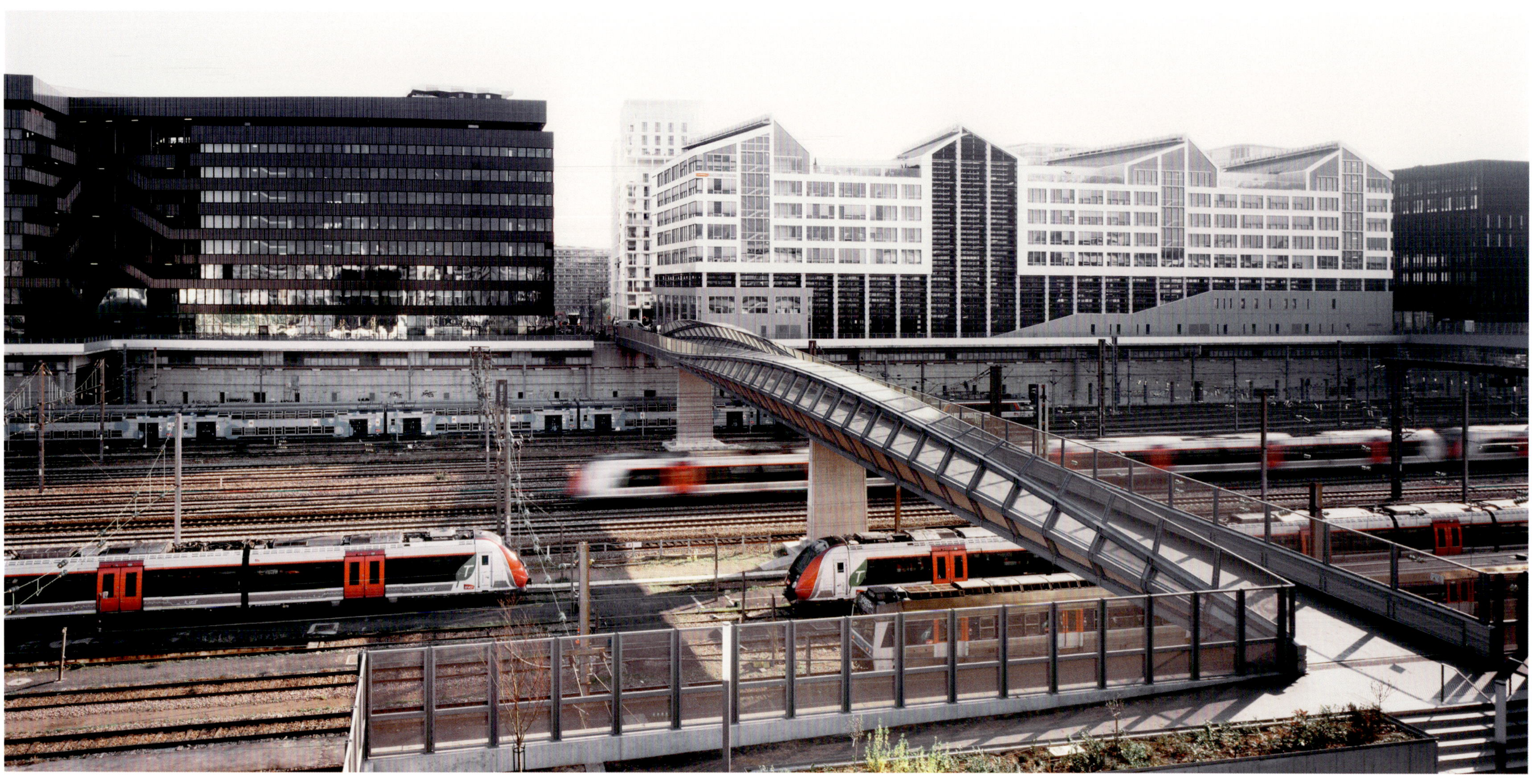

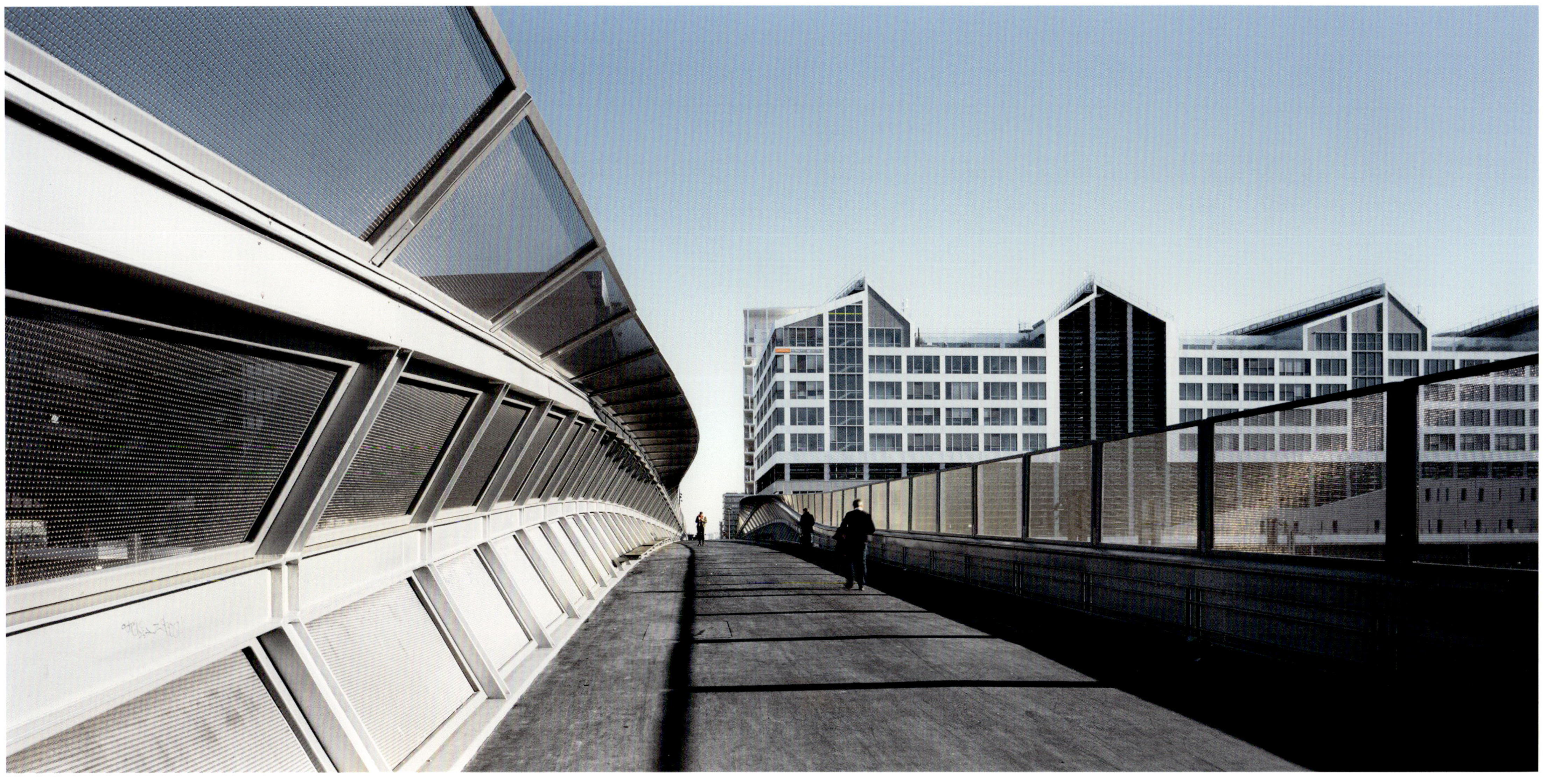

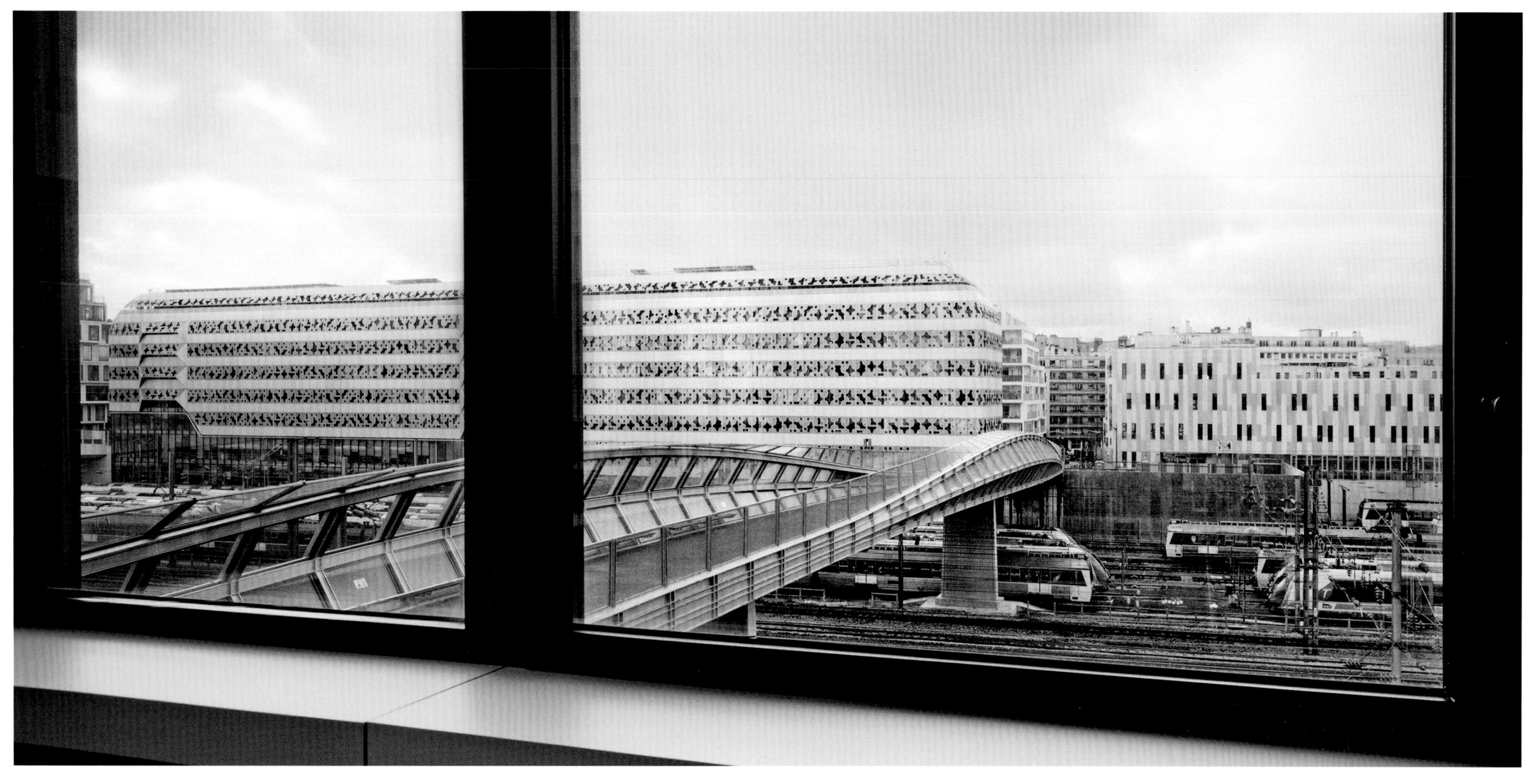

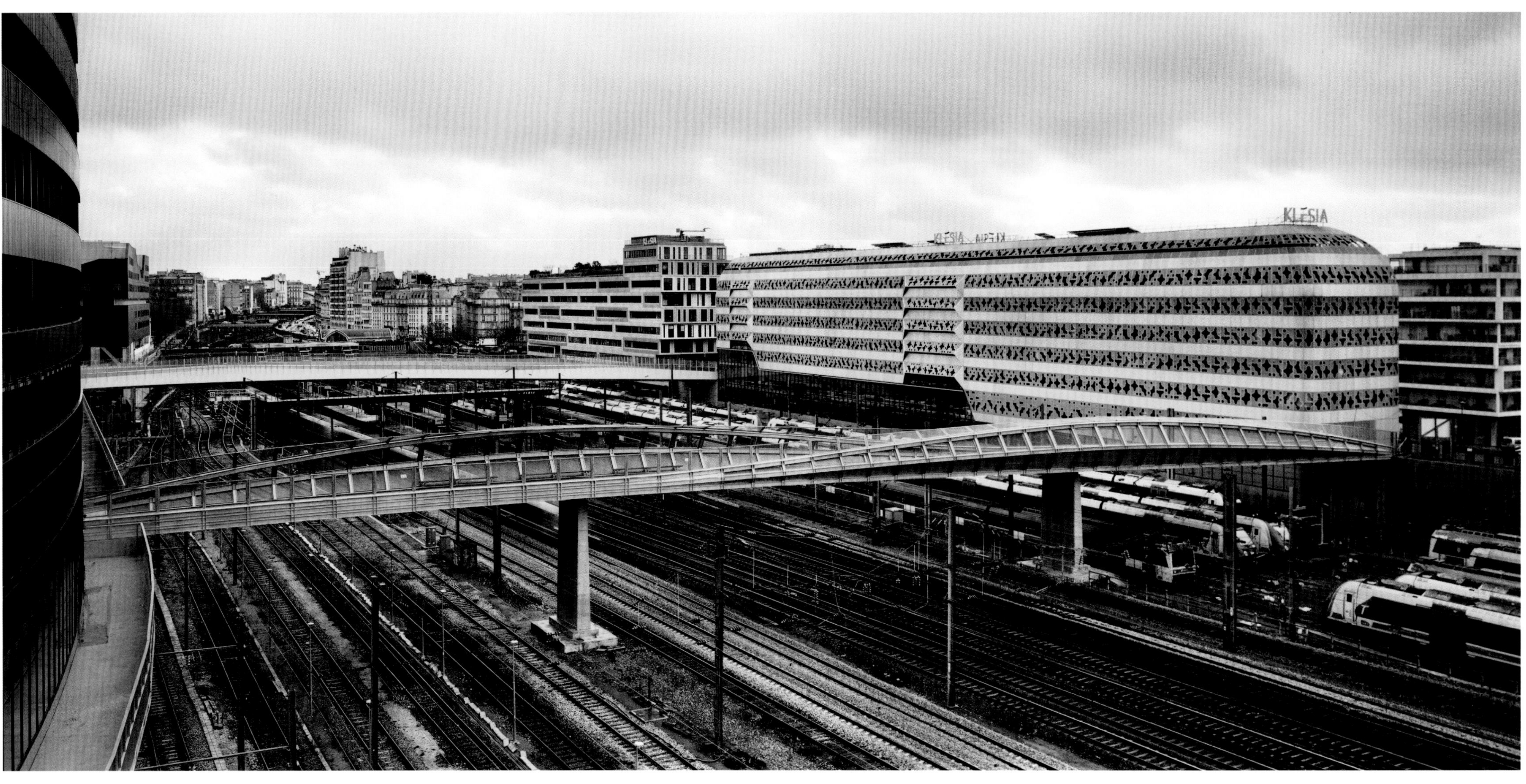

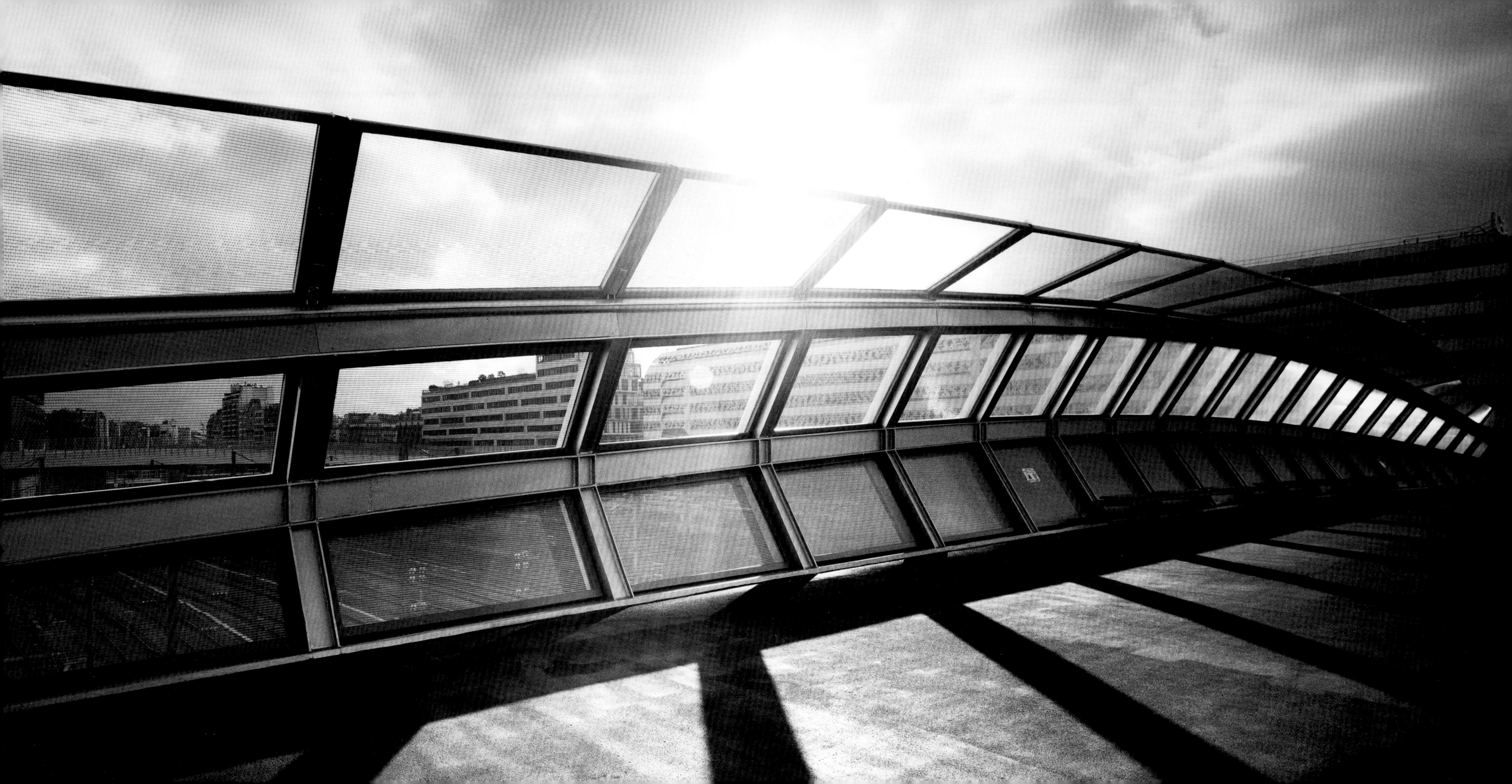

Pôle Nautique de Mantes-la-Ville
Mantes-la-Ville, France

The new swimming pool at Mantes-la-Ville forms part of the urban development and landscaping scheme around the station. The urban character of the swimming pool is an important condition of its architectural development. The aim was to provide a water sports facility preserving the need for an element of privacy, without impinging on the pleasure derived from the play of light on the water.

The pool opens out onto the surrounding gardens, its entrance being completely transparent. The roof of the pool is conceived as something providing comfort. It forms a delicate canopy allowing swimmers to appreciate the seasons' changing light and casting reflections of rippling water and light on the façades of the neighboring buildings.

The wide glass walls running between the main beams allow the light to filter through, giving form to the space and setting up vibrations throughout the pool area reflecting the rhythm of the light. The varying shape of this curved roof means that the pool areas have a quiet acoustic without unpleasant echoes.

Opening towards the south, the complex is flooded with light. The design of the roof further contributes to the effects of light, being constructed so as to capture the warm and reddish evening light from the west as it falls on the curving roof without dazzling the swimmers.

We conceived the roof as providing large volumes sheltering beneath the leaves of broad rounded palm trees dividing up the spaces and permitting variations to be made to the variable light sources.

The structure fades into the background, allowing the contours of the wood-clad double curvature surfaces to develop continuously between the façade and the roof. The building's volume seems to have become broken down in the disjunction between the opaque wood surfaces and the transparency of the glass, in the discontinuity between structure and light. It is a place that enhances the pleasure of water beneath a broad expanse of sky, bringing together the pleasures of the site, the landscape, and of the emerging town.

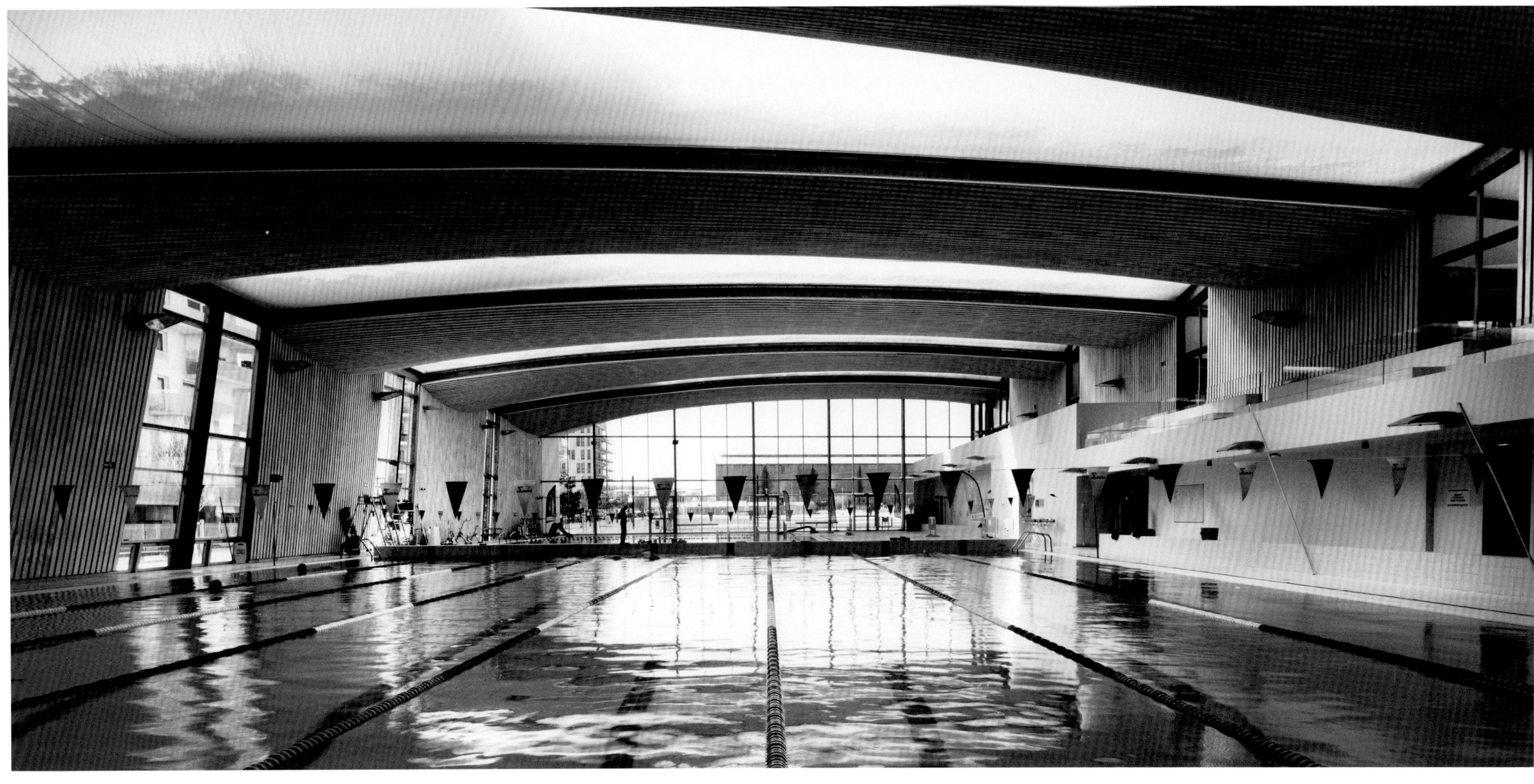

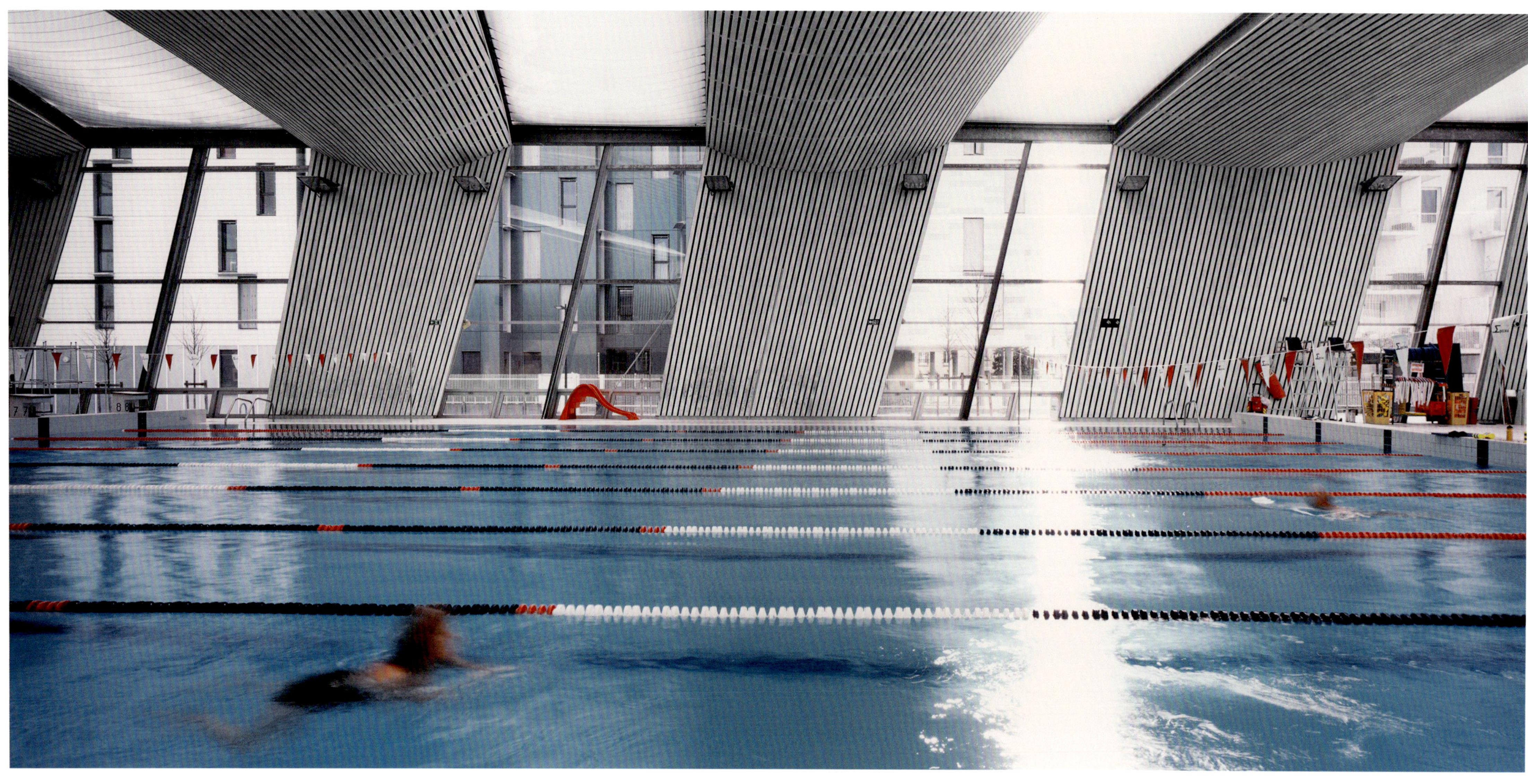

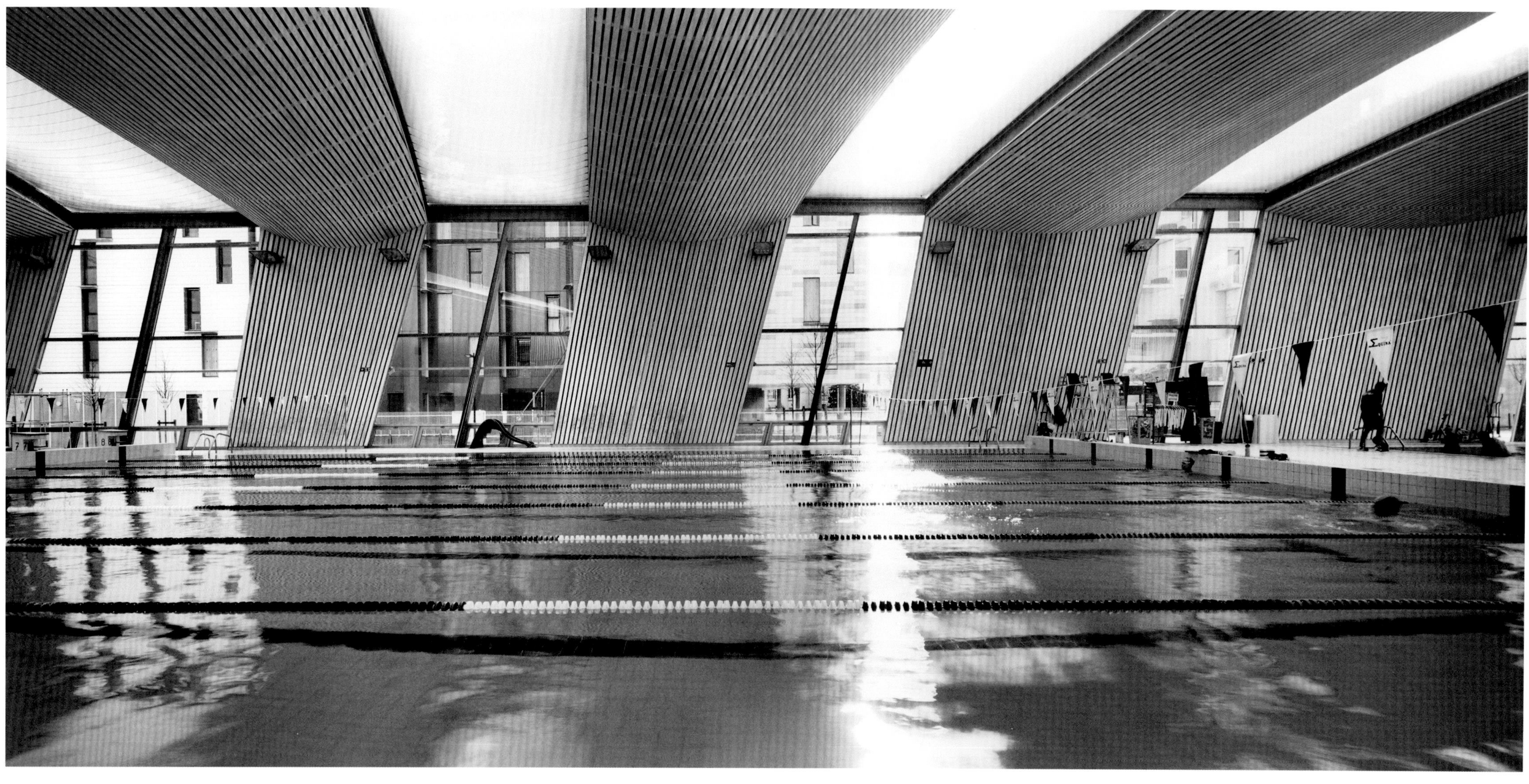

Pôle Nautique, Mantes-la-Ville, France

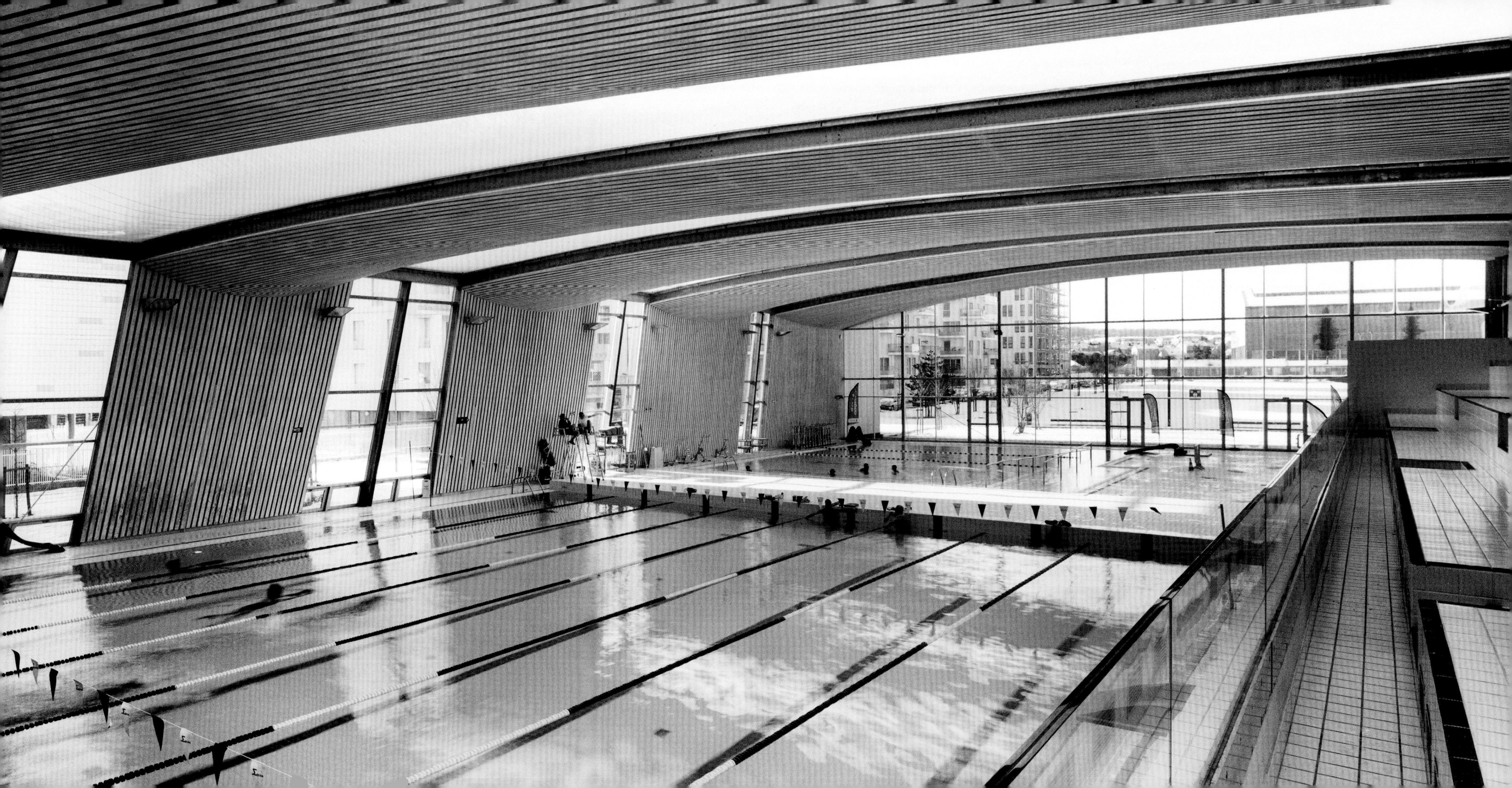

Montpellier Railway Station
Montpellier, France

Because they form part of the territorial network of railway infrastructure, train stations seem to have to be "delocalized"; detached from their fixed site so as to be incorporated into the network. We set out here to approach the project in an entirely different way: to make the new station, the Montpellier station, its own site, a Mediterranean station.

Trains and railway lines are, by their nature, territorial on a grand scale. The aim is to increase speed and save ever more time. But this speed that acts overall on the areas covered by the infrastructure also makes it possible to have access to the local dimension and the points of departure and arrival. The station can thus be seen as the meeting place between the absence of the distance covered and the presence of the place, that of leaving and arriving. This is where the local meets the global. A station anchors a journey through the land, making a significant mark on the geography of the place.

A Mediterranean station is one that takes account of variations in light and climate. Instead of enclosing space with a screen of glass, here shade is manipulated so as to guide the strong light through an opaque filter. The traveler is protected and the structure of the covering encourages the play of light and shade.

The pleated aspect of the covering incorporates the main entrance and also allows for an easily found entry to the station from the south, the multimodal hub, and the gardens outside.

This leaf-like double curve is constructed out of a lacy skin made of ultra high performance concrete (UHPC), a mineral material that both gives it the desired structure and allows the light to filter through.

The vast structure of the roof offers the pleasure derived from filtered light, shelter from sun and rain, and a panorama over the landscape, while accommodating the wind-powered system regulating the bioclimatic environment in the ticket hall.

Entering the station the traveler is immediately struck by the presence of both light and shade, by the calm, peaceful atmosphere created by the vast ribbed roof reflecting the changing seasons and providing a protective shelter.

This project represents a first in that it combines in a single piece two generally distinct elements: structure and roof.

Each of the 115 UHPC palms has a span of 18.4 meters (60.4 feet) with an average thickness of 4 centimeters (1.6 inches). Thanks to the density of the concrete and its low porosity, no sealing was required for the shells. Glass inserts were added to the double-curved surfaces of the concrete palms. The large palms of the roof possess a strong inertia thanks to the resistance of their form ensured by curving and folding. A long period of development was required for this roof both for the calculations and for experimental trials in the prefabrication factory.

It was made possible by the close relationship we developed between structure and architecture. More importantly, it was this relationship that made it possible to work closely with the client and the builder.

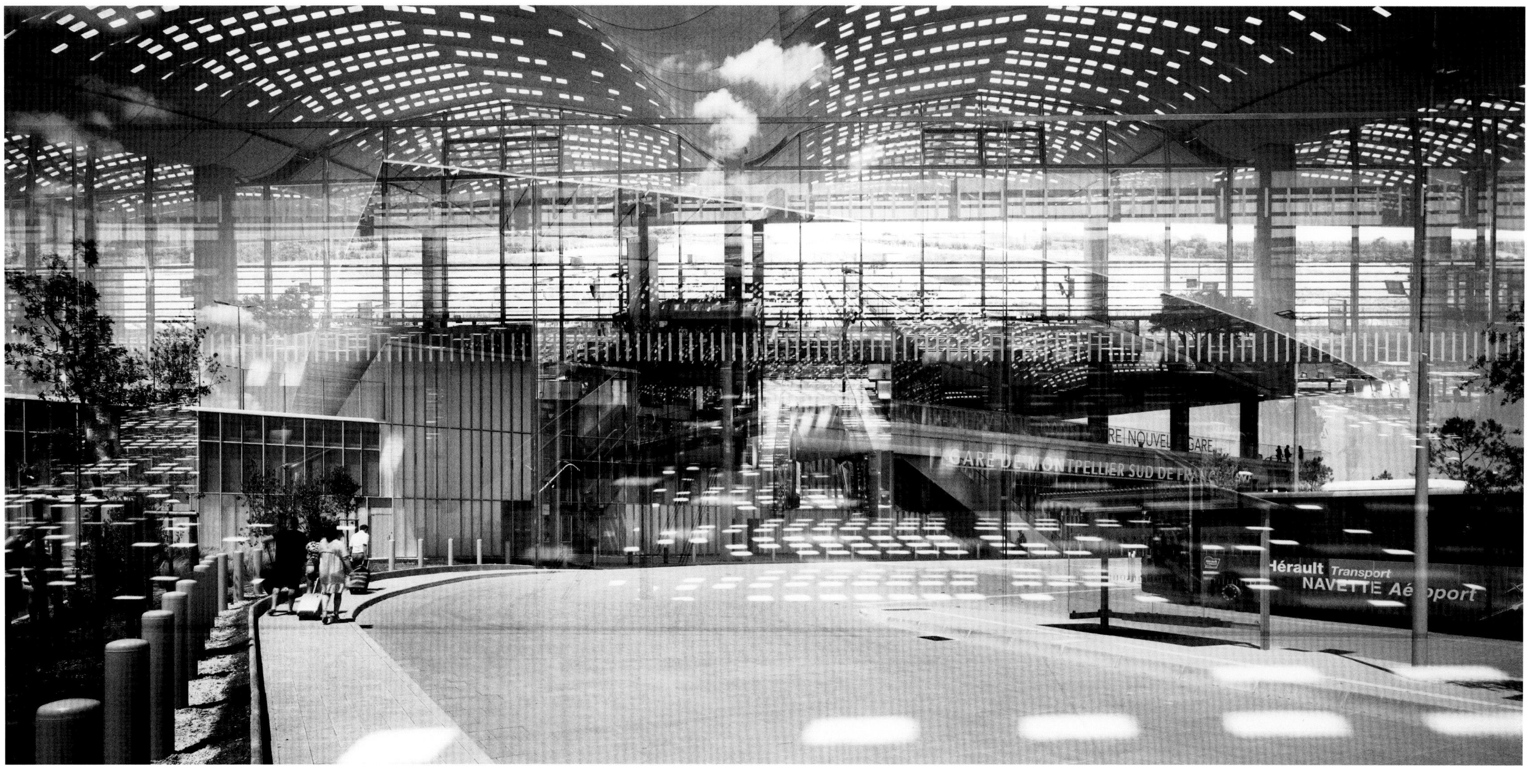
GARE DE MONTPELLIER SUD DE
Hérault Transport

Characteristics intrinsic to the material and its rheology involve static calculation. The preparation of the formwork molds followed experimentation in making these very delicate and slender elements. The geometry of the palms took into account both the resistance requirements and those relating to transport and lifting. The form of the structure emerged from these coinciding constraints, so different and even divergent in nature.

The architecture simultaneously evokes the wealth of variations in light and the austerity of an effective structure. The worksite has invited itself to the project table, making consistency a requirement: a dialogue with the wider landscape as well as with the people of the prefabrication plant, with the mechanics of the structures as well as with the interplay of the diffracted light, with the differential geometry of the folded surfaces as well as with the rheology of the fiber-reinforced concrete.

The success of the project is due to this experimental convergence. We wanted to make a station of the senses, of emotion, based on attention to light and shade, and to Montpellier's climate. A station dedicated to the pleasure of the place and the sentiments of the travelers.

Today, to see travelers passing beneath the glancing sunlight penetrating the roof-structure is to gaze again into the mirror of memory, recalling a project enhanced with shared pleasures that run through it like a red thread.

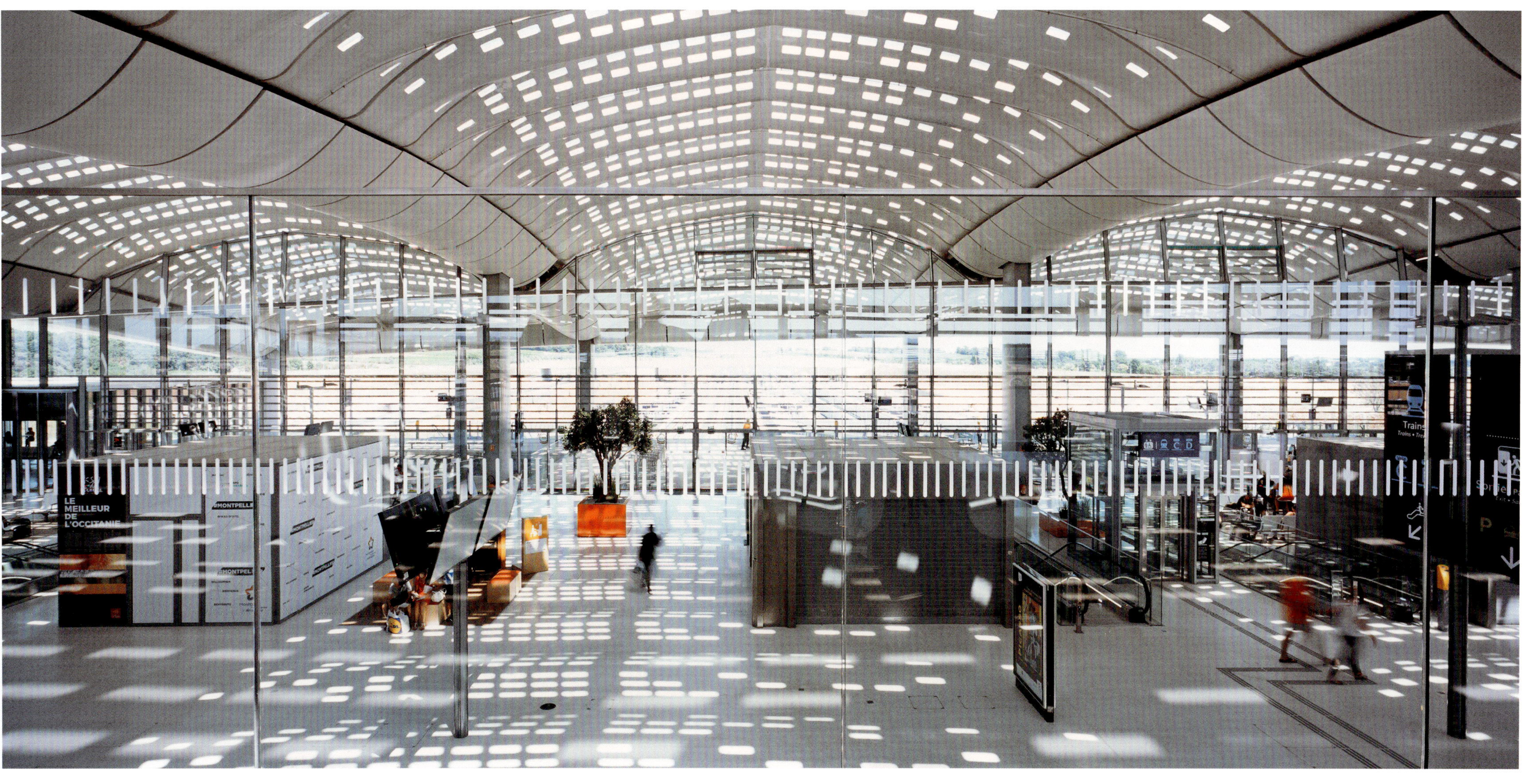
LE
MEILLEUR
DE
L'OCCITANIE

Montpellier Railway Station, Montpellier, France

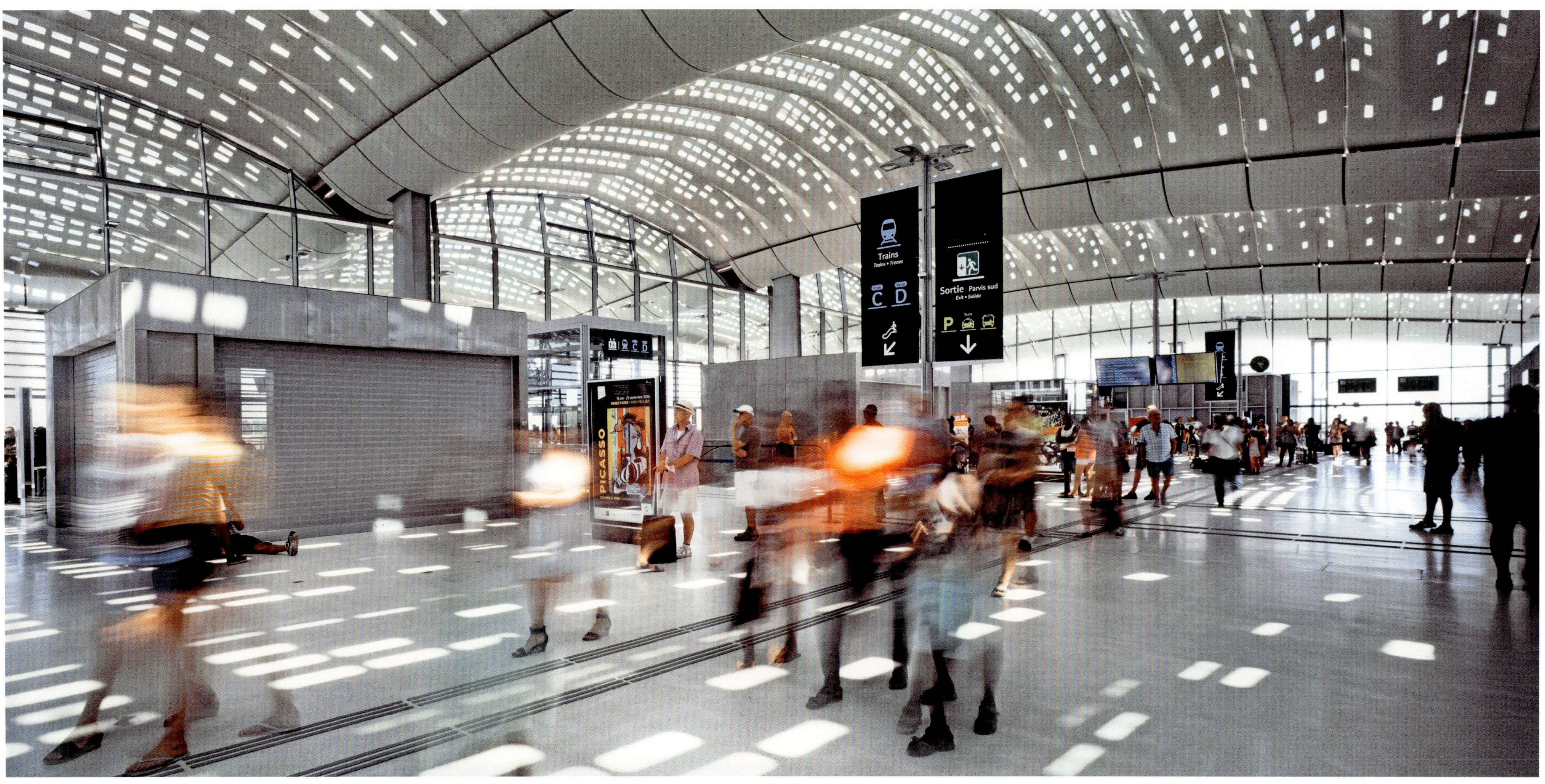

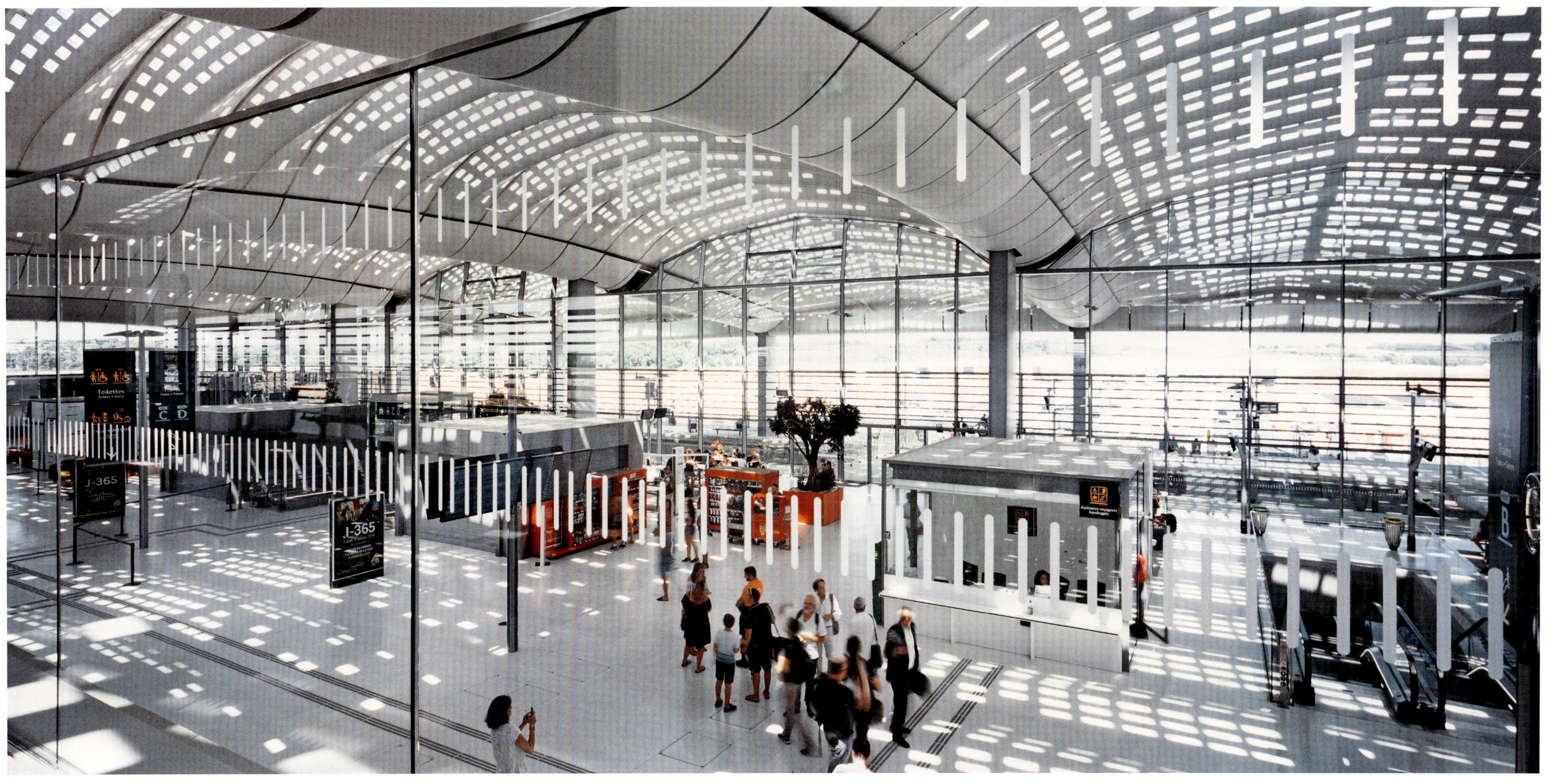
Toilettes
C D
J-365
J-365

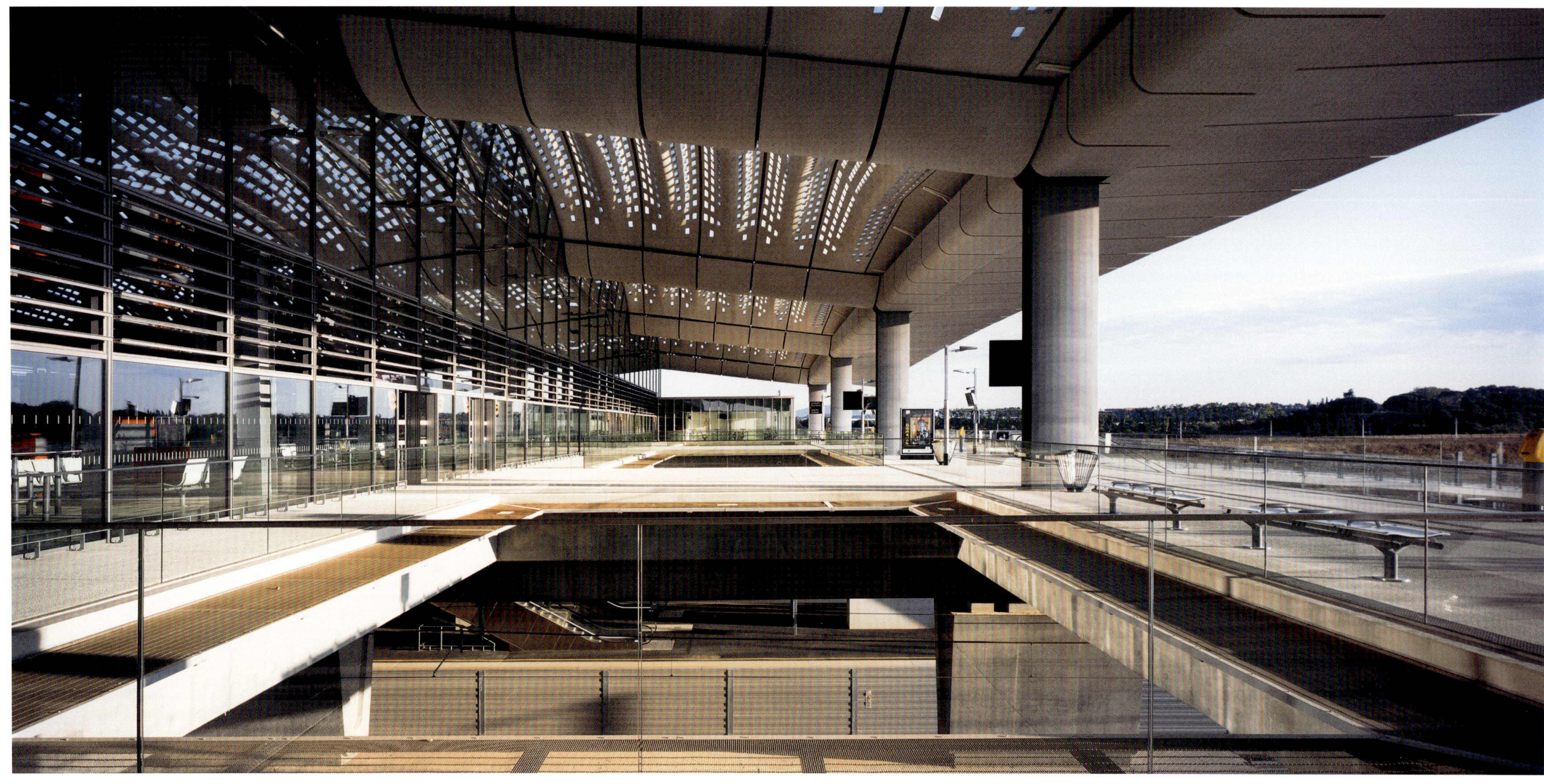

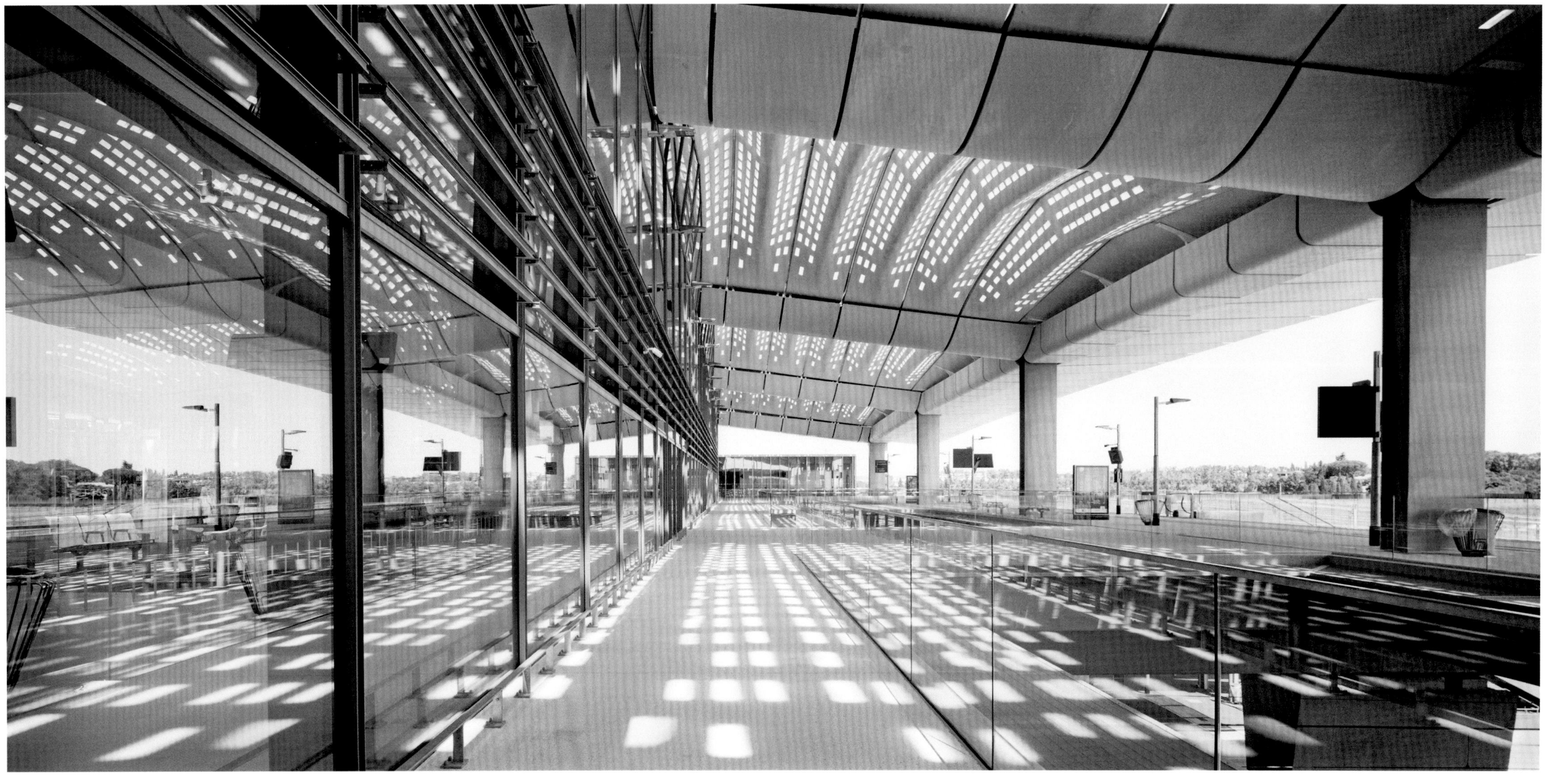

Montpellier Railway Station, Montpellier, France

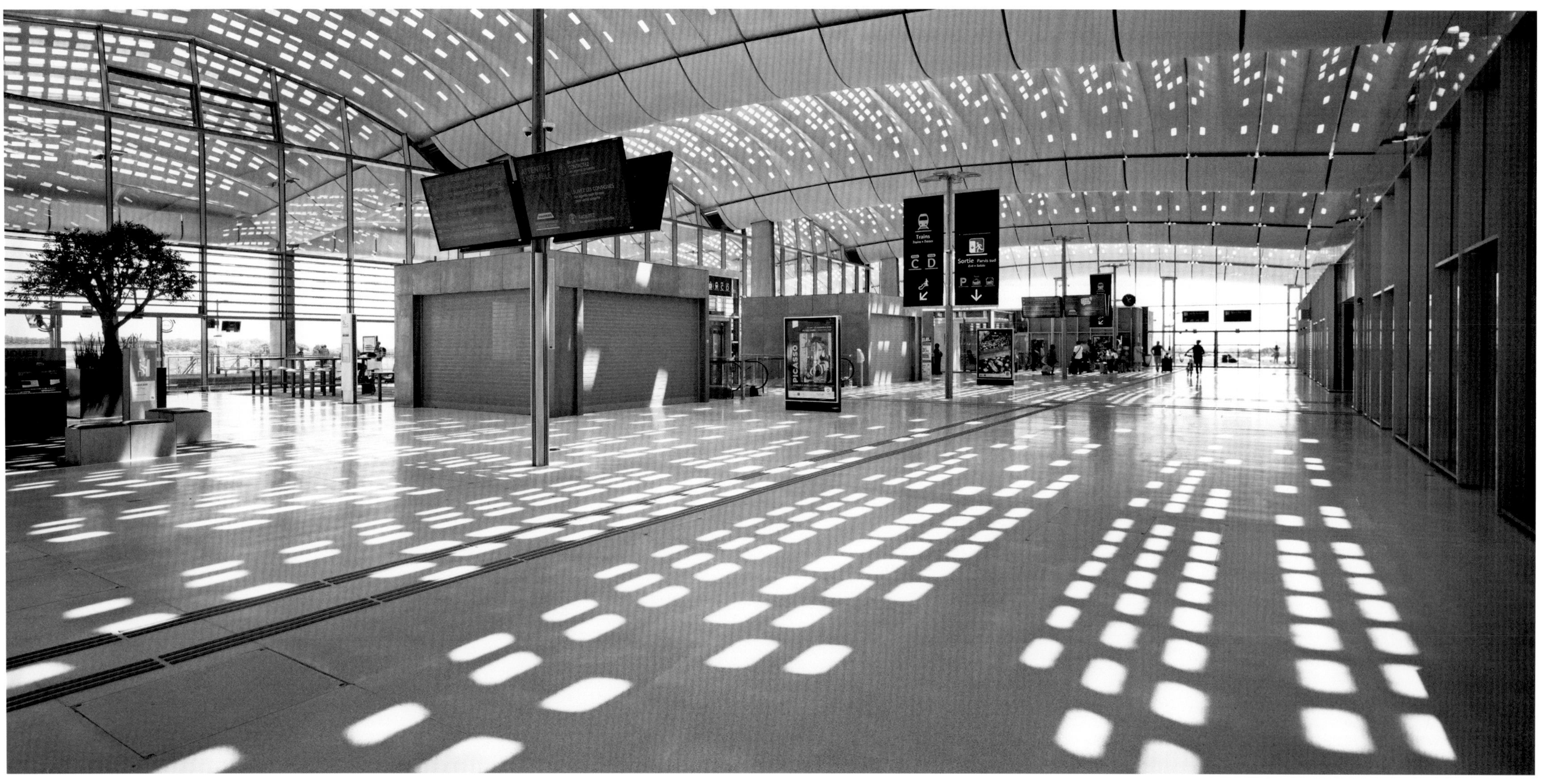

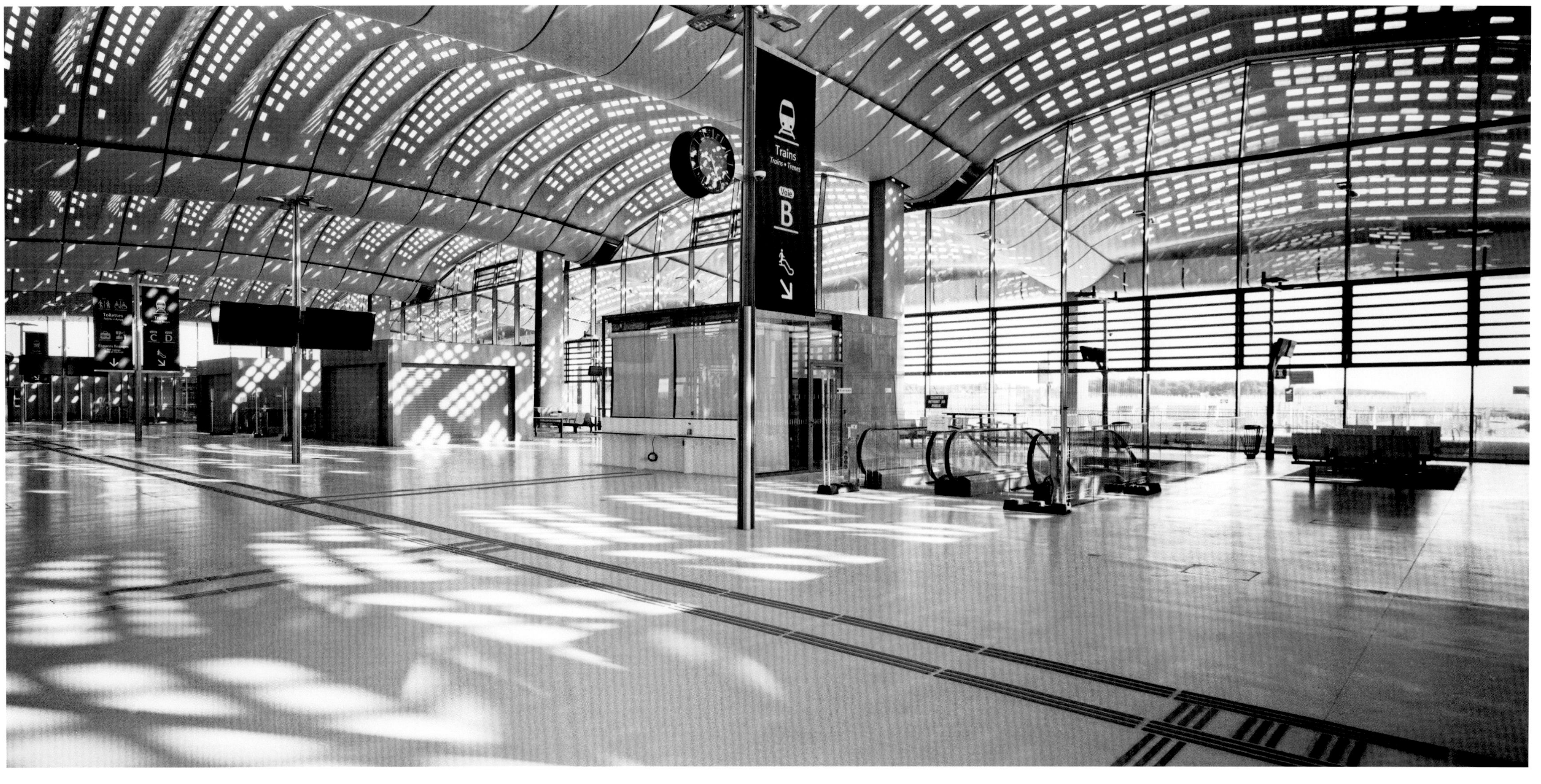
Trains
Voie
B
Toilettes
C D

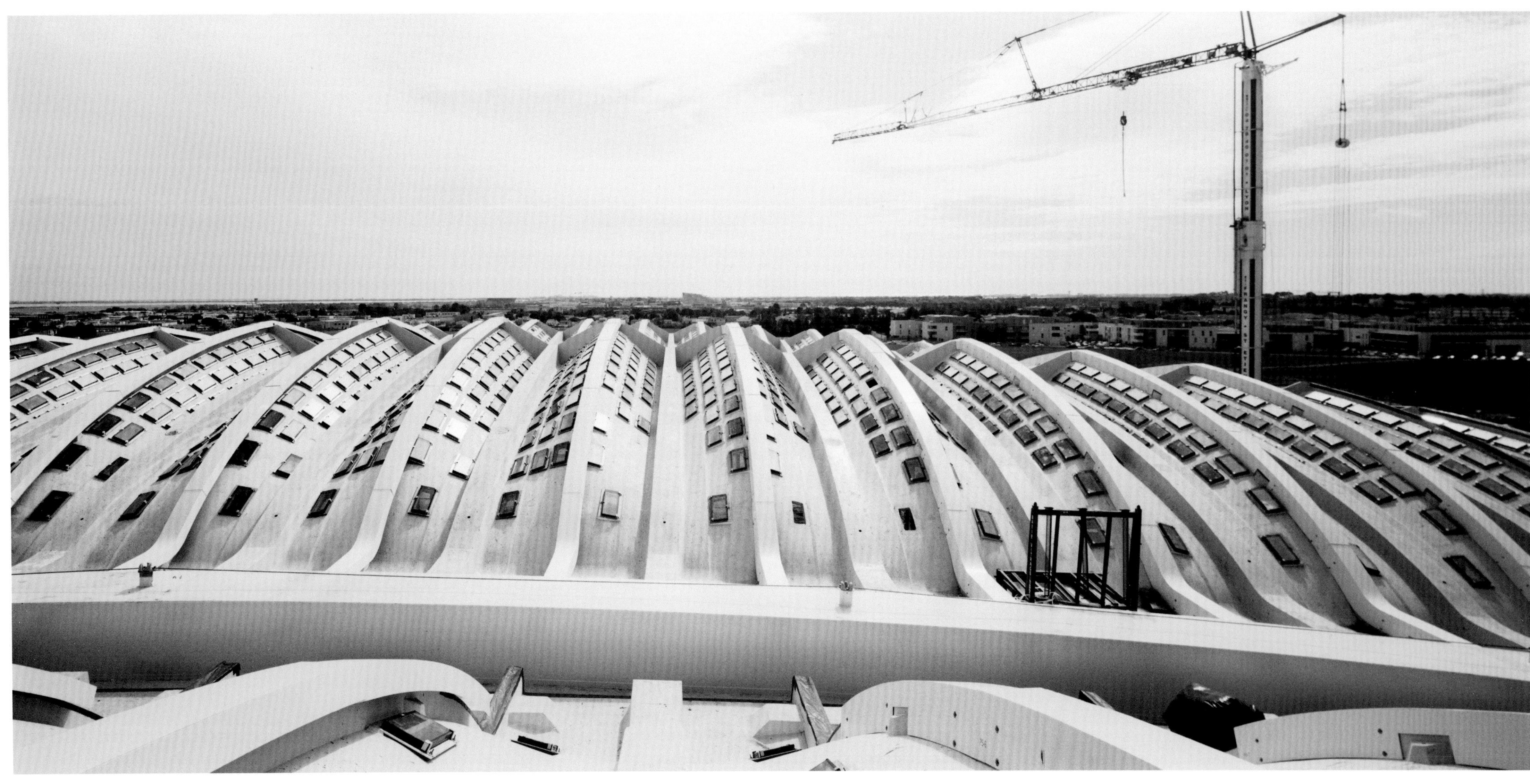

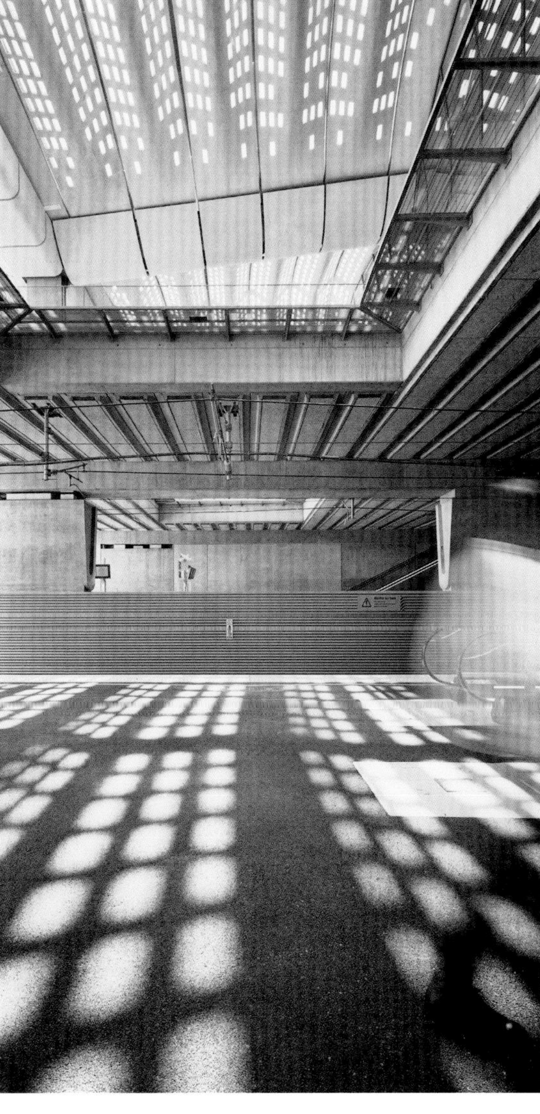

Montpellier Railway Station, Montpellier, France

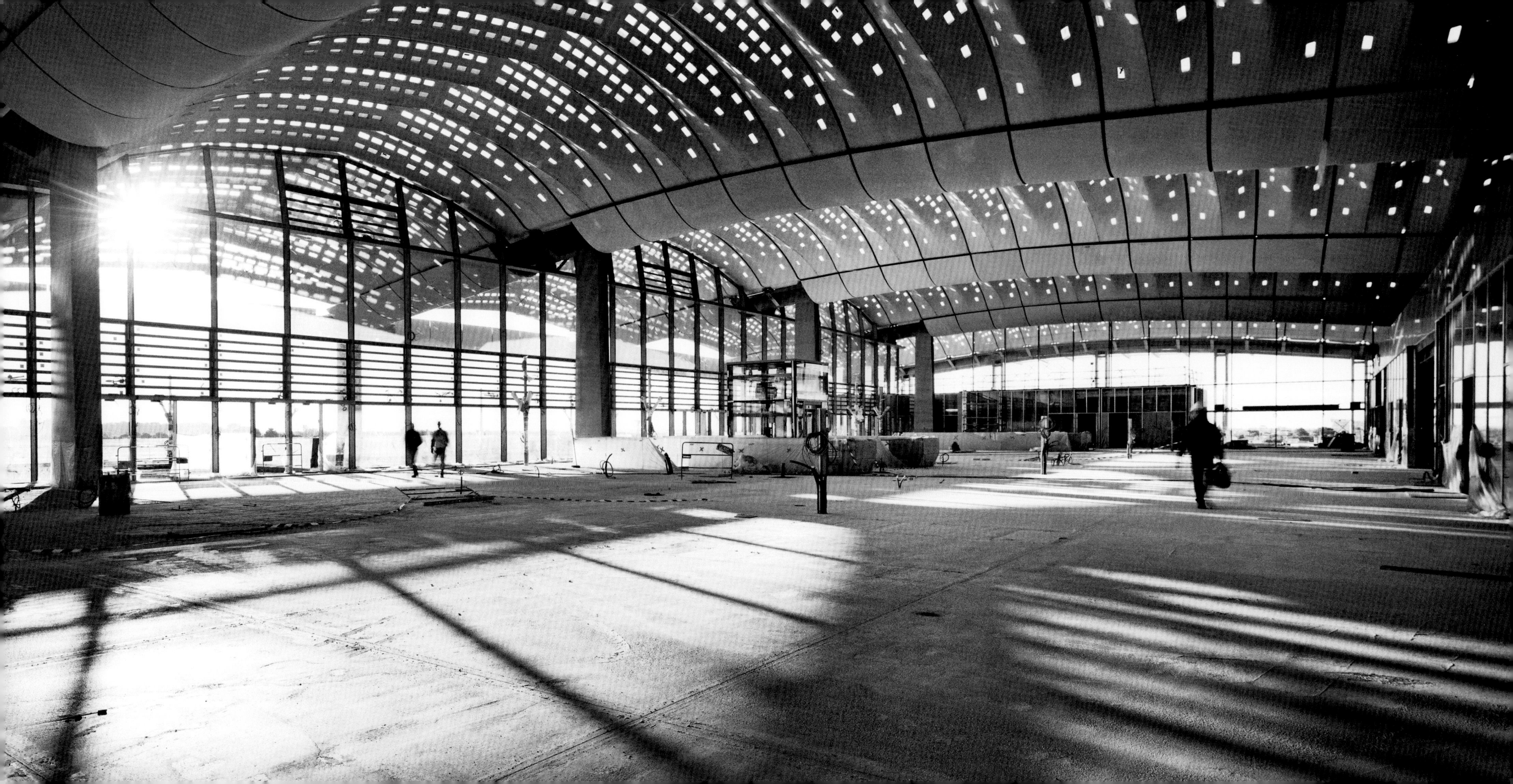

Amédée Saint-Germain Armagnac Bridge
Bordeaux, France

The new Amédée Saint-Germain Bridge is first and foremost designed to be an essential urban improvement for the regeneration of the Saint Jean Belcier district in Bordeaux.
The central feature of the project to open up Bordeaux's districts, the bridge can be understood as a tool in the dialogue with the infrastructure—the station, the train lines—that we prefer to see in a positive light as a service for the city where the railway lines flow like a river.
It presented a significant challenge, involving local attitudes to public spaces and decisions about the siting of the new development.
The project is above all a celebration of public spaces, achieved by the creation of a generous cantilevered walkway for pedestrians and bicycles, independent of and divided off from the section with lanes for motorized vehicles.
Regard for the quality of public space is a priority for the project. In collaboration with the station, Gare St. Jean, our aim is to design it so that it becomes part of a continuity of the public space, of the land, and of the zones to be improved.

A Unitary Project within an Urban Context

We made the structure's unity of design the main focus of our project, concentrating particularly on a continuous route with walkways for pedestrians. The result is an asymmetric structure with, on one side, a wide walkway and, on the other side, intended for vehicles, a narrow service sidewalk. We reflected this asymmetry of the lanes in the asymmetry of the deck of the whole. In seeking to address these requirements, the project's design falls into line with the pleasure of the place and the development of a multi-use public space.

A Light and Delicate Structure

The structure expresses both the transverse asymmetry of the structure in its functionality by highlighting the separation of pedestrian and cycle traffic and, longitudinally, the flow of forces in the continuity of the bridge over its two central piers.
In the center of the structure is an open space at the point where the forces are the lowest. With the distribution of moments on supports being maximum, we have created two superstructures made of curved arched frames above and box girders below. The two frames thus formed are filled with a diagonal mesh divided into compressed and tensioned bars.
Like eyes looking down on the river of train lines, these two structures represent a remarkable example of variable inertia.
The variable geometry of the curved superstructure gives an elegance of design to the bridge whether viewed from the public spaces or, in the distance, from the station.
The economy and frugality of materials are here the guarantee of an enduring attention to the development of this structure.
The new bridge is part of the public space it shapes, creating a notable fluidity. An urban landmark on different levels, its design is sensitive not only to the pedestrians who cross it, who live nearby and who value it, but also to its more distant appearance in the urban landscape that it has transformed.
The structure can be read explicitly, both in the geometry of its design and in its daily use.
Taking root in its urban context with its softly curved structure and continuous and slender silhouette, the bridge offers a new and welcome link.

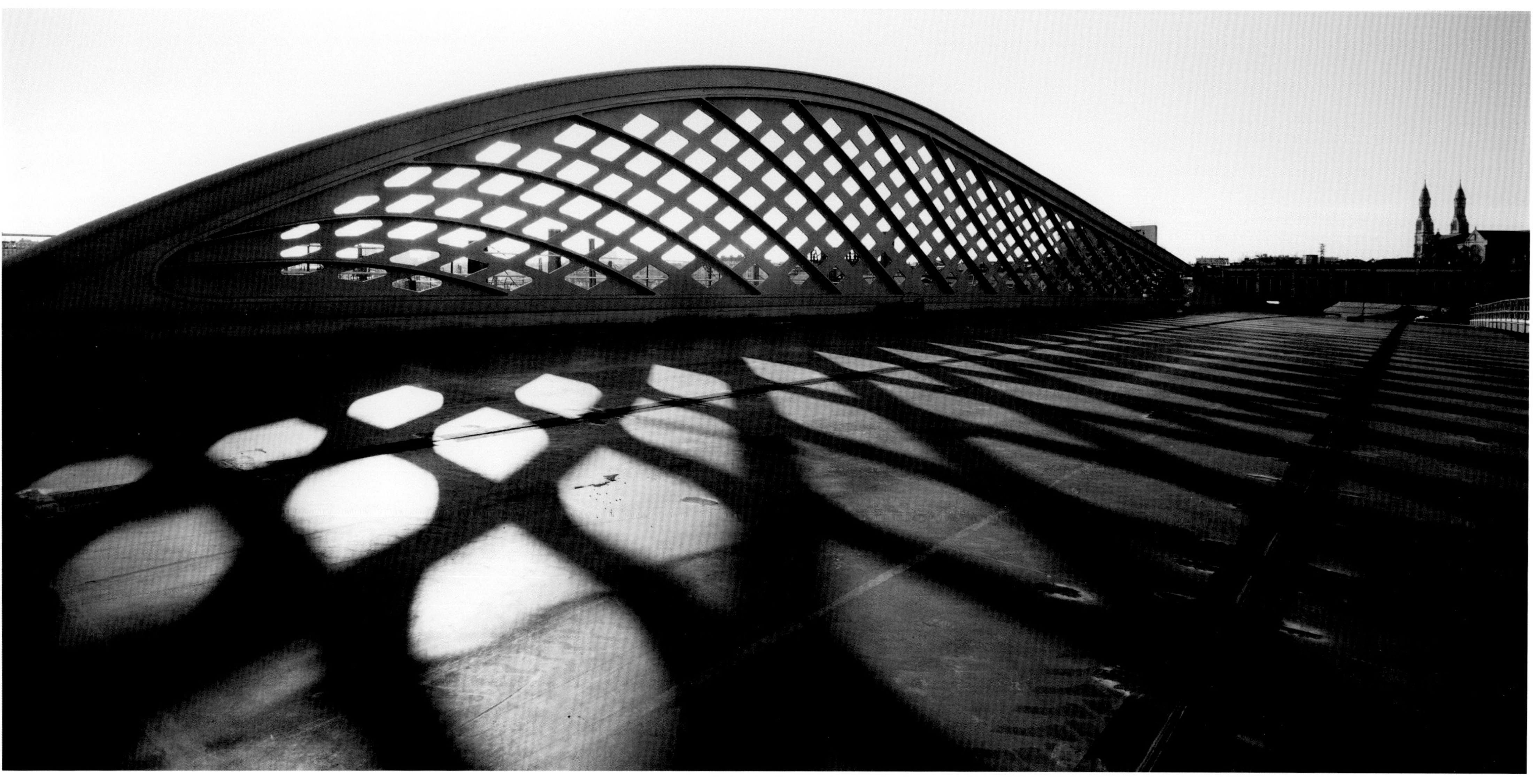

Amédée Saint-Germain Armagnac Bridge, Bordeaux, France

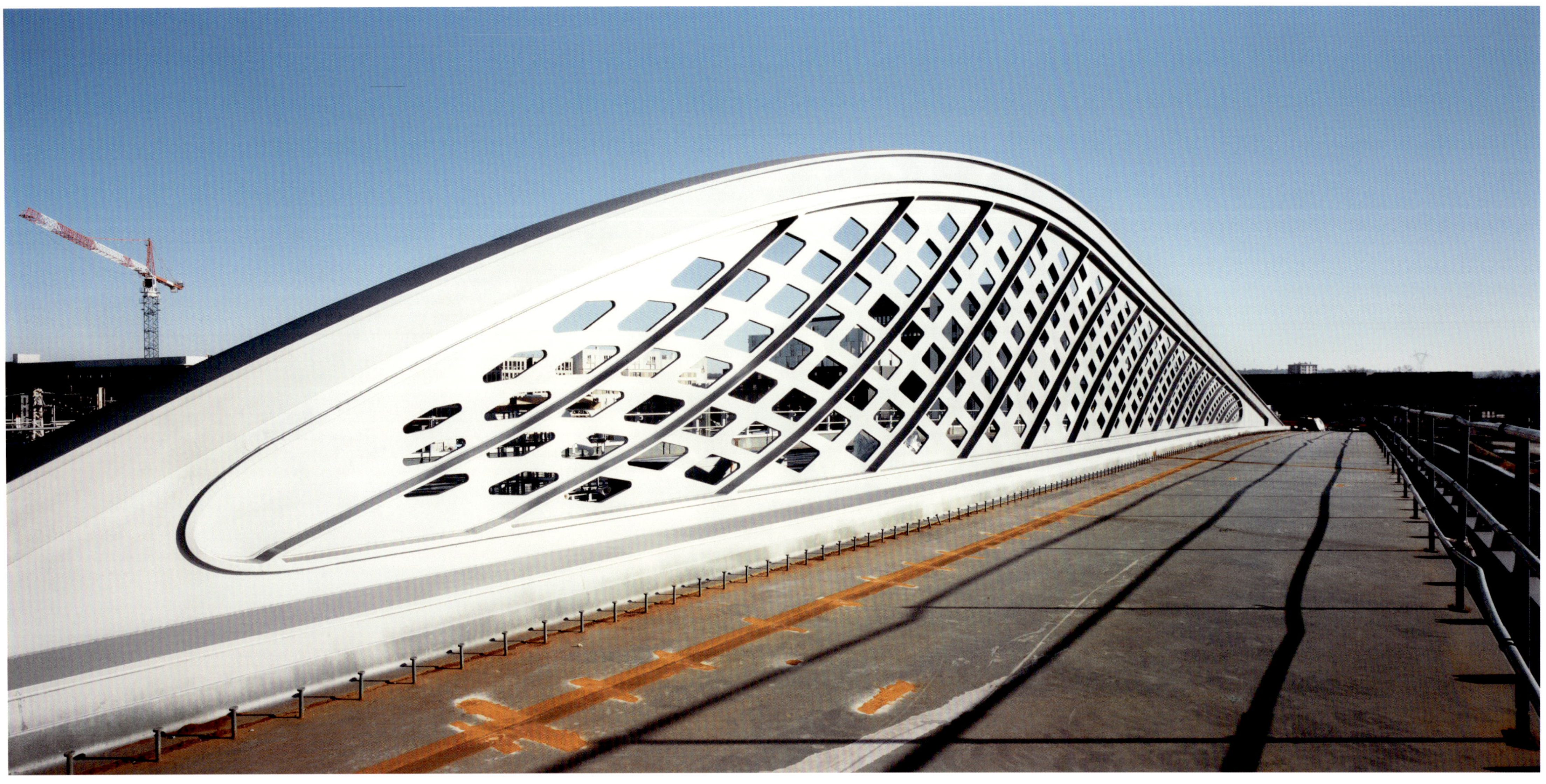

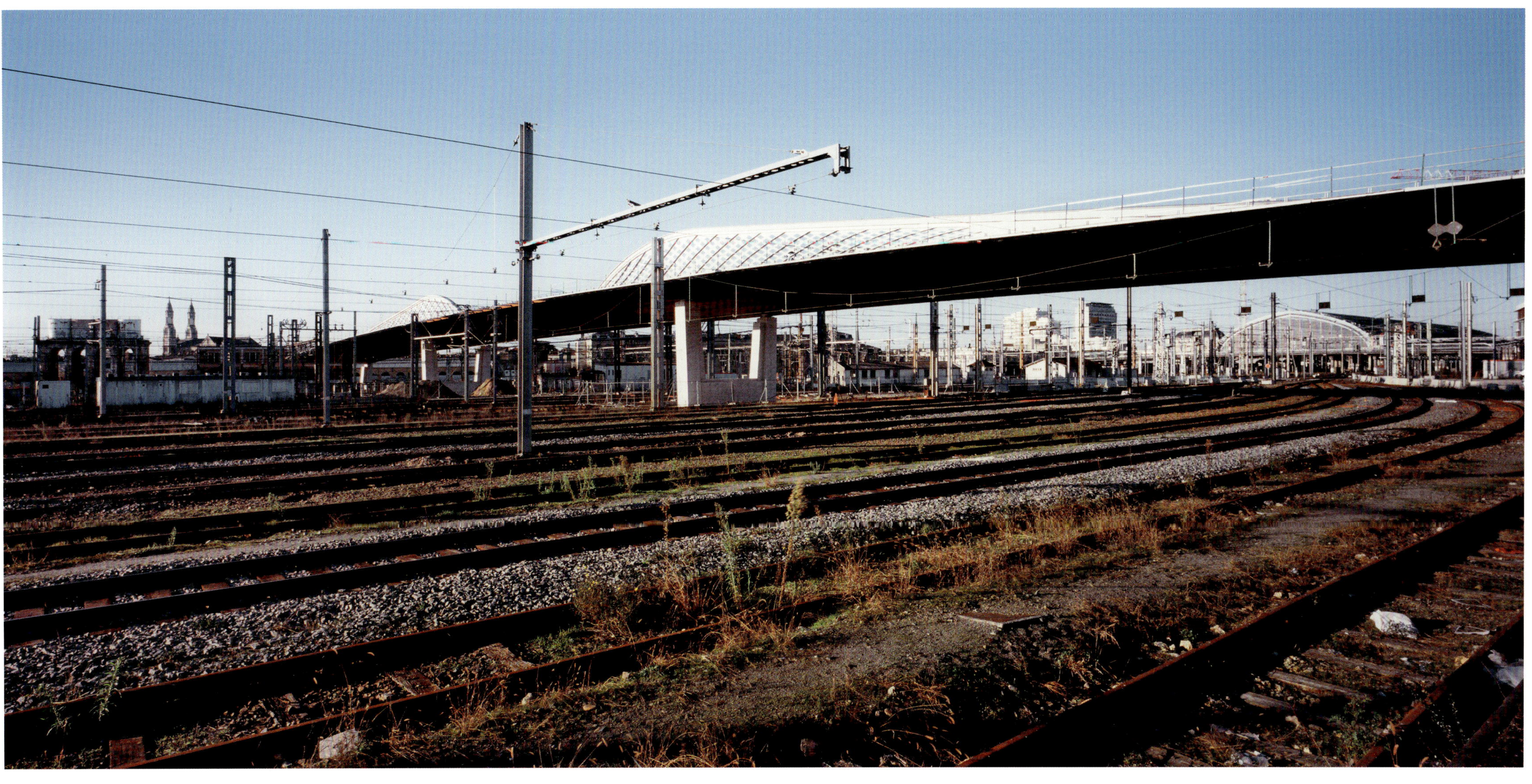

Amédée Saint-Germain Armagnac Bridge, Bordeaux, France

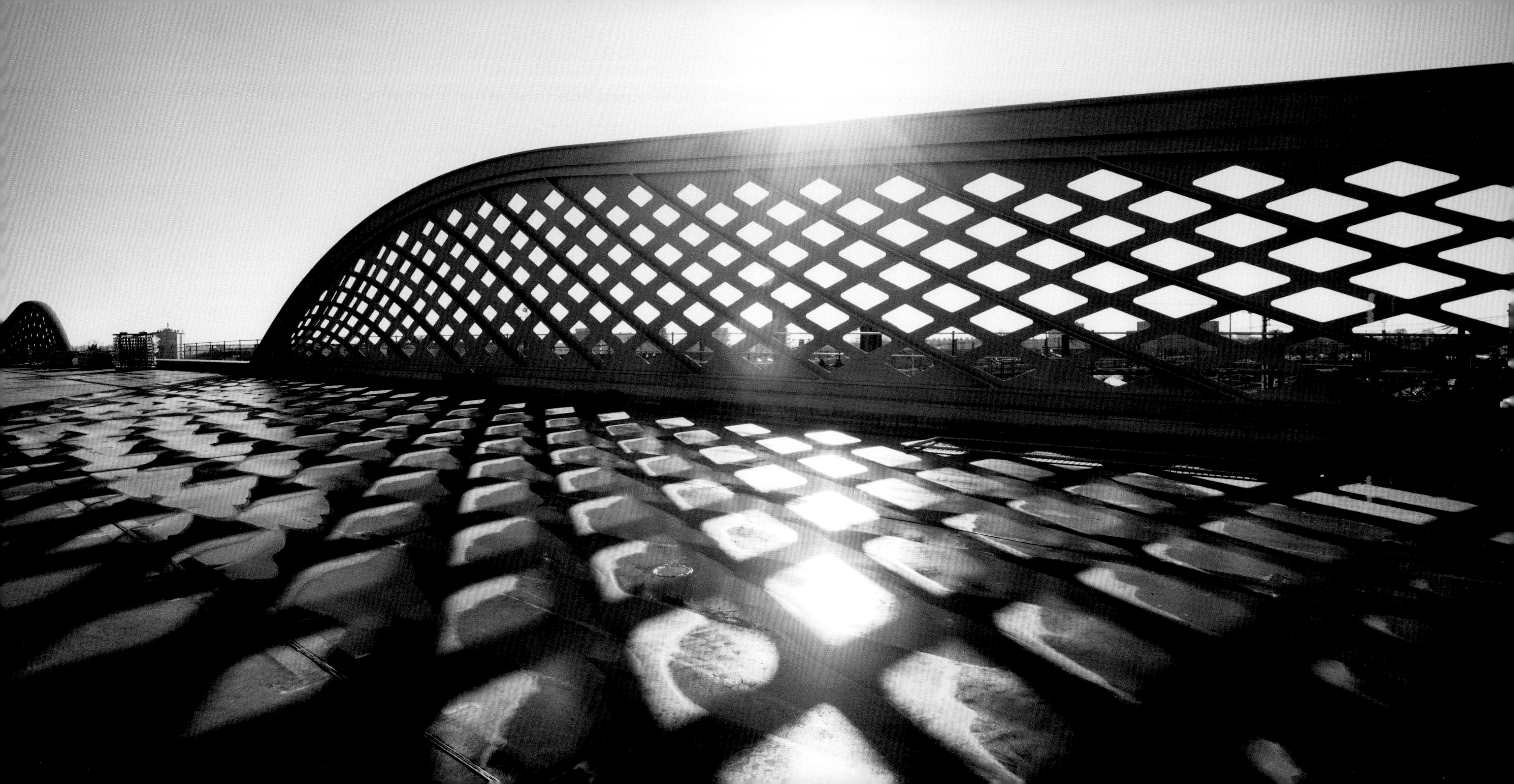

Airtime Building
Paris, France

Flowing like a river between the Avenue de France and Halle Freyssinet are the railway lines, now wider, now merging together.
Here, to the right of the Airtime building, the possible area without intermediate supports is fifty-eight meters. Everywhere else the buildings being erected over the railway network have been constructed on a thick platform, a table of concrete on which any collection of buildings conforming to the rules of urban development can be erected at random without planning ahead of time. Urban planners have abandoned the idea of the *tabula rasa* in favor of a *tabula nova*; a platform waiting to be developed. This approach is irrational and wasteful.
Our proposal reverses the question. Instead of installing an initial platform, we suggested suspending the platform forming the roof over the rails from the bridging building. This new approach changes the economic equation, allowing the cost of the invisible platform structure to be integrated with that of the superstructure of the building.
As designed, the building thus becomes a bridge-building resting on either side of the tracks which are fifty-eight meters apart, its 16,000 tons being suspended above the trains. The effect of this structural arrangement is liberating, making it possible to use gravitational stresses to our advantage. Since the stresses are concentrated in the floors forming the bridging structure, the other parts of the building are free. Suspended from or resting on the main structure, they can vary in thickness and embrace elements such as terraces, balconies, loggias or mezzanines—all different ways of expanding the working space depending on orientations and views.

The architecture gains in coherence and the structure itself is implied without drawing attention to itself. Tomorrow, the railway lines below will disappear along with the whole network beneath the new construction, but the extraordinary method used will continue to evoke their presence. The beams of the main bridging are concentrated in the floors with façades pierced with a pattern recalling the Vierendeel beams used. The terraces included on the suspended or supported floors are freely varied.
We decided on an approach that uses gravity in order to create a “stabilized equilibrium,” a suspended building. The bridging structure was not simply the result of the need to span a wide area. It was also a liberating element where the directions of the protruding main beams offer multiple aspects and arrangements. The structure here serves the dialogue between urban life and usage: it liberates the panorama and that brings about a variety of usages.
The suspended mass leads us to think about gravitational forces, but in a way that is more sensitive to the pleasures of the place and more generous in respect to the pleasure to be taken from being there. The offices open onto long terraces that extend the working areas in all directions over the city, near and far: benches, plants, and electric sockets will open up the office spaces, too often isolated from the rest of life, making them more homely and more empathetic.
This building is not standard, nor should life at work be standard. In the transparency of the inner courtyard, the suspended spaces float above a garden, the trains passing invisibly below.

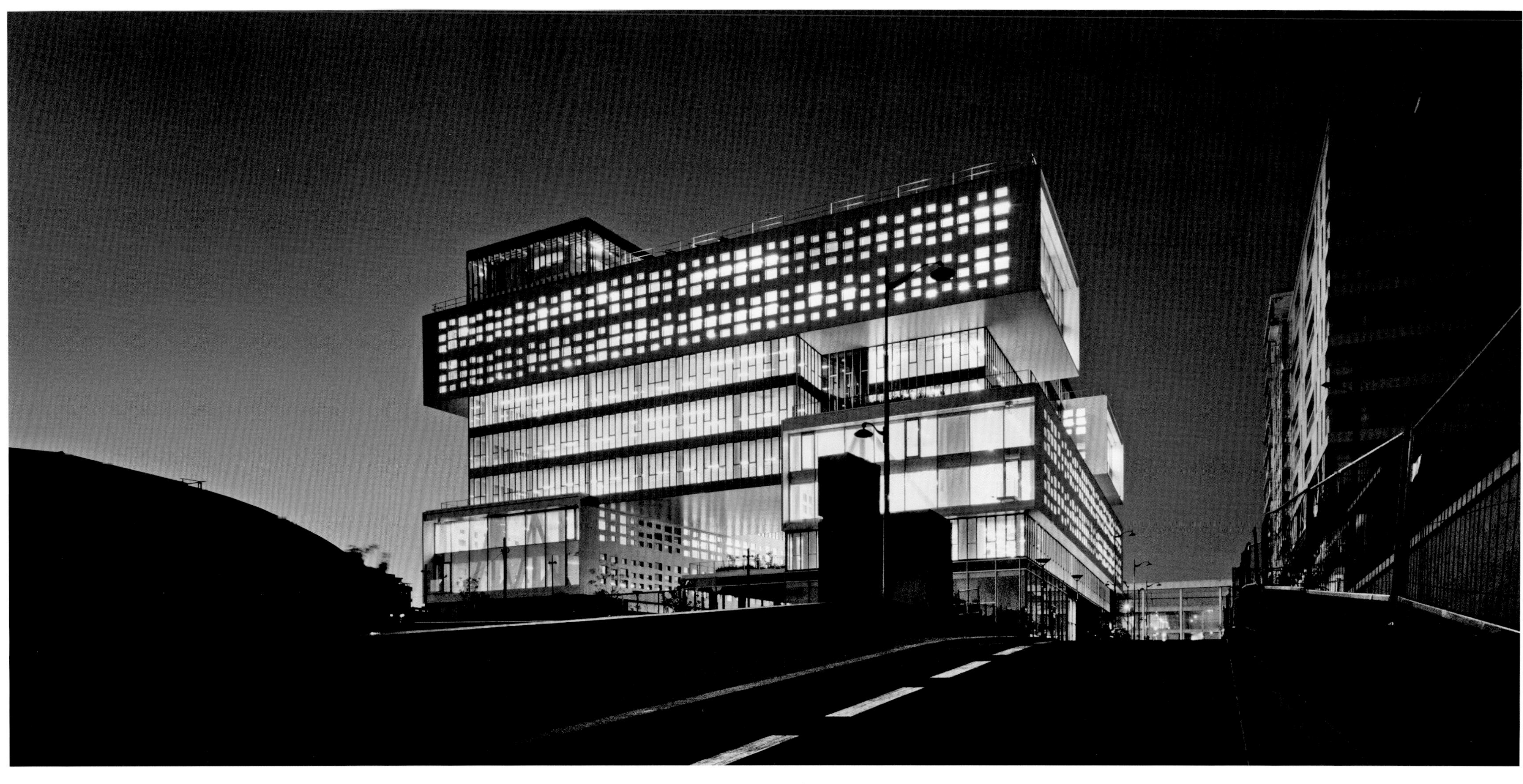

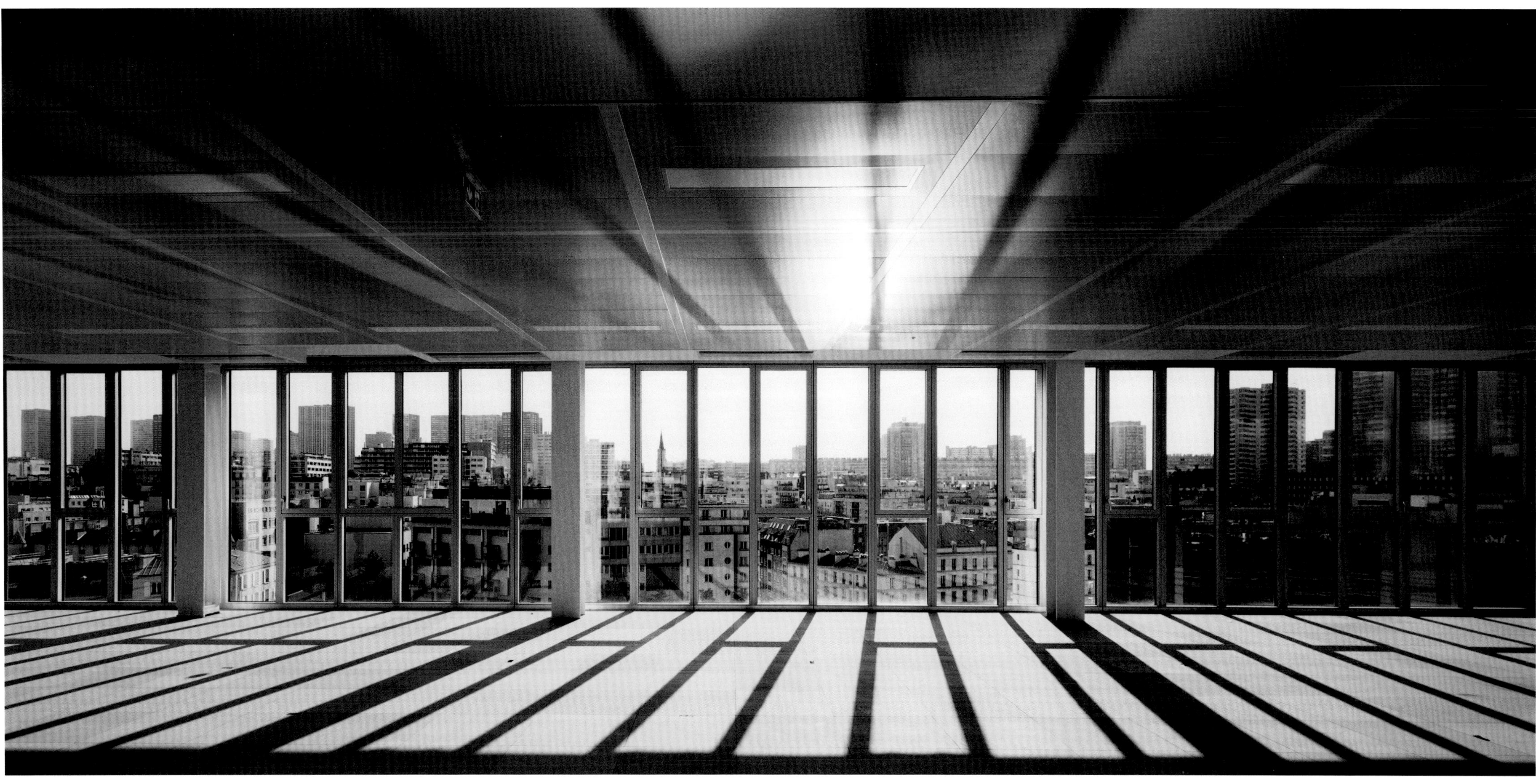

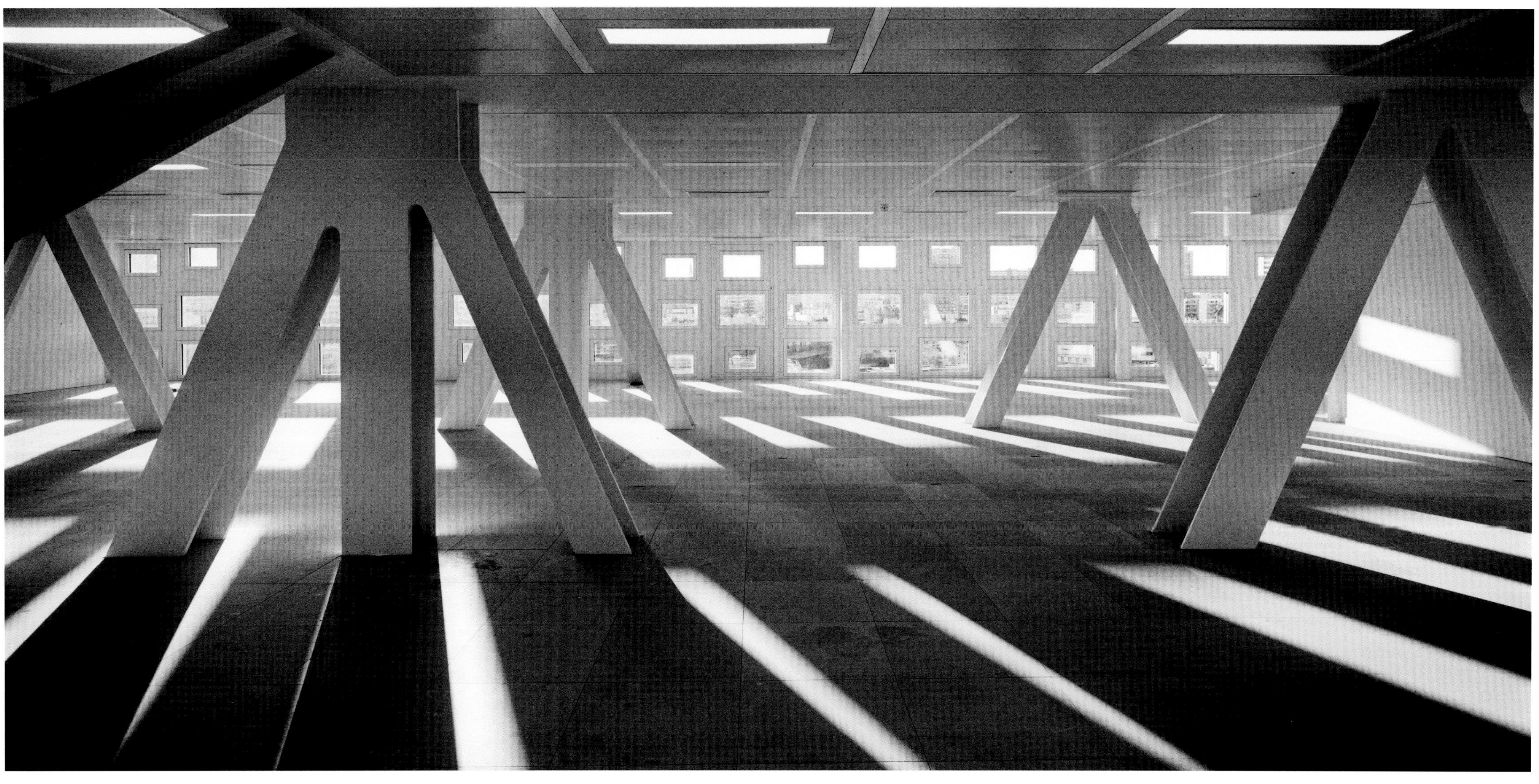

Airtime Building, Paris, France

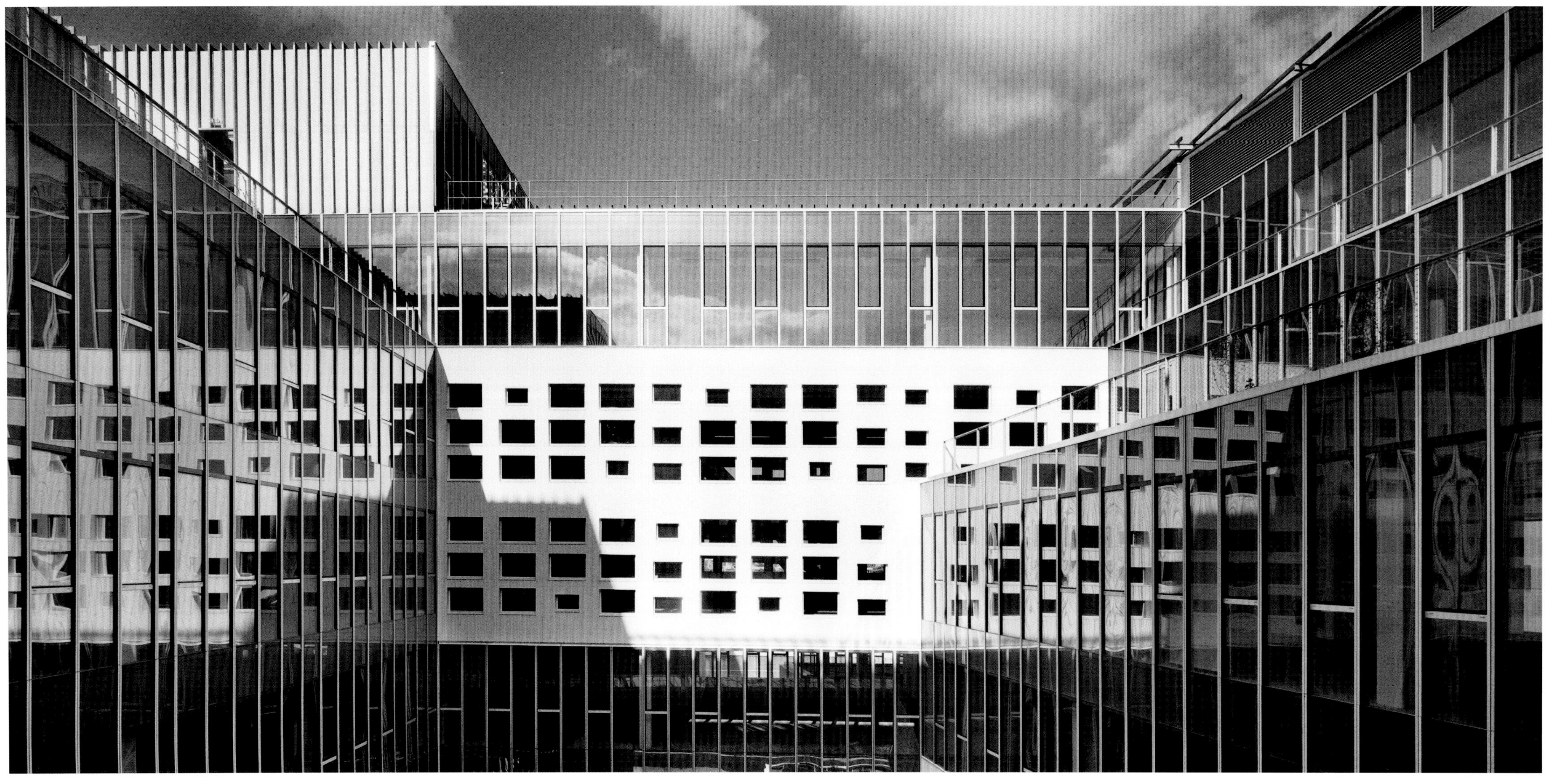

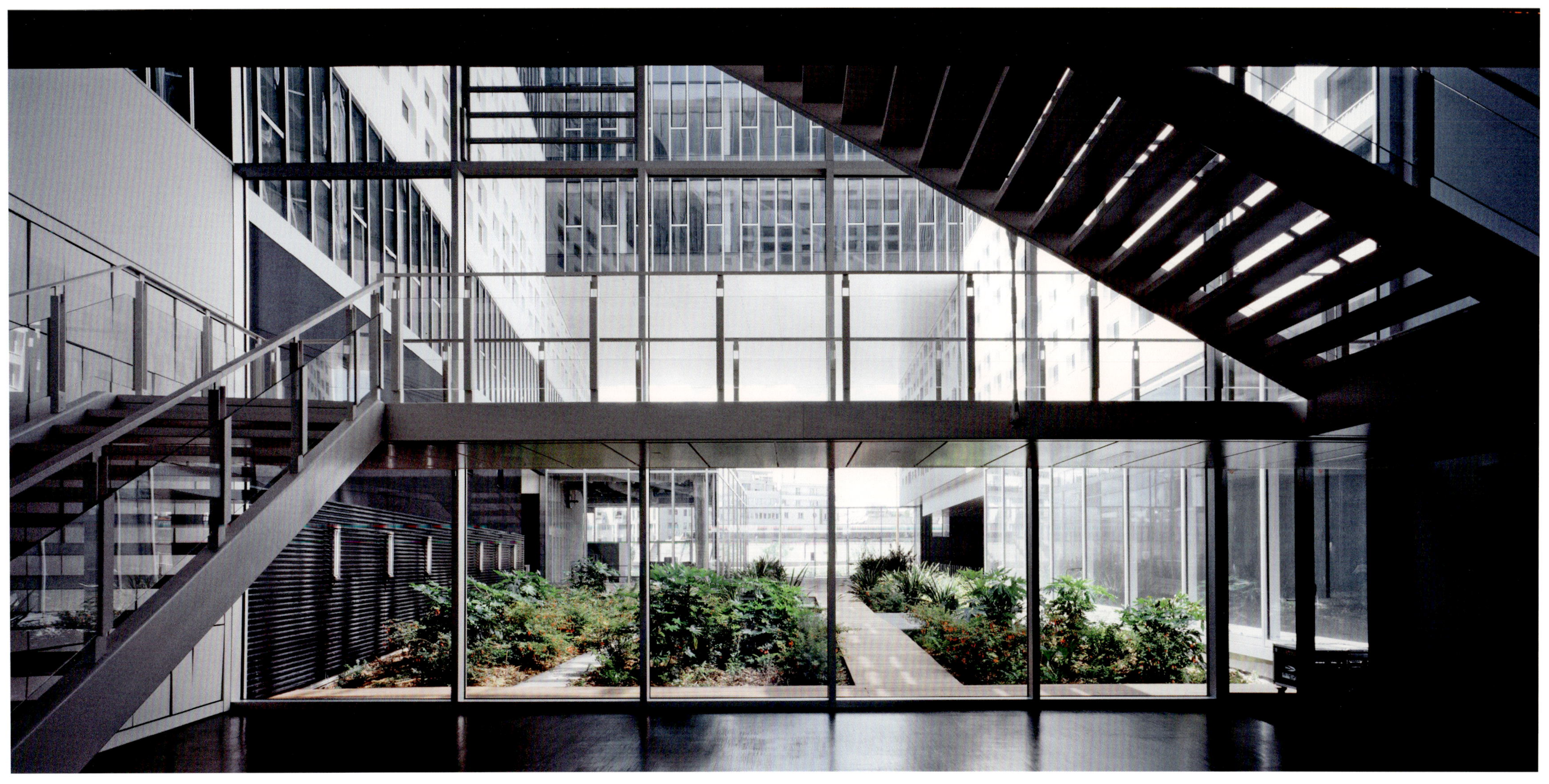

Airtime Building, Paris, France

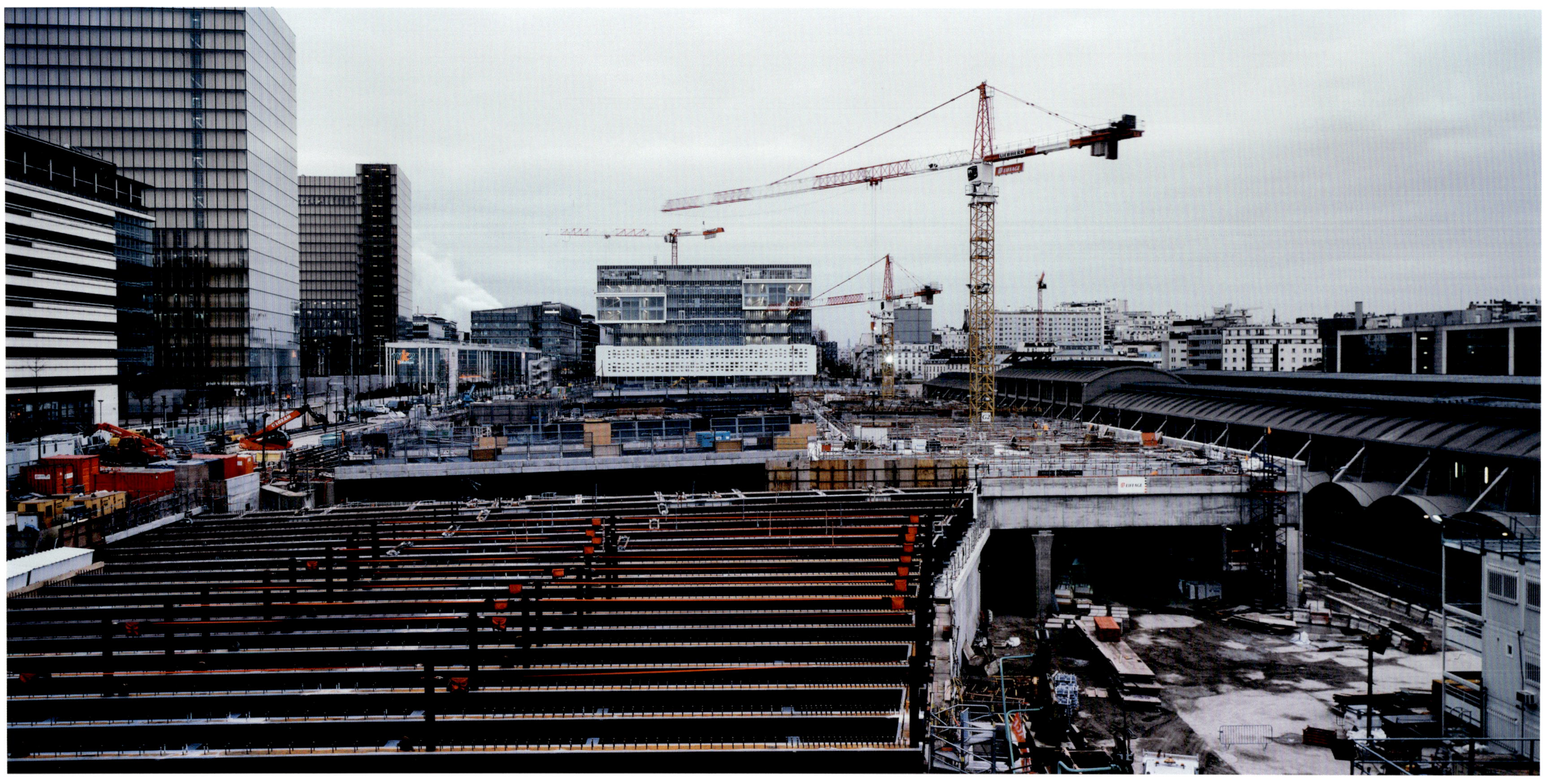

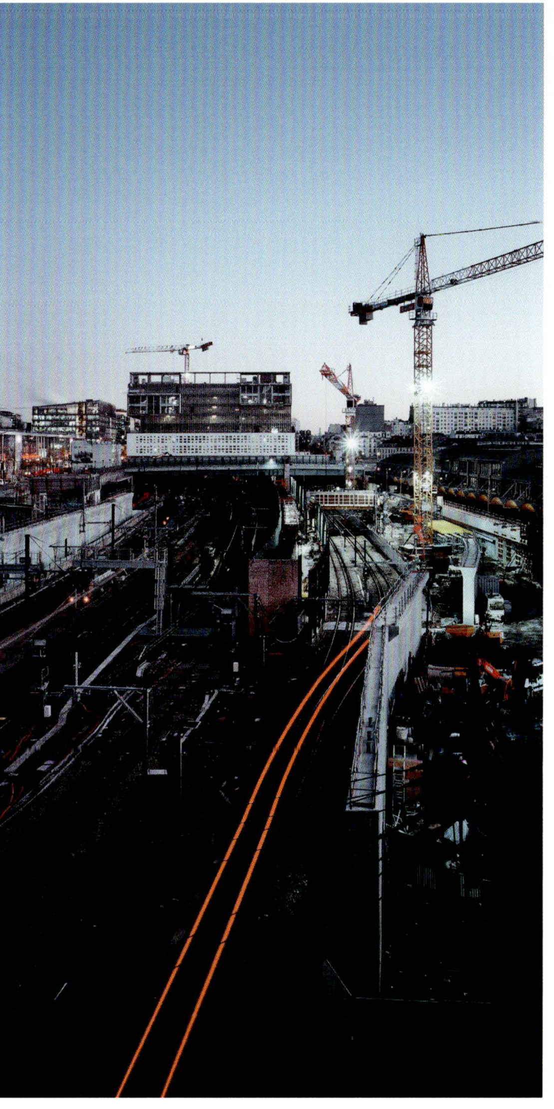

Airtime Building, Paris, France

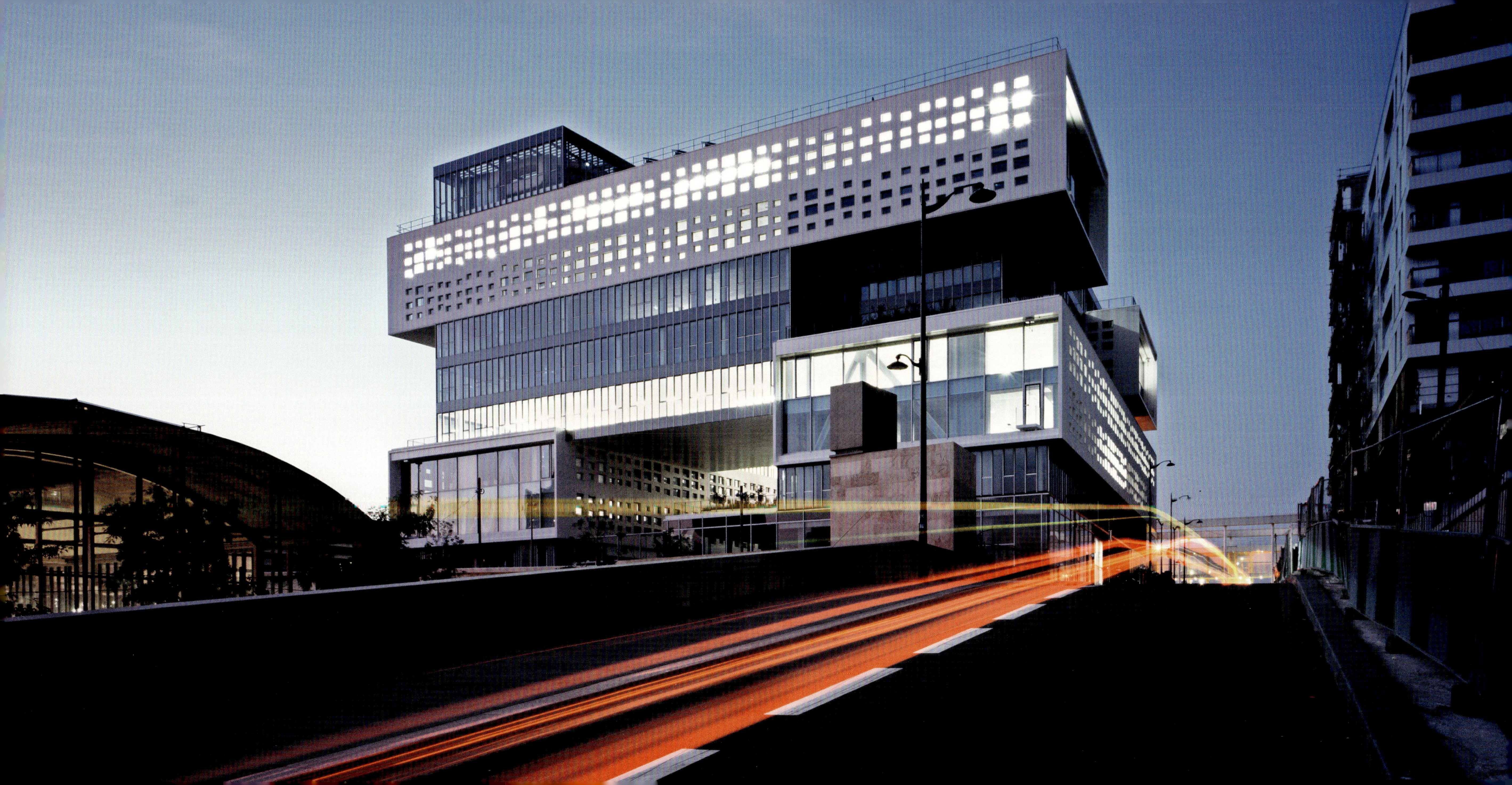

Strasbourg School of Architecture
Strasbourg, France

A School in the City

The new school of architecture in Strasbourg is in the heart of the city. Although not the only example, nevertheless the deliberate choice of site for an architecture school means that a unique dialogue is established between the city and the teaching of architecture: our project represents this dialogue.
The project consists of two buildings. One is old and was converted from a 1930s garage; the other is new and is called the Moll Building. This building is inspired by the idea of openness. The ground floor consists of a public space, becoming a huge vertical hall with four levels, allowing easy access between the different disciplines involved in the study of architecture.
In order to achieve this the building is raised as if balanced on stiletto heels so as to free the spaces from limiting structures and throw them open to the city.
In its volumes the building is able to maximize what is allowable to the greatest extent: while abiding by the limitations of urban legislation—respecting alignments, observing dimensions, and following the recommended attic standards—it offers the maximum constructed volume.
Here, the design takes advantage of the constraints to create three building elements, each of two stories, placed one on top of another, opening up spaces for communal activities looking out over the city.
These three units, required by building regulations to be divided up, thus form three constructed units structurally superimposed on one another in an apparent stabilized balance, unified by a single envelope that changes in appearance according to position or the movement of light.
This structural envelope, rigid and with a high amount of inertia, means that the teaching rooms can do without load-bearing points, exposing the connection between support and surface, making the void in the structural envelope habitable.

The management of the relationship to the exterior, the view, the city, and the light is of the greatest importance. From the interior, the views, depending on the use of each room, seem to extend the spaces over the city, providing ample accessible terraces. Having thus opened itself up to the city, the building's load-bearing structure simply arranges itself according to the requirements of gravity, exploiting the effect of the large pierced cladding sheets that give unity to the appearance of the structure.
The metal and glass envelope unifies the whole without concealing the true construction of the building. The distribution of load frees up the transparent ground floor that opens up towards the city. The care with which the building is designed is not intended as a lesson for students, but rather as a rational expression of the potential offered by the interplay of materials and structure.

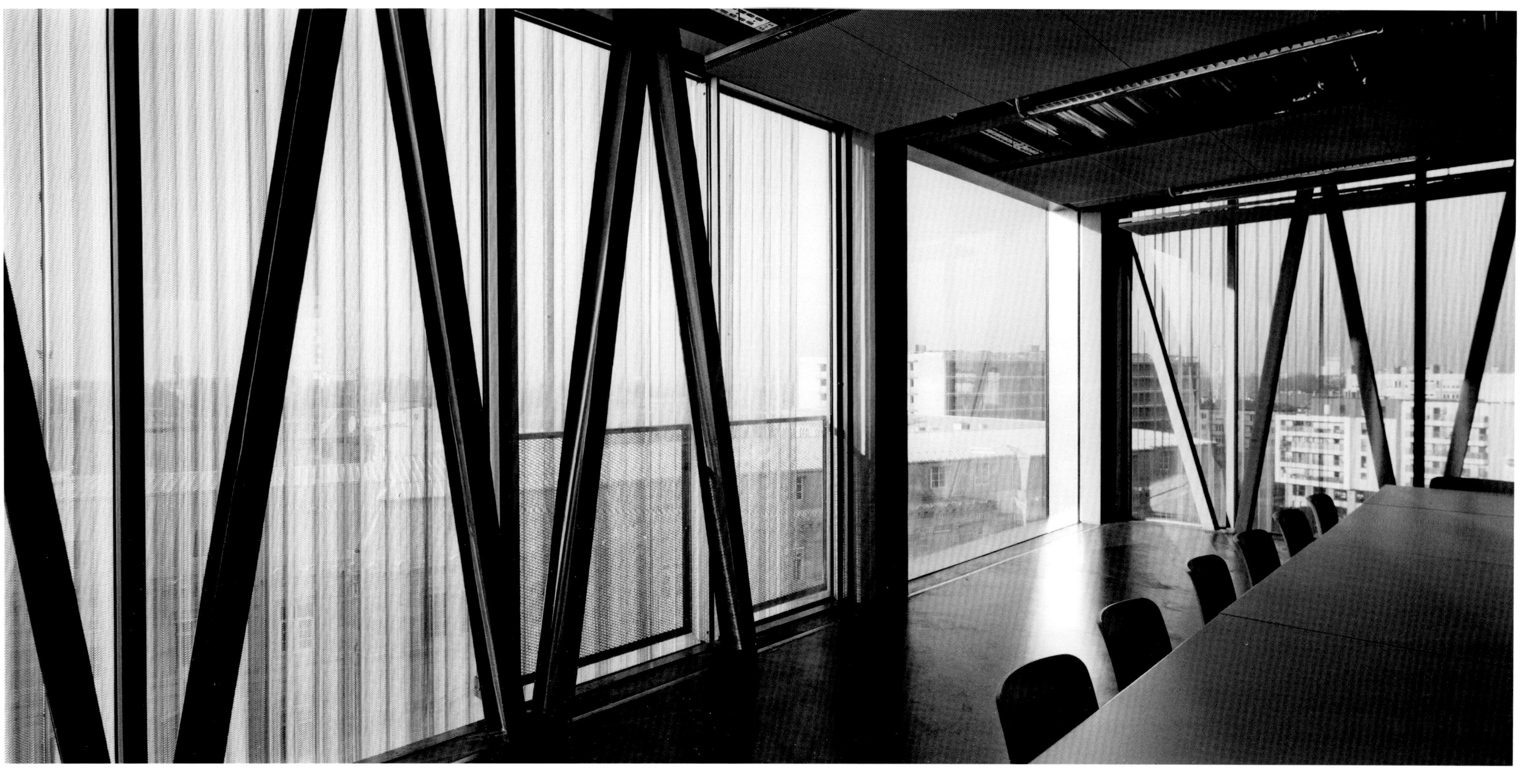

The load-bearing façade consists of a framework of varied steel struts constructed according to the stress passing through them while at the same time opening up broad bays over the city: a building that is both visible and instructive.
Forming an external skin, a metal curtain allows light to filter through to the interior. At nighttime, like a stage curtain, the light flows in the opposite direction, revealing the weight-bearing structure in all its variety.
Counterpoising material with structure, pedagogy with urban life, the two buildings, linked by a delicate footbridge, suspended by its upper beam, stand as representatives of the dialogue between the contemporary and the historic.

In the City: Permanence / Modernity

The new school of architecture finds its logic in the links it forms between the city, education, and the material world.

It seeks to express belonging and sharing.

The buildings belong to the city whose history they continue through the constructed stratification of buildings placed together for the purpose of teaching and learning. They are open, ready to discuss architecture not only with students, but also with the inhabitants of Strasbourg.

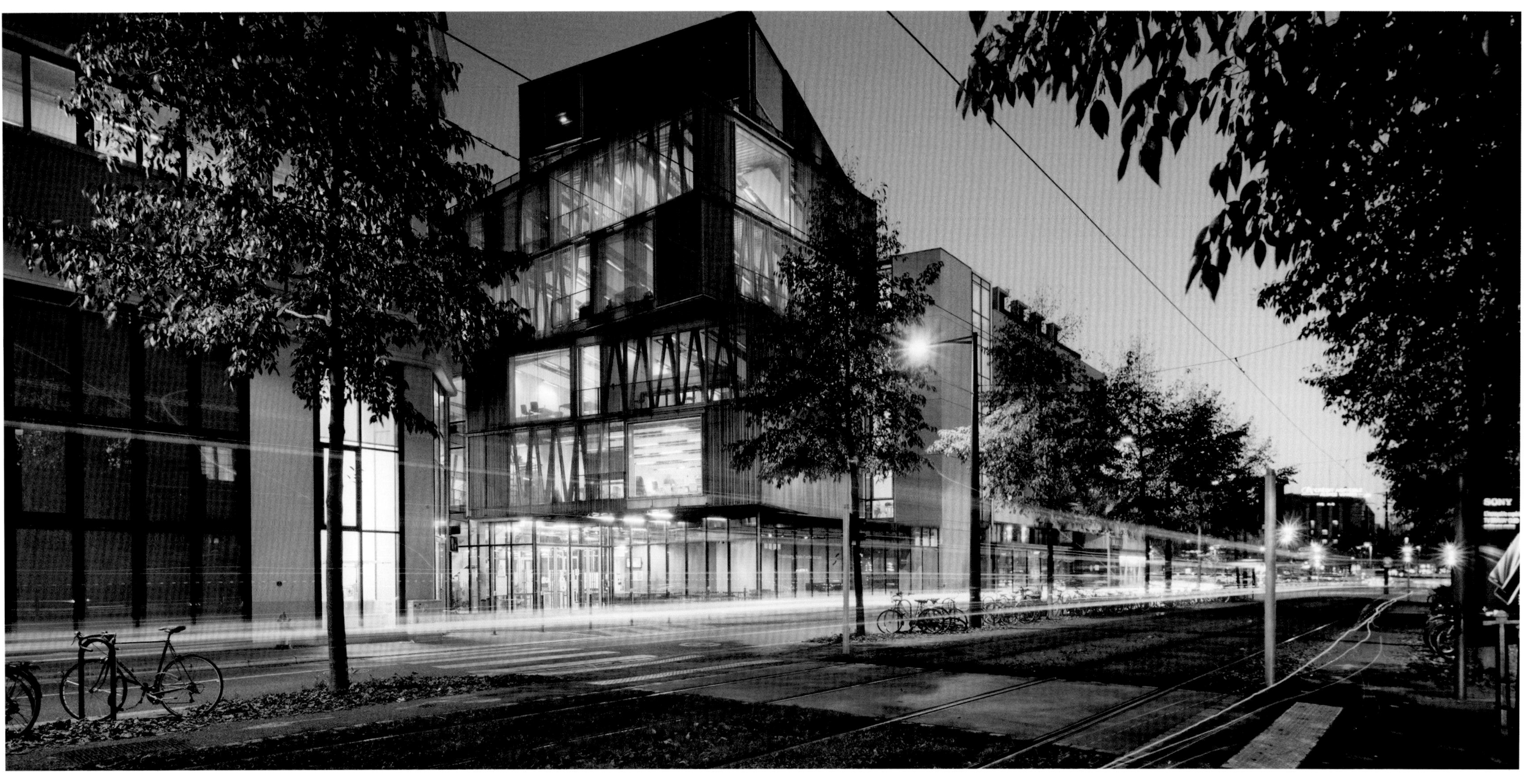

Roland-Garros: The Simonne-Mathieu Court,
The New Greenhouses Court
Paris, France

When the landscape designer Michel Corajoud put forward his plan for improvements to the Roland-Garros site for the international tennis tournament, his intention was to open it up, creating a link with the city. This necessitated opening up an extensive public space and the construction of a new court accommodating 5,000 visitors in the adjacent garden where not long before some poorly constructed greenhouses had been added. The garden is notable not for these greenhouses, but rather for its fine botanical hothouses designed in 1898 by Jean-Camille Formigé, and which were naturally never under threat.

Taking its inspiration from these hothouses made of glass and cast iron so characteristic of the nineteenth century, the new tennis court will be partly below ground level, surrounded by a terraced concrete platform, surmounted by a steel structure, and wrapped with botanical greenhouses designed to meet the highest technical specifications.

These new greenhouses form a glass backdrop, a case within which plants from four continents can flourish. They refer to the design of the nearby hothouses and are inspired by, without imitating, steel architecture that, since the construction of the Crystal Palace in London in 1851, still inspires with its delicate relationship between light and structure, as the perfect model of airiness and economy.

It was necessary to provide double-glazing and much more effective insulation than that of the poorly constructed greenhouses they referenced. Rather than creating a simple surface of smooth glass the design makes use of fragmented scales of glass, their edges arranged in two different directions. In this way the skin of the construction changes as the light alters as a result of diffraction, and vibrations are set up by the reflections on the irregular, broken up surfaces. The steel of the glasshouses gives rhythm to the whole, echoing the balanced structure of the terraces that rise up to the gallery running around the top of the building.

The play of light, shadows, and transparency on the structure continues the characteristic effects of nineteenth-century architecture while at the same time integrating contemporary techniques in oxy-fuel cutting and welding.

Just as Michel Corajoud wished, a dialogue between gardens and sport, botany and tennis, technical and physical performance has emerged from a shared space.
The presence of structures from the past in no way inhibits this confident contemporary architecture—quite the contrary. The different activities intersect in time; the tennis tournament is an integral part of the development of the botanical garden. The Simonne-Mathieu Court is a good illustration, if one were needed, of the need for the pleasures of urban life to adapt to an ever-increasing combination of different uses.

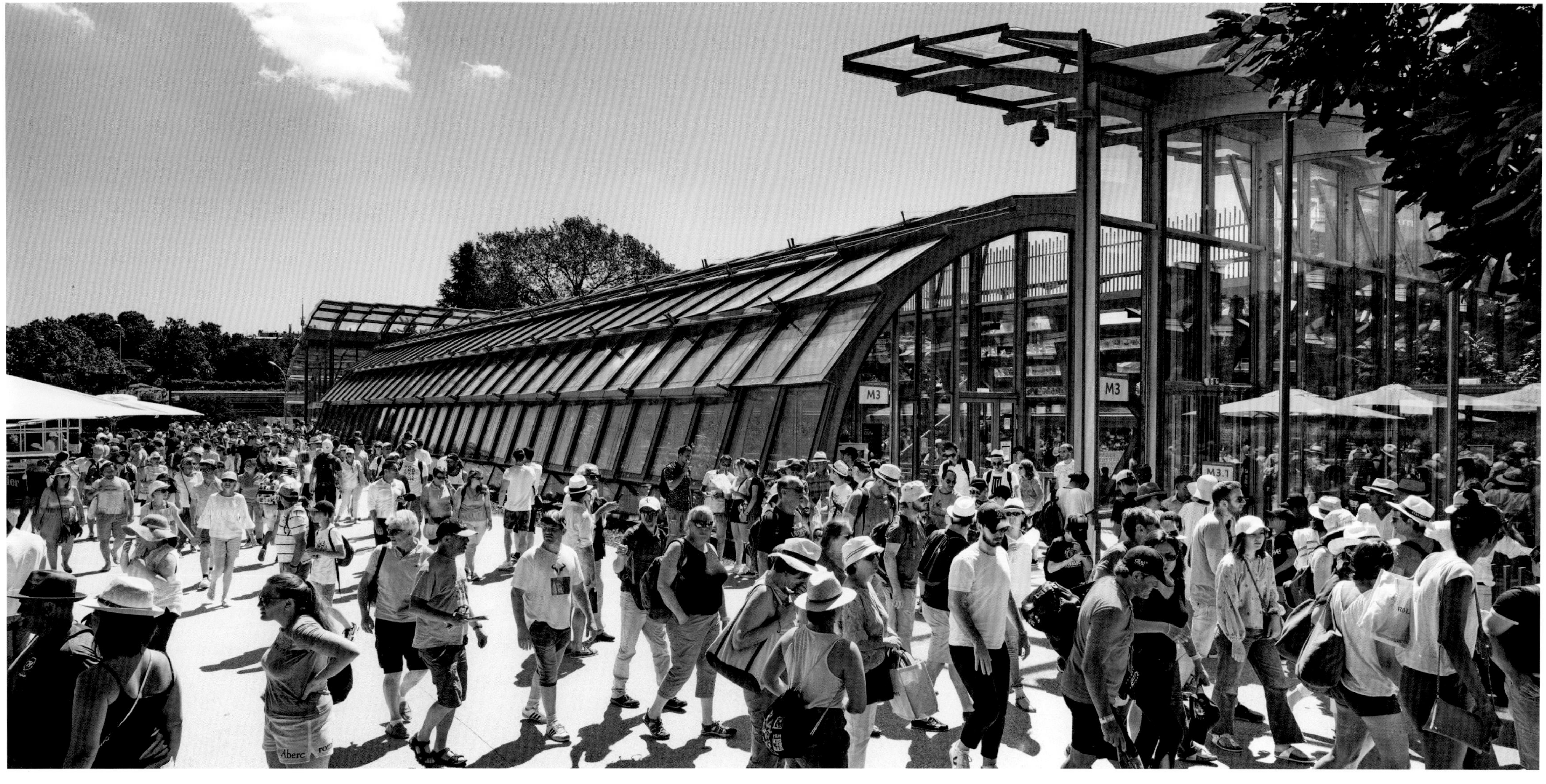
M3
M3
M3.1

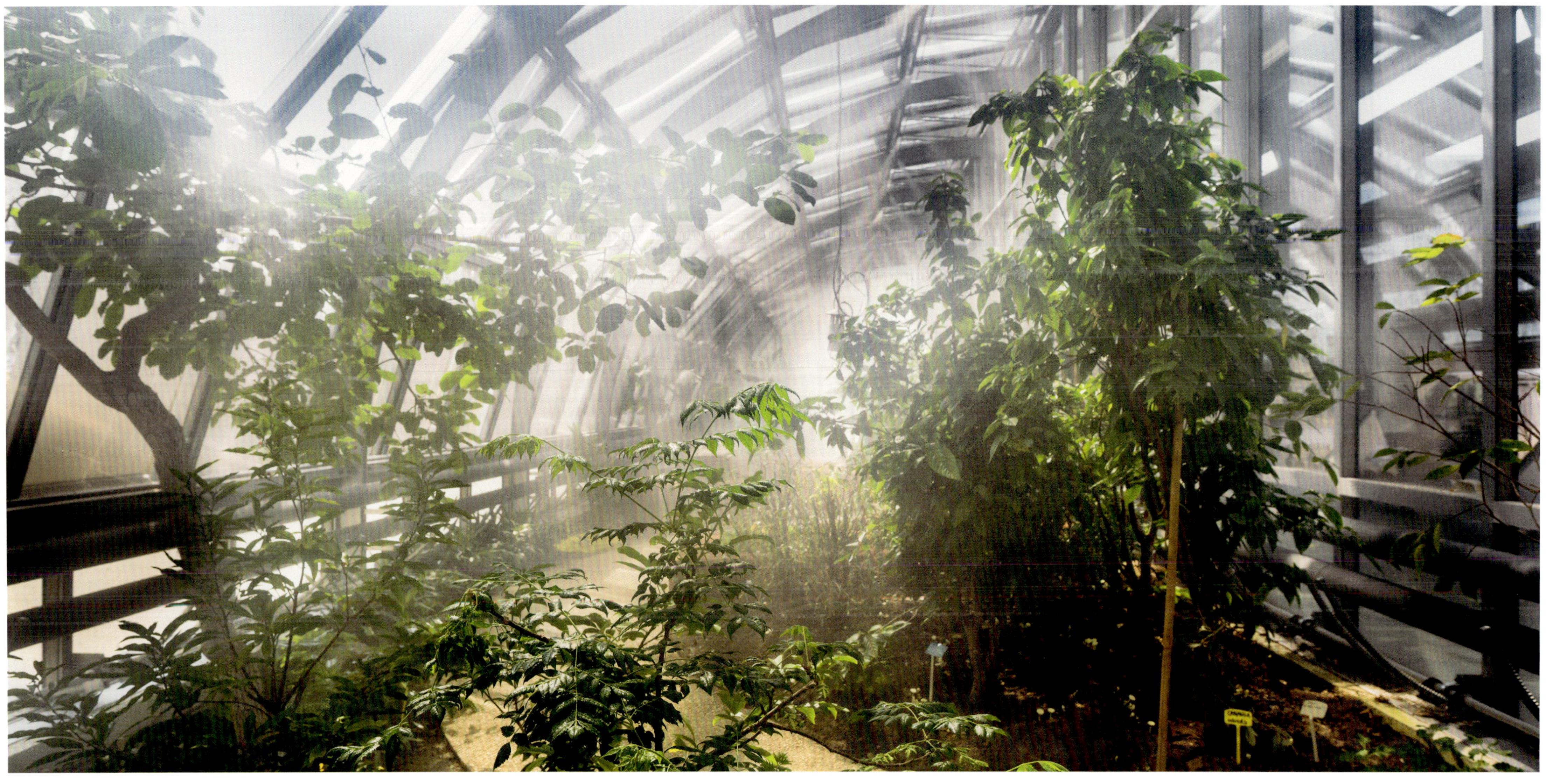

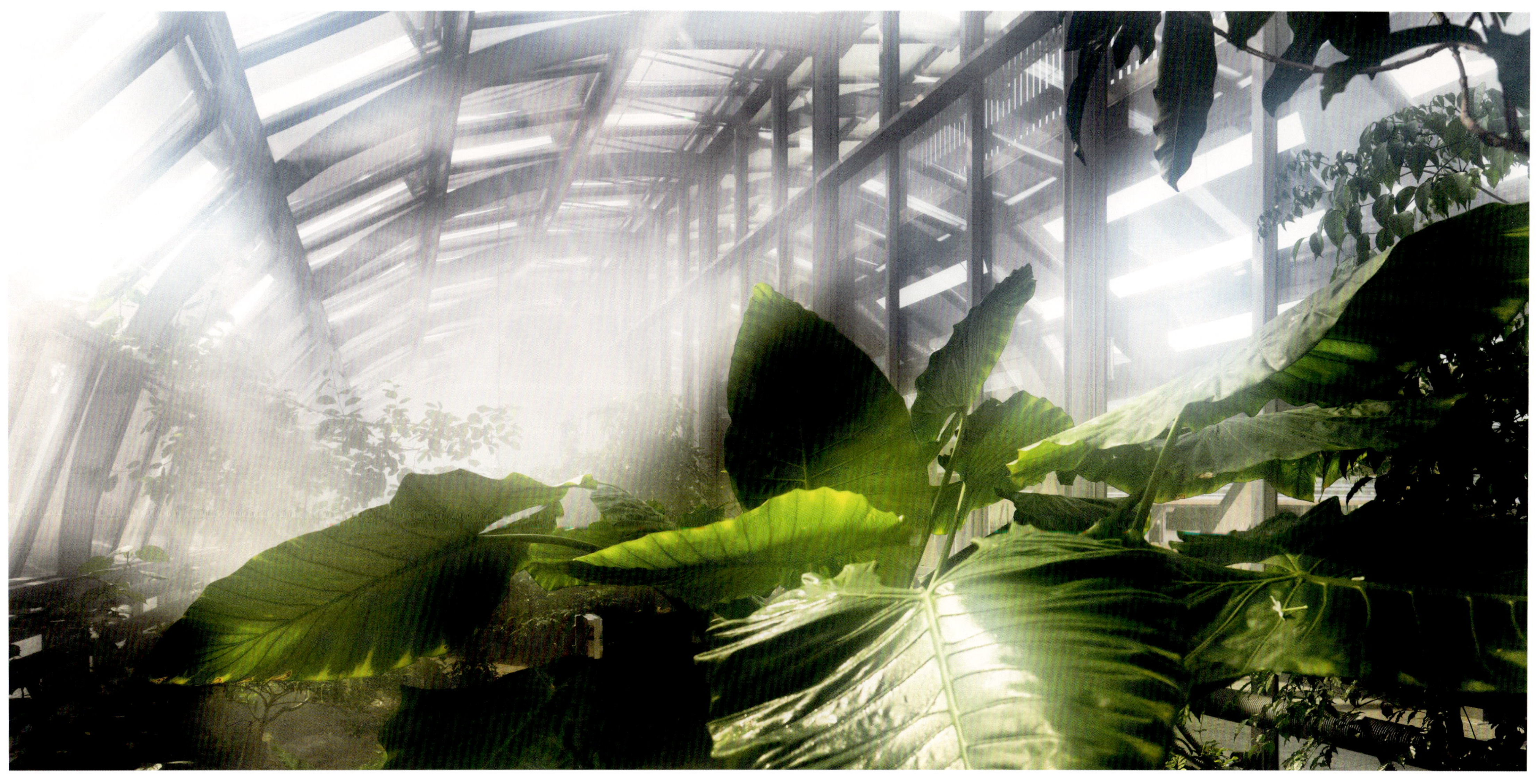

Roland-Garros: Simonne-Mathieu Court, Paris, France

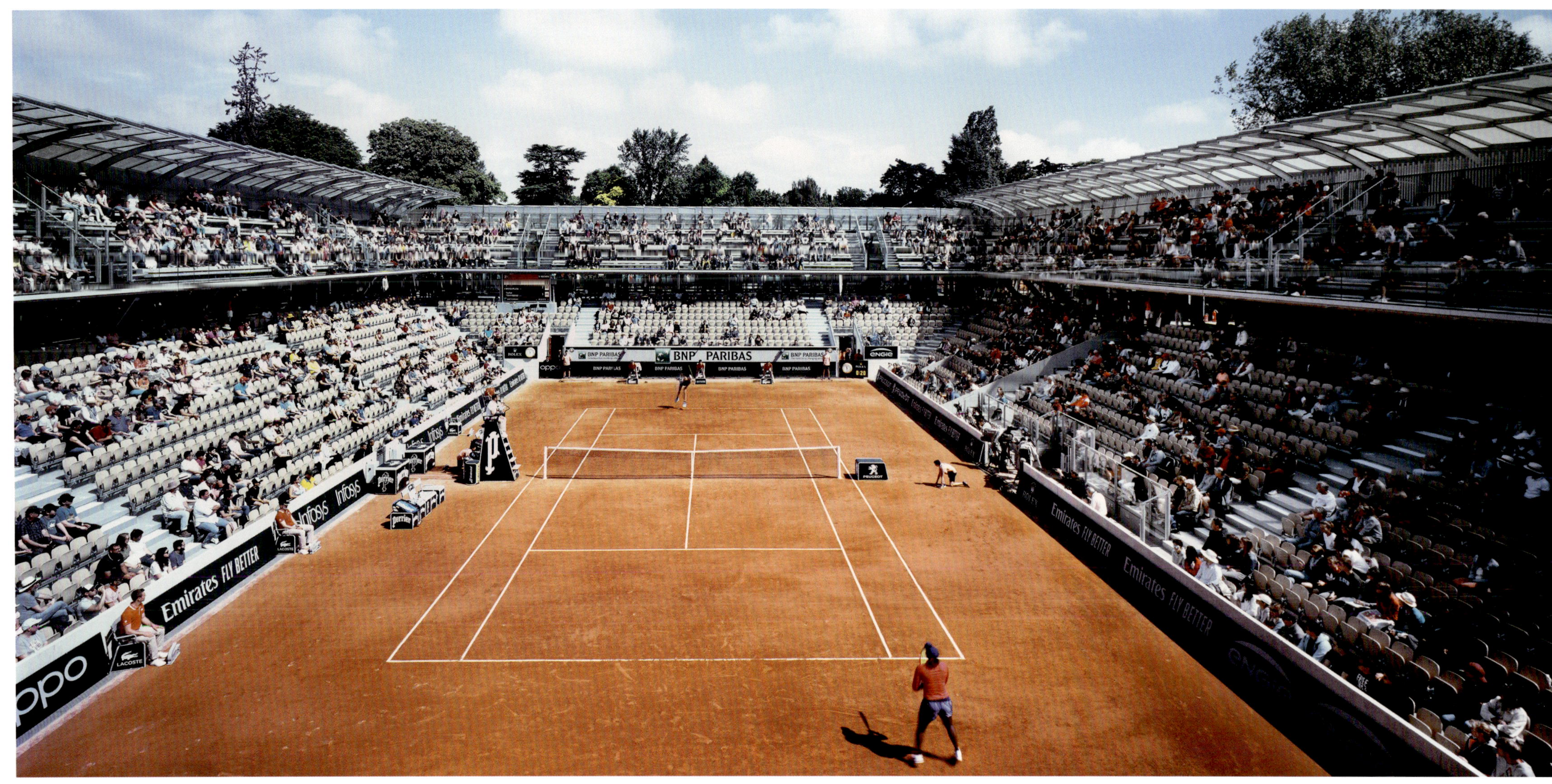

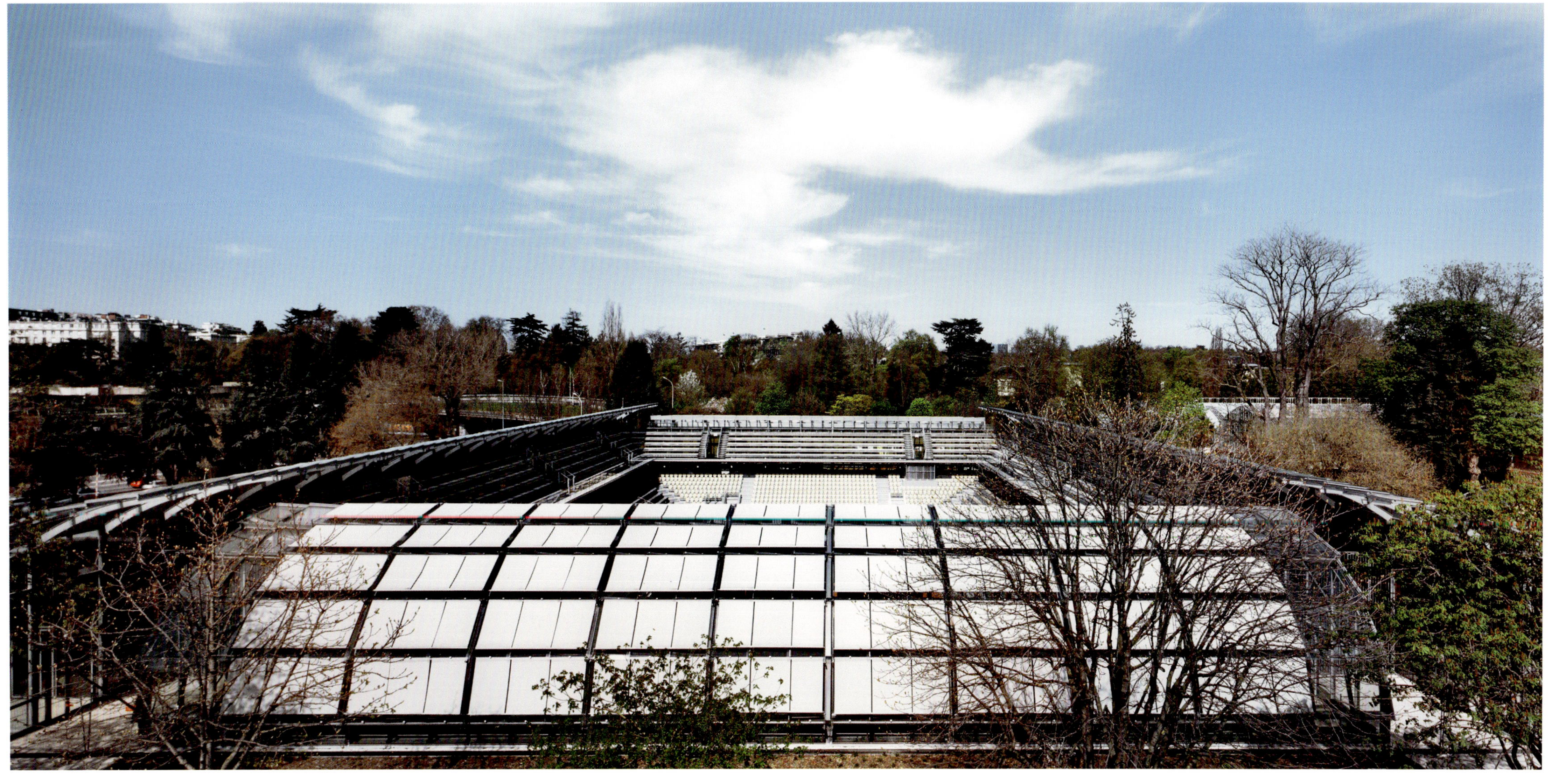

Roland-Garros: Simonne-Mathieu Court, Paris, France

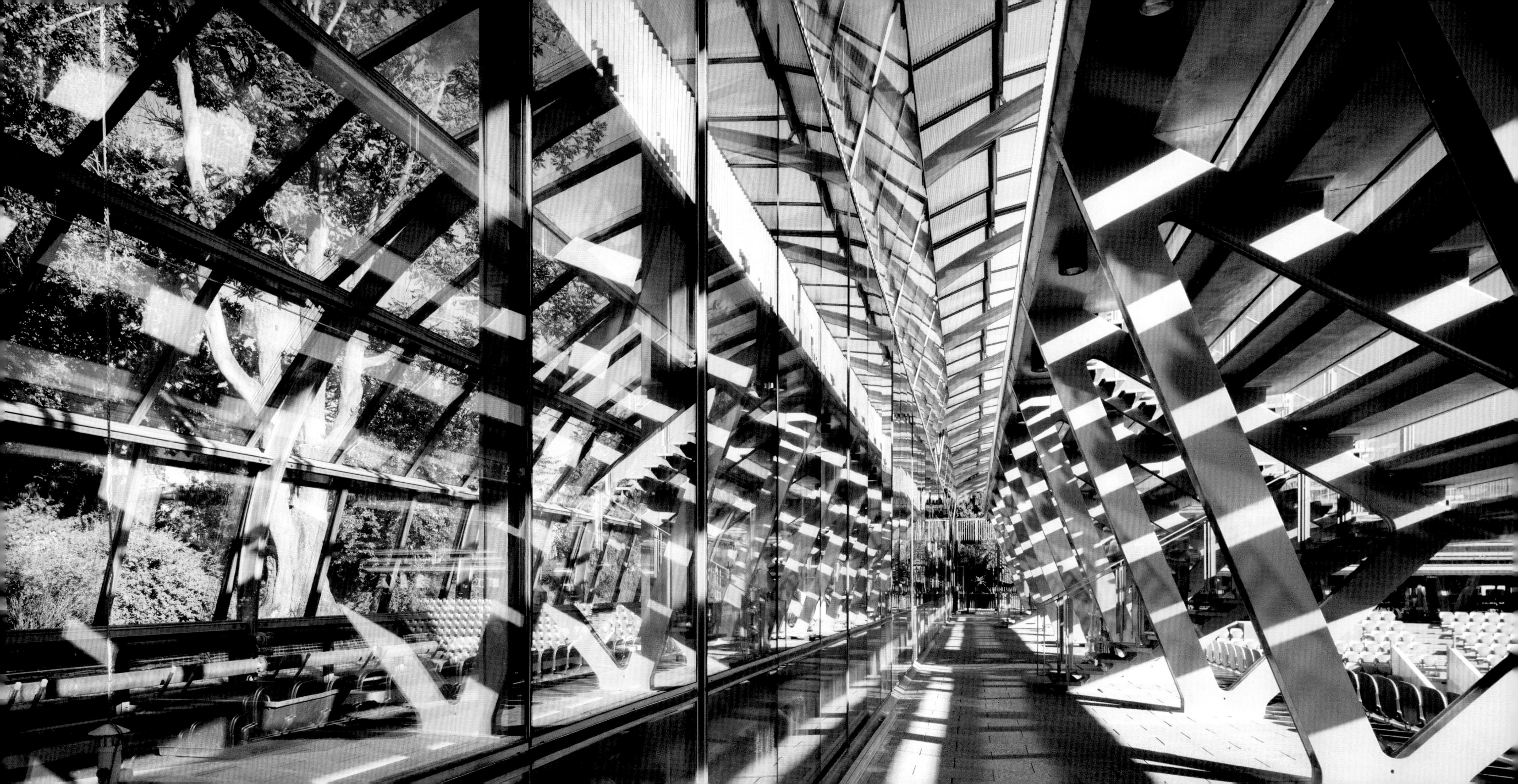

Two-Banks Footbridge
Strasbourg—Kehl, France—Germany

A Project Anchored in the Geography of the River

The new footbridge over the Rhine springs entirely from the geographic and geometric logic of the gardens on either side of the river.

Rather than regarding the river as a gap to be crossed in some abstract way, it is what molds the geography that gives the place form, life, and meaning.

The project set out to provide a meeting point between these two anchoring points of the riverbanks, then extending above the embankment along the circular walkway. The bridge is designed as a double bridge, offering a variety of ways of crossing and a meeting point in the middle of the river.

Here geography prevails over history and the public space passing above the old frontier makes a visual link between the shared territory between the Black Forest and the Vosges. The place created at this meeting point soars over the Rhine, soothing us with its distant views and reminding us of the proximity of this single landscape.

A Structure that Opens into the Landscape

The river enters into a dialogue with the bridge thanks to the deceptively delicate crossing and the interplay of curving forms standing out against the sky.

The bridge is supported by cables, allowing the intersecting decks—one a horizontal curve, the other a vertical curve—to be detached from the main supporting structure. The walkways seem to trace a Möbius strip, something that can be seen as symbolizing Franco-German relations.

In a landscape that opens up to the sky, the footbridge presents slim structural lines that intersect to offer a multiplicity of paths and meeting points with the Rhine.

Far from seeking to obscure the horizon or place massive anchoring points in the landscape, the aim is rather to make a link that is tenuous and delicate, like the thread running between the two shores of a geography marked by a history that, while painful in the past, has today seen peace.

With its multiplicity of possible routes and the lightness of its web-like structure, the footbridge pays tribute to the river that runs beneath it, offering a timeless symbol of a delicately balanced meeting between nations.

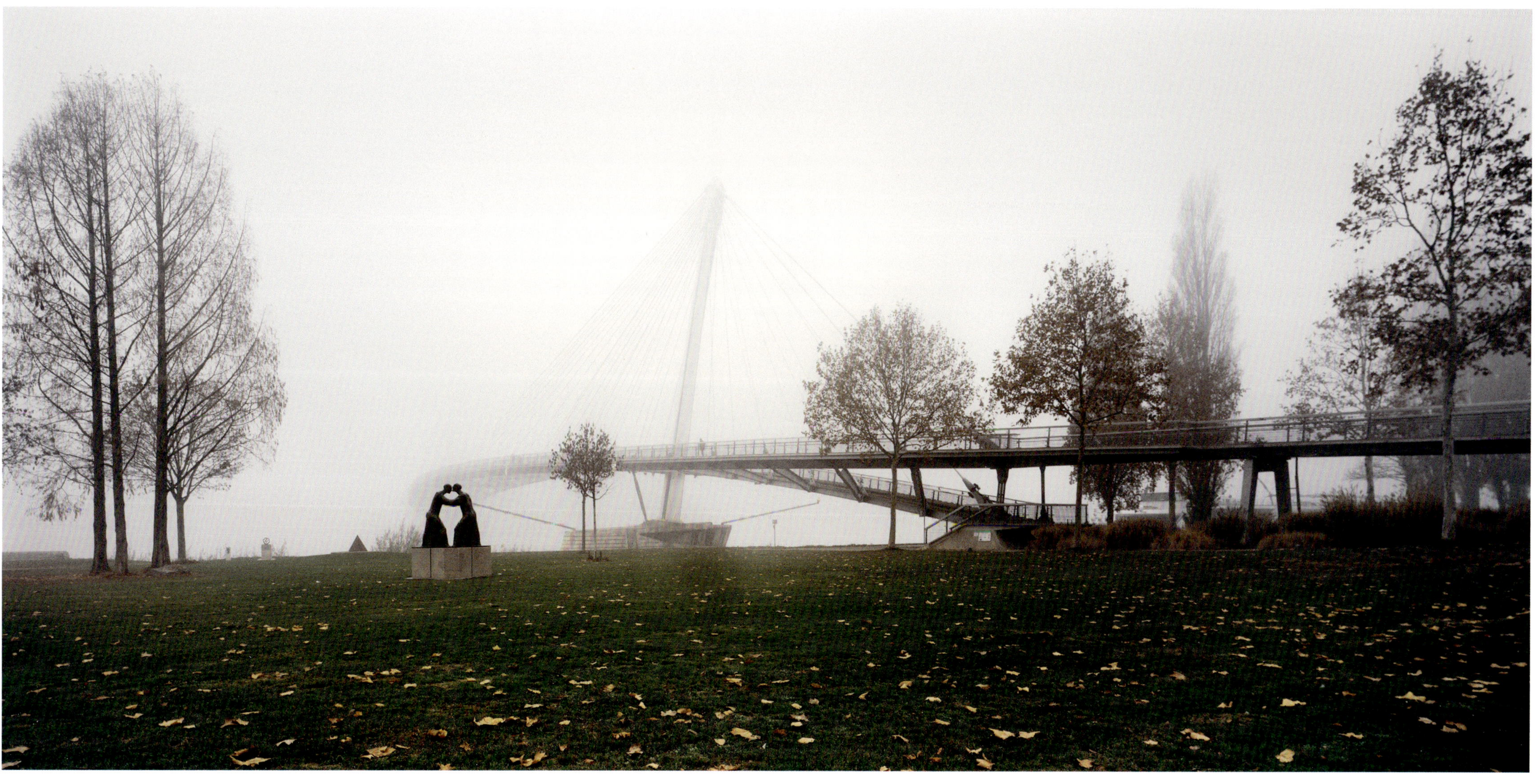

Two-Banks Footbridge, Strasbourg—Kehl, France—Germany

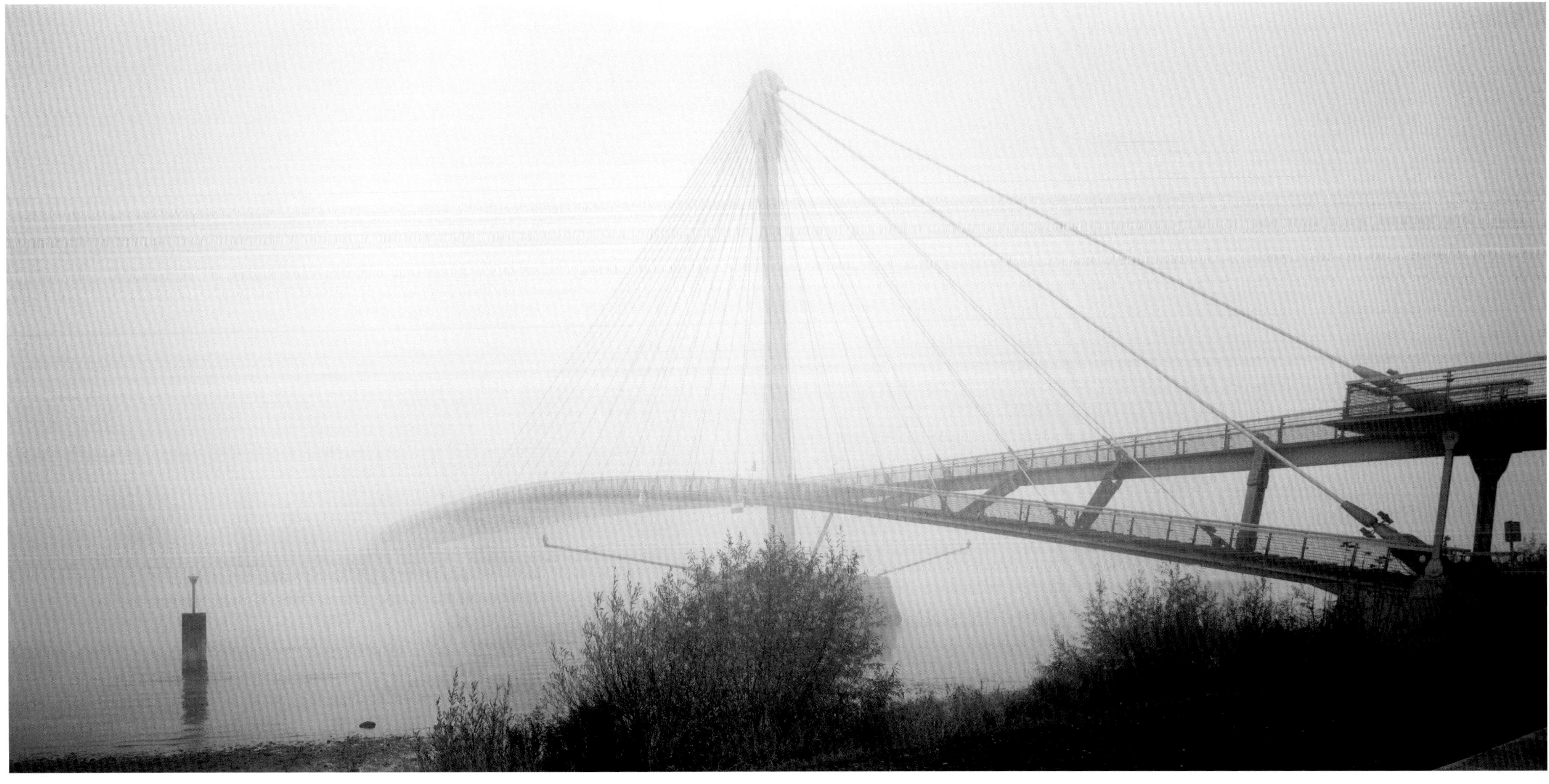

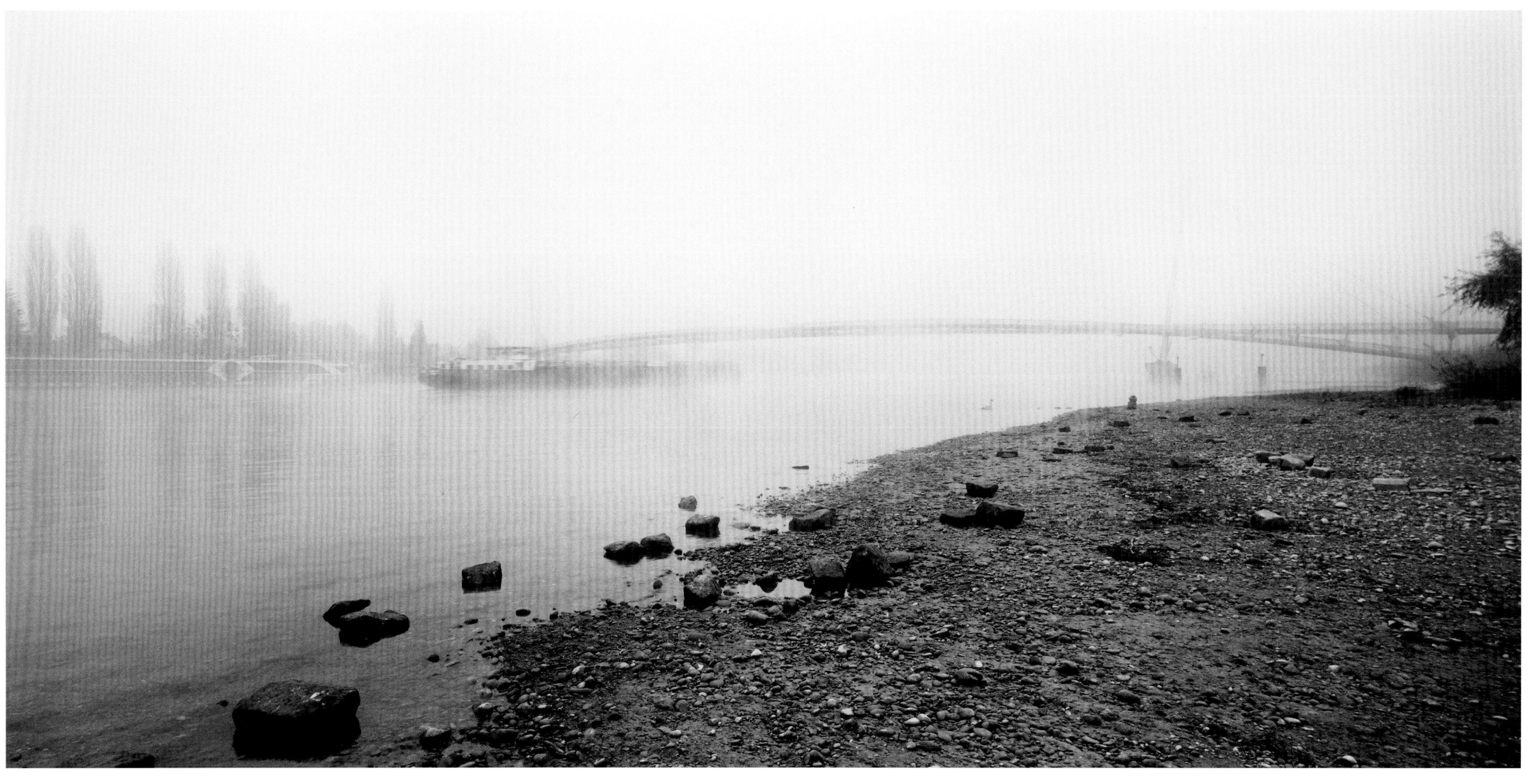

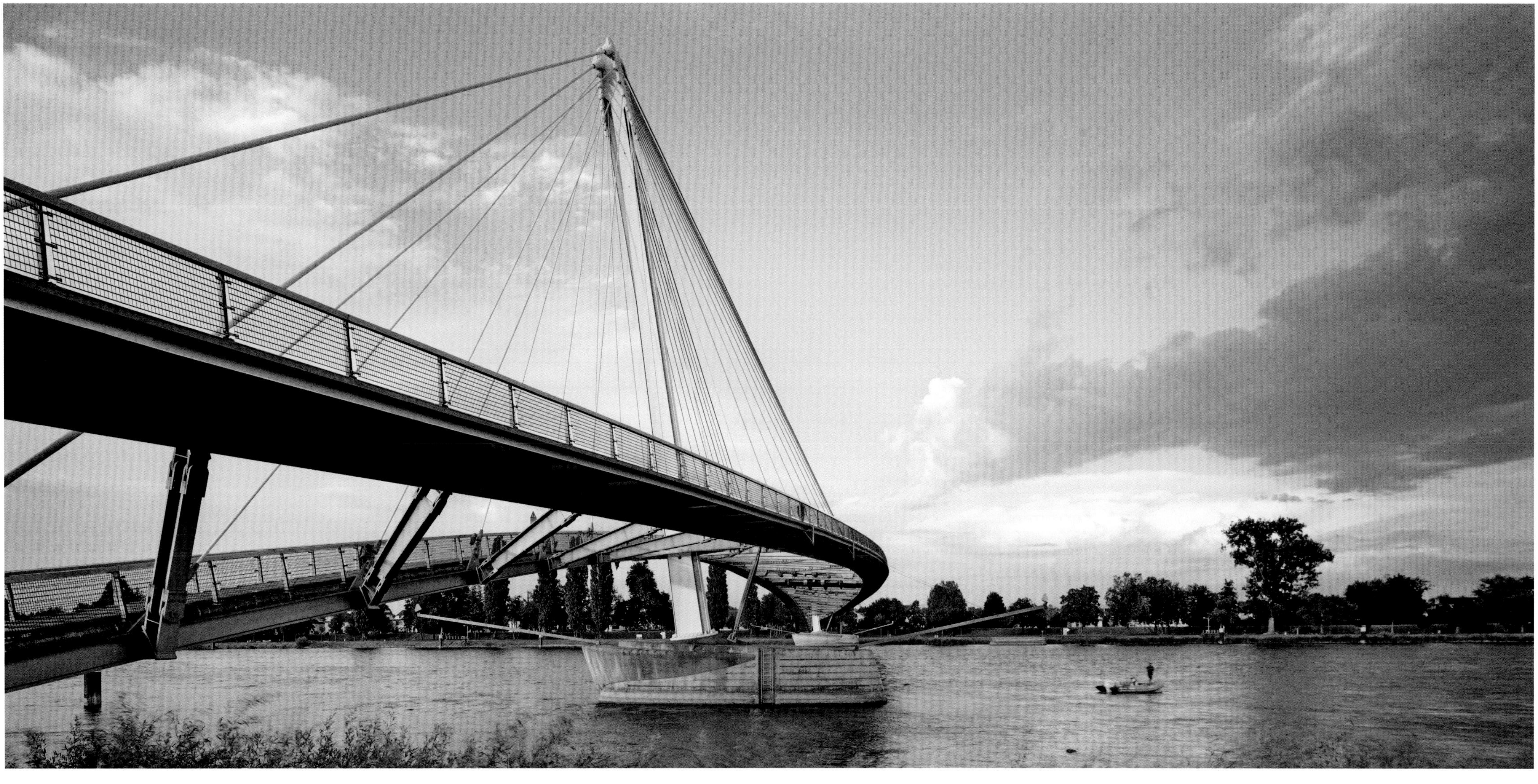

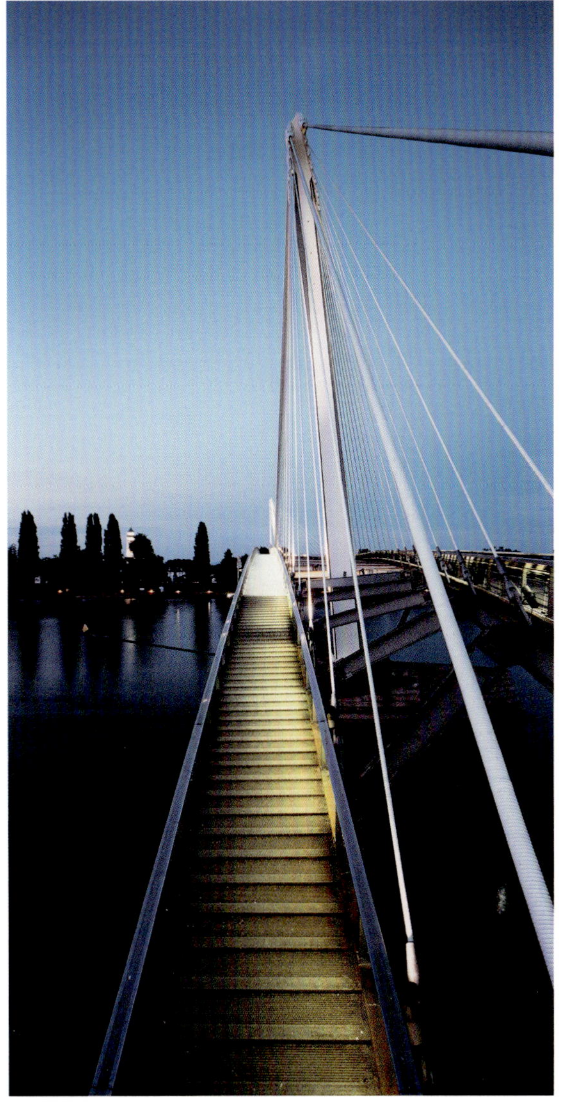

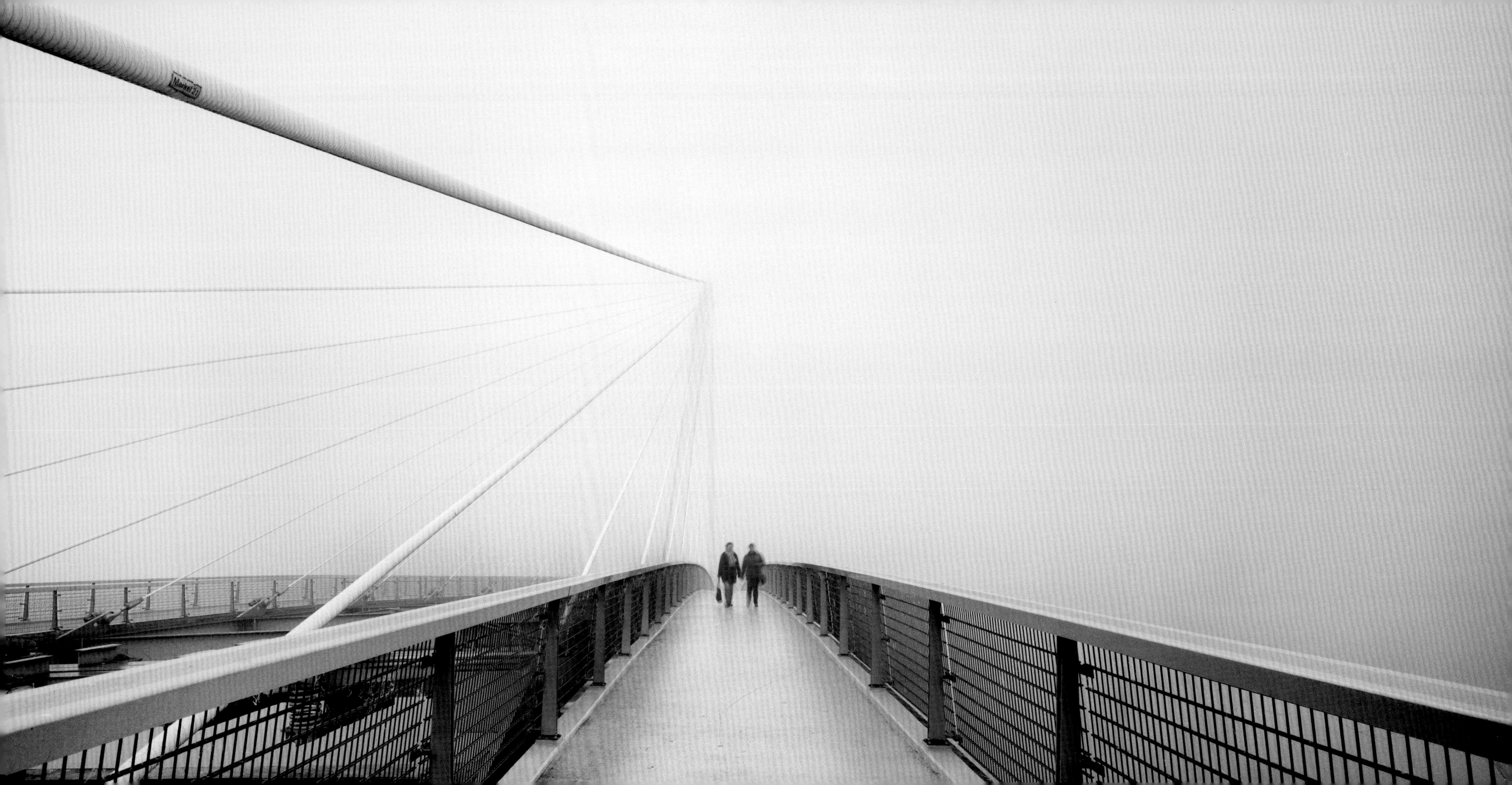
Merkel 21

Three Bridges in China

When I carried out my first project in China fifteen years ago Chinese society was beginning to change, but no one could have anticipated the urban explosion that was to accompany it. People still went about on bicycles and Beijing had only two ring roads—today it has six. This metamorphosis of Chinese cities has, naturally, been accompanied by a massive development of urban infrastructures and, as a result, of civil engineering projects.

We opened an agency in Tianjin, home of Liu Chengyin, who is our local director in China. This city of fifteen million inhabitants forms part of the megalopolis that, from Beijing to Binhai, links the capital to the sea. We designed numerous projects in this area, on the Hai River, at the Tianjin Economic-Technological Development Area (TEDA), in the port of Tanggu, and in the new town, the Sino-Singaporean eco-city where the Zhong Sheng Da Dao and Jin Liu Lu bridges were constructed. This new city has set itself up as a model of sustainable urban development based on technology and infrastructure. Making water and water treatment central to its conception, the city has been constructed around a lake crossed by the two bridges.
In this urban explosion the Chinese administrative authorities have often highlighted the symbolic role that engineering structures can play. Rather than restricting them to their functional place, they are made, in the race for the development of cities, a symbol of a particular attention to public works—the attribute of an assumed modernity. While this conception has sometimes resulted in formalistic, mannered, or historicist excesses, it also opens up a field of experimentation of which we have often taken advantage.

Two Bridges on the Artificial Lake

The lake is central to the sustainability inspiring Tianjin's eco-city. There are no constraints as to form or span. The theoretical challenge here is to enter into a dialogue with this artificial landscape, evoking the relationship with the water by analogy with the floating bridge.

The Zhong Sheng Da Dao Bridge

The bridge consists of two parallel decks made up of five concrete arches, each with a span of fifty-four meters. These hollow volumes, formed of double-curvature surfaces, possess a high level of inertia thanks to the effectiveness of their form's resistance. The apparent massiveness of the bridge is contradicted by the structure's floating character, while the reflection of the arches in the water makes it yet more enigmatic. The gravitational direction is neither ordered nor hierarchical, but the continuum of the concrete surface ensures effective load transfer. Massive but floating, opaque but pierced, a dialogue emerges with the surface of the water in relation to the horizon, the line of gravity between the sky and the land.

The difficulty in carrying out the work lay in the need to divide the complex surface into sections of shuttering that could be combined, manipulated, reused, and reassembled symmetrically twenty times. The plan for the shuttering was geometrically and constructively regulated using a digital model available both to our office and to the builder, the building site and the geometric tool being central to the project.

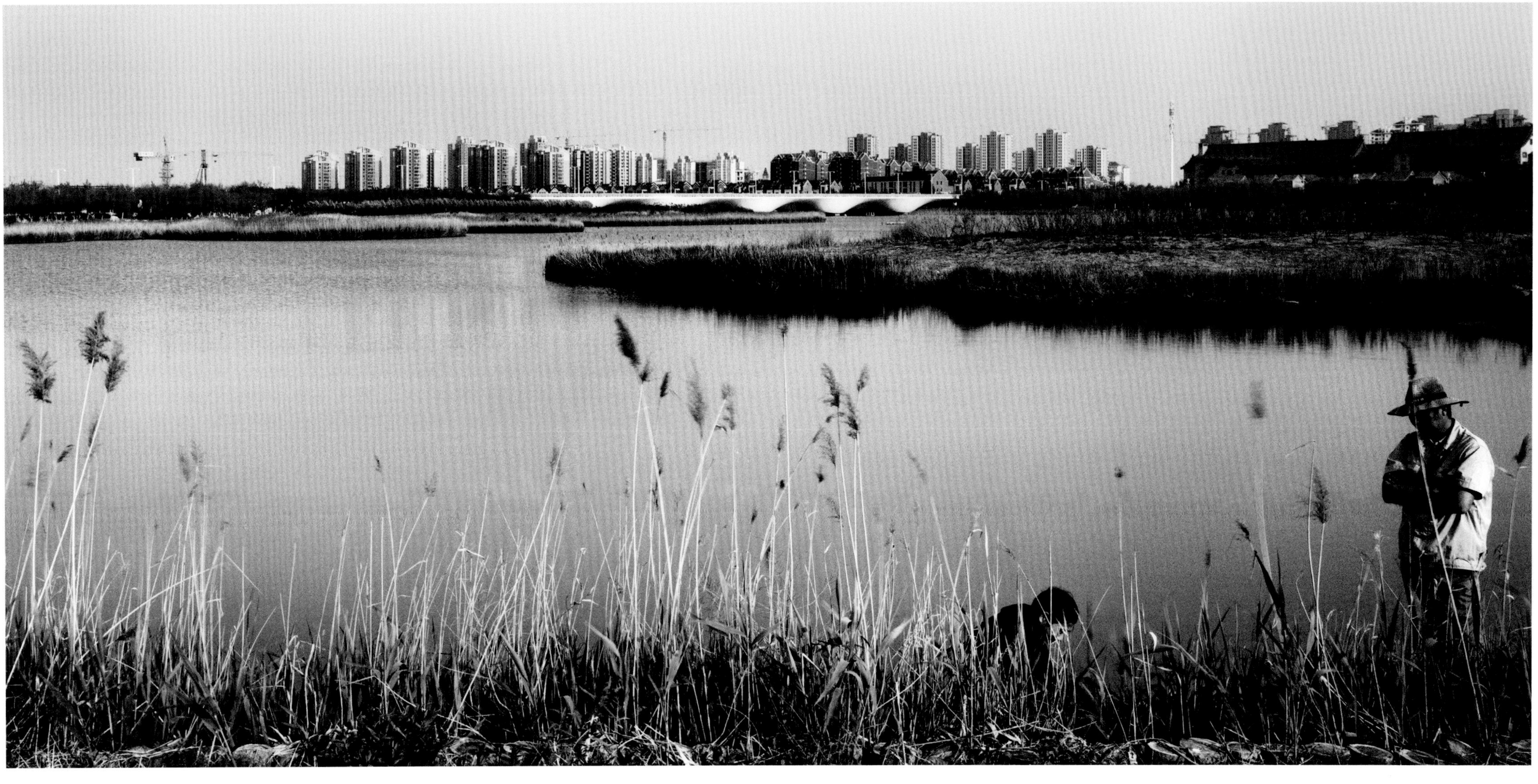

The concern of the new city for sustainable development makes me think of the Roman she-wolf, associated with the legend of Romulus and Remus, whom she nurtured with her own milk. She could be once more a founding symbol for this forward-looking urban venture.

The Jin Liu Lu Bridge

This bridge followed on from the Zhong Sheng Da Dao Bridge. The approach here was to find a solution that related to the latter, so instead of opaque massiveness we started from hollowed-out surfaces. The line of arches is exactly the same, but here the inertia is qualified by the voids, by the distance between the deck and the variable ribbon. This ribbon is formed of a double-skin steel surface, the side wings of which vary in size, rising and curving, echoing the static scheme and responding to the direction of gravitational forces. Instead of a raised mass, a concrete continuum floating on the lake's horizon, here we see a steel leaf framing empty spaces through which can be seen the ever-changing play of light. The double curvature of the steel sheets draws on techniques from the shipbuilding industry, the metalwork of the arches evoking another kind of floatation.

The Liu Shu Footbridge in Yangzhou

The construction used for this footbridge was fundamental in the principle developed for the Jin Liu Lu Bridge. Here, in less than six months, and including initial studies, we were asked to design a project commemorating the anniversary of the city of Yangzhou. This port is home to one of the country's most important shipbuilding industries. The mayor, secretary of the Communist Party, allowed me to make use of these skills in a project that, compared with the tonnage involved in the enormous ships under construction, was very much limited in scope.

It was with enormous pleasure that we were able to transpose the highly developed technology of shipbuilding to the creation of this delicate footbridge! The metal sheeting produced, shaped, and bent in a double curve closely follows the static scheme. Through the variation in inertia, the structure reflects in its form the distribution of the moments of flexion of an arch embedded at both ends in the abutment of the structure. The steel sheets were cut with an automated oxy-fuel cutter following the outline of shaped templates created by a complex digital tool making it possible to assemble non-developable surfaces.

The link between shipbuilding and the metal construction of this light structure, making it possible to have continuous steel surfaces rather than metal struts often developed as a framework, is indicative of the extent to which the building site informs the project that, starting from the schematic diagram, shapes the metal until it takes on its delicate form created by the gentle undulations of the curved surfaces.

The name of the footbridge evokes the leaf of the willow trees that grow on the lake edges; the locals see its form reflected in the shape of the bridge.

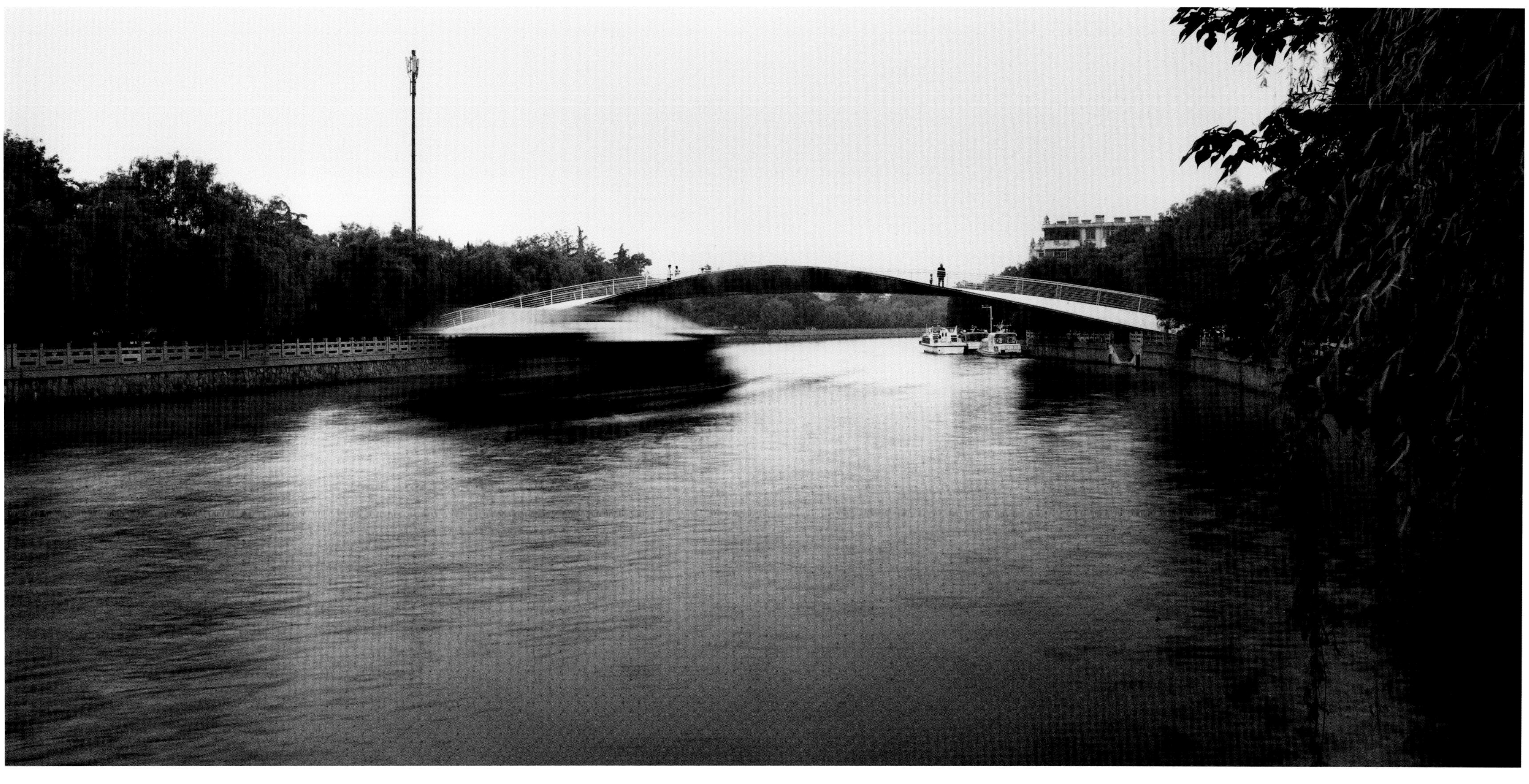

Jin Liu Lu Bridge, Tianjin, China

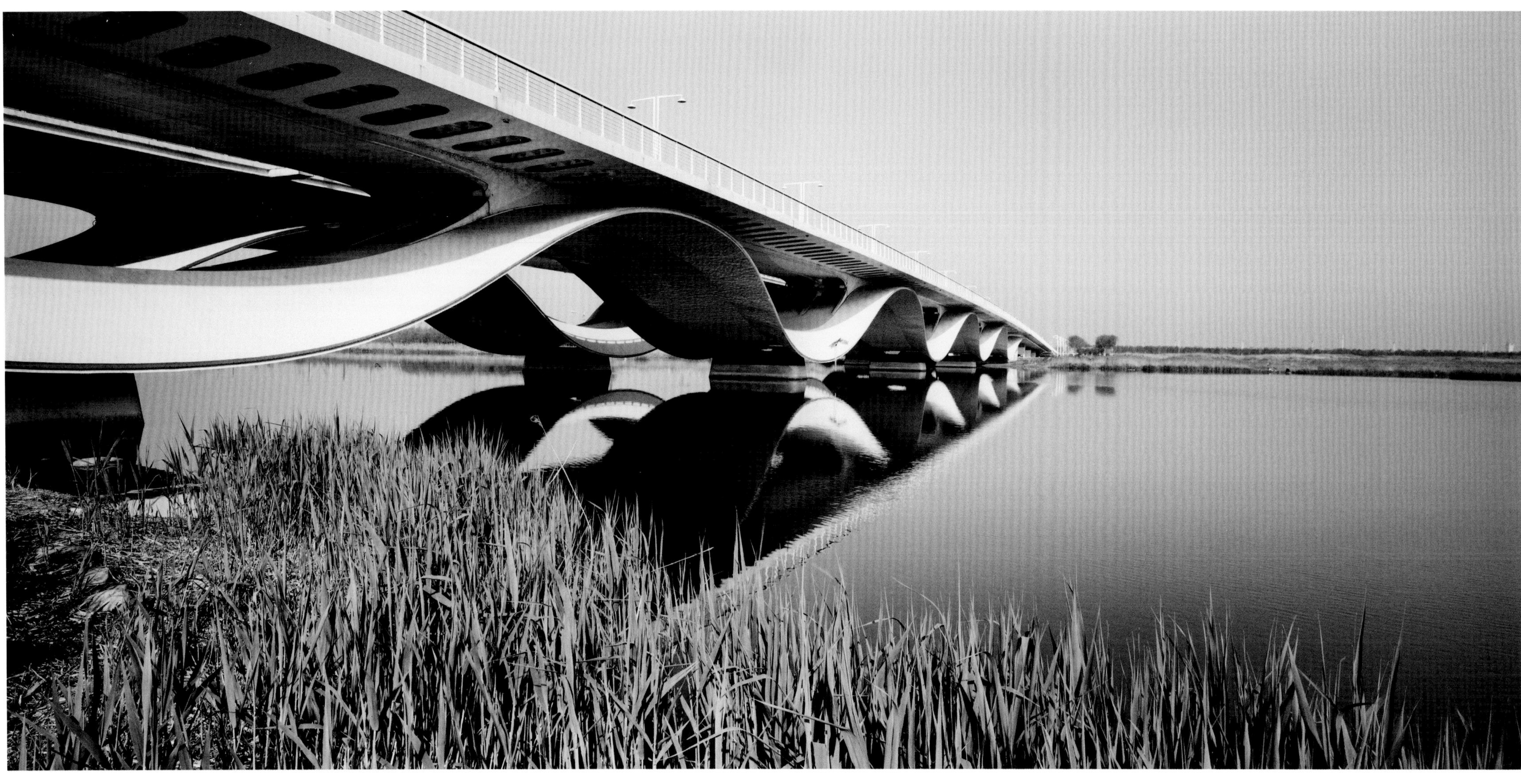

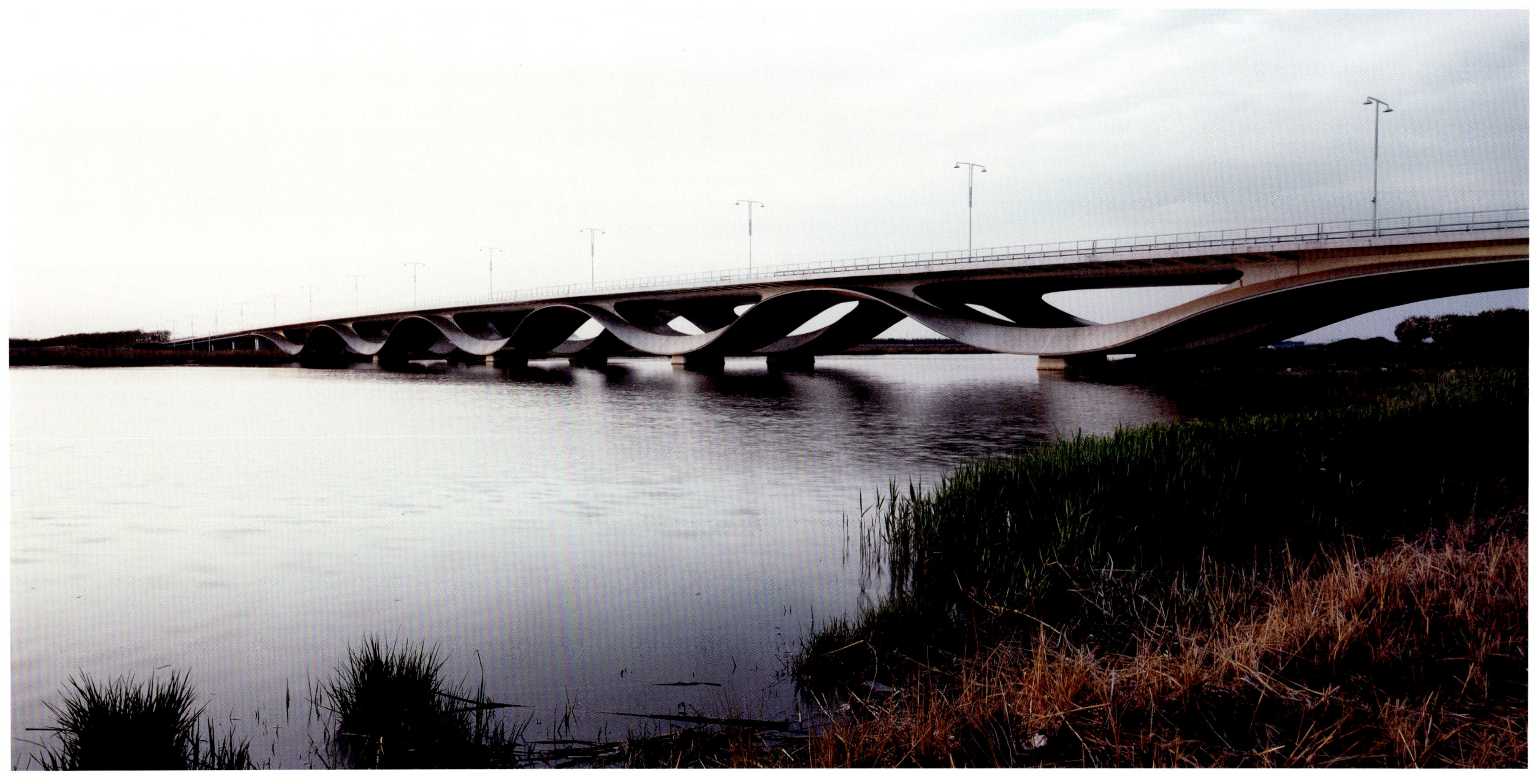

Jin Liu Lu Bridge, Tianjin, China

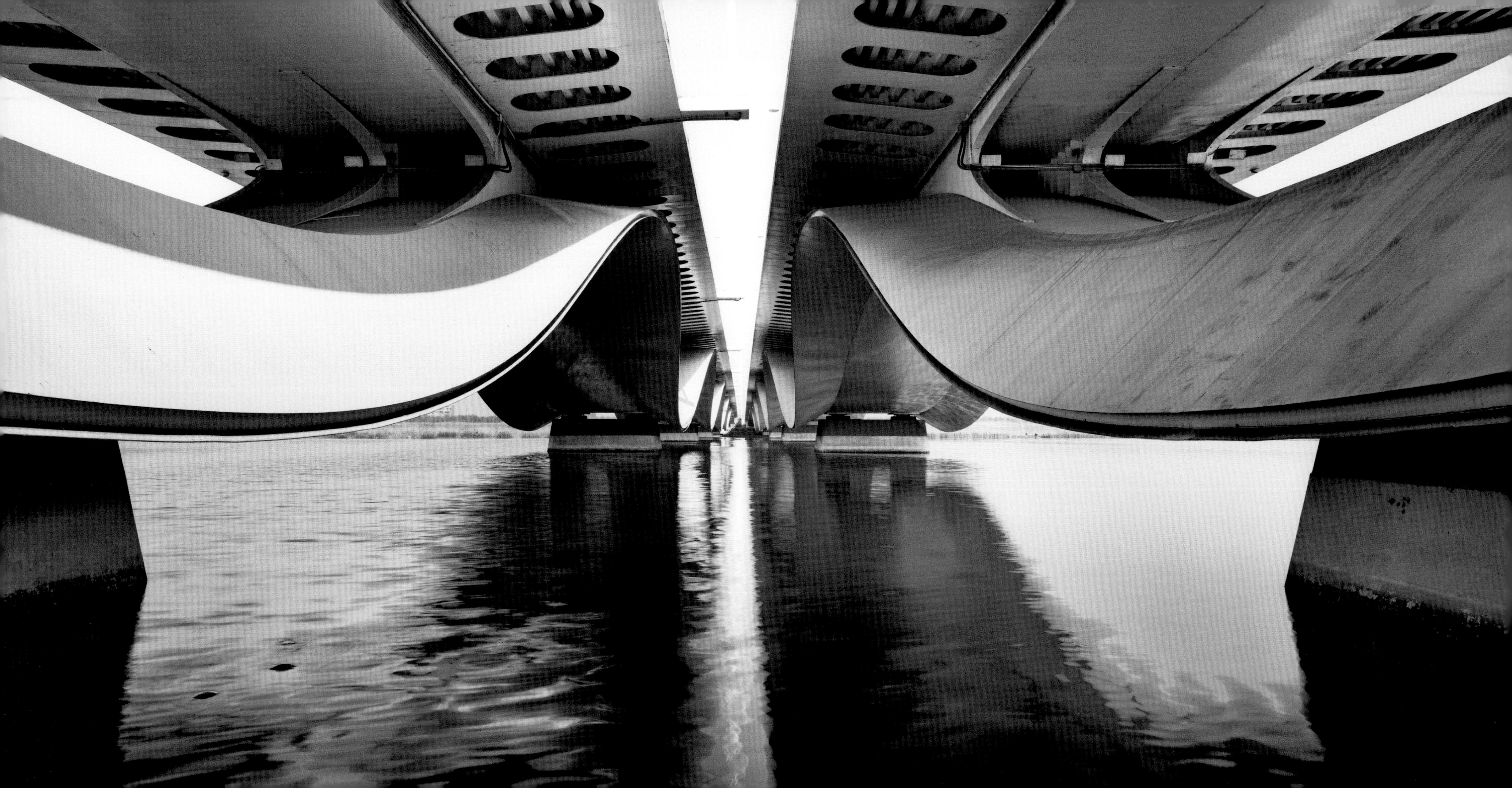

Zhong Sheng Da Dao Bridge, Tianjin, China

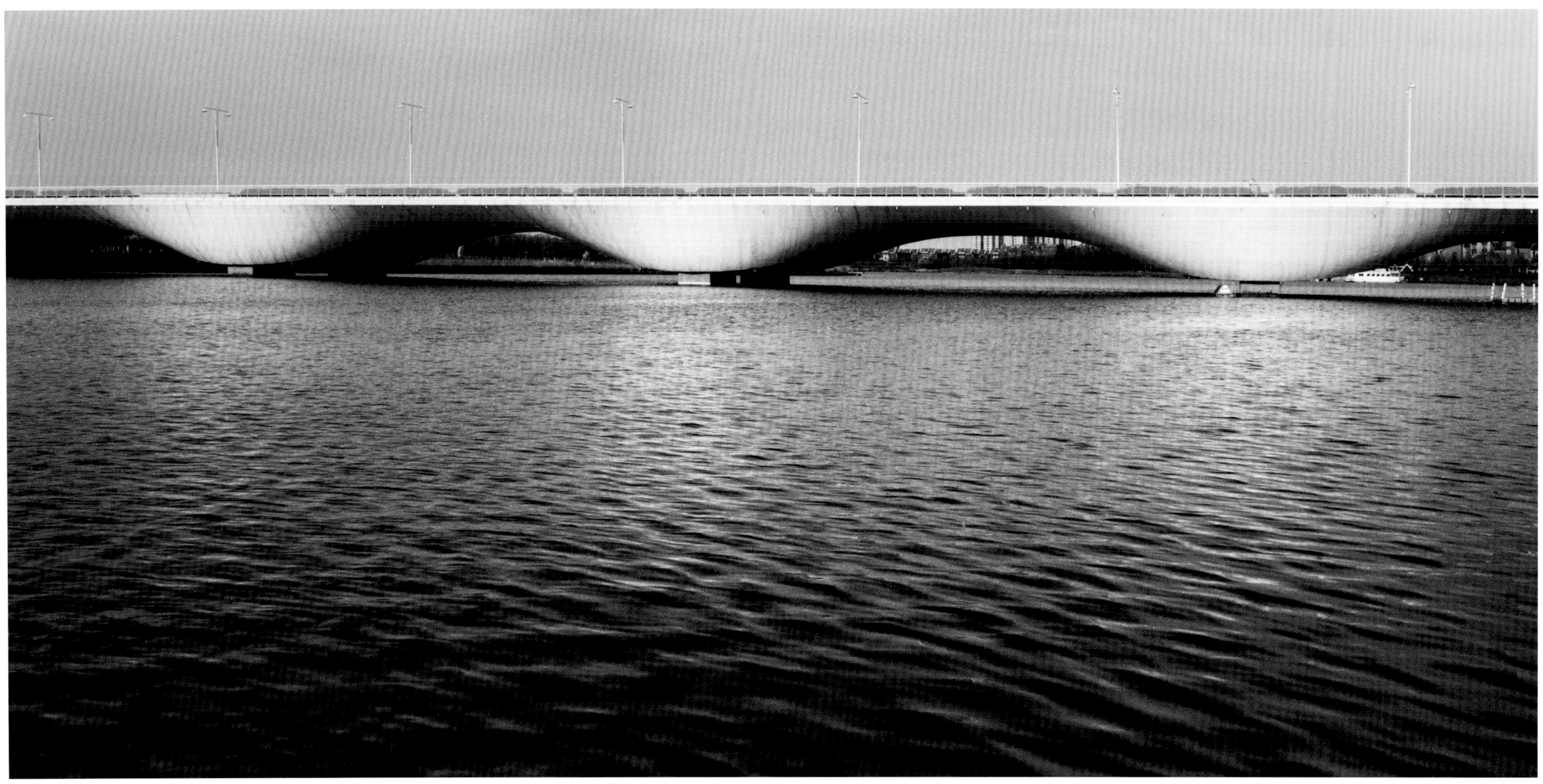

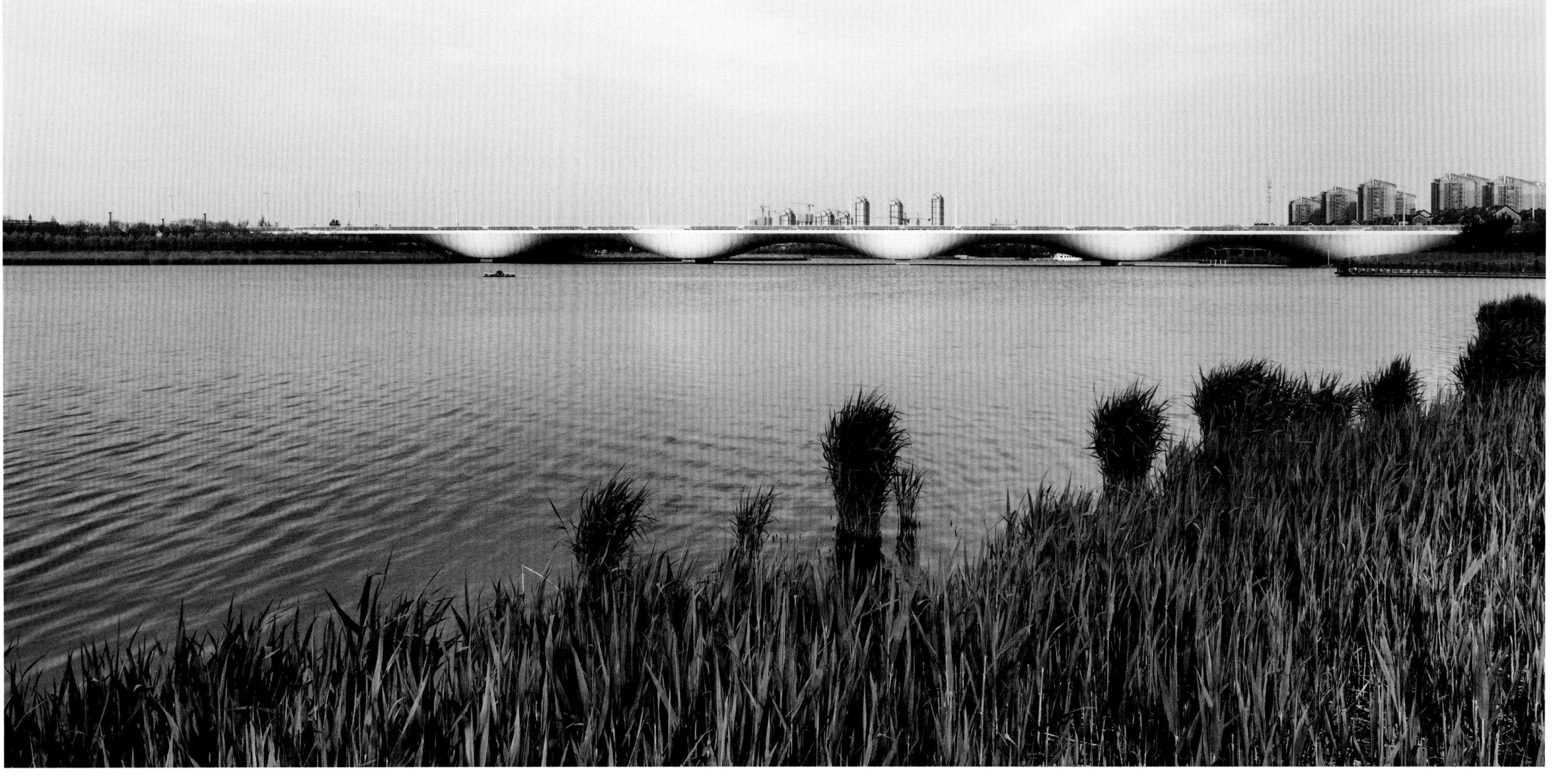

Zhong Sheng Da Dao Bridge, Tianjin, China

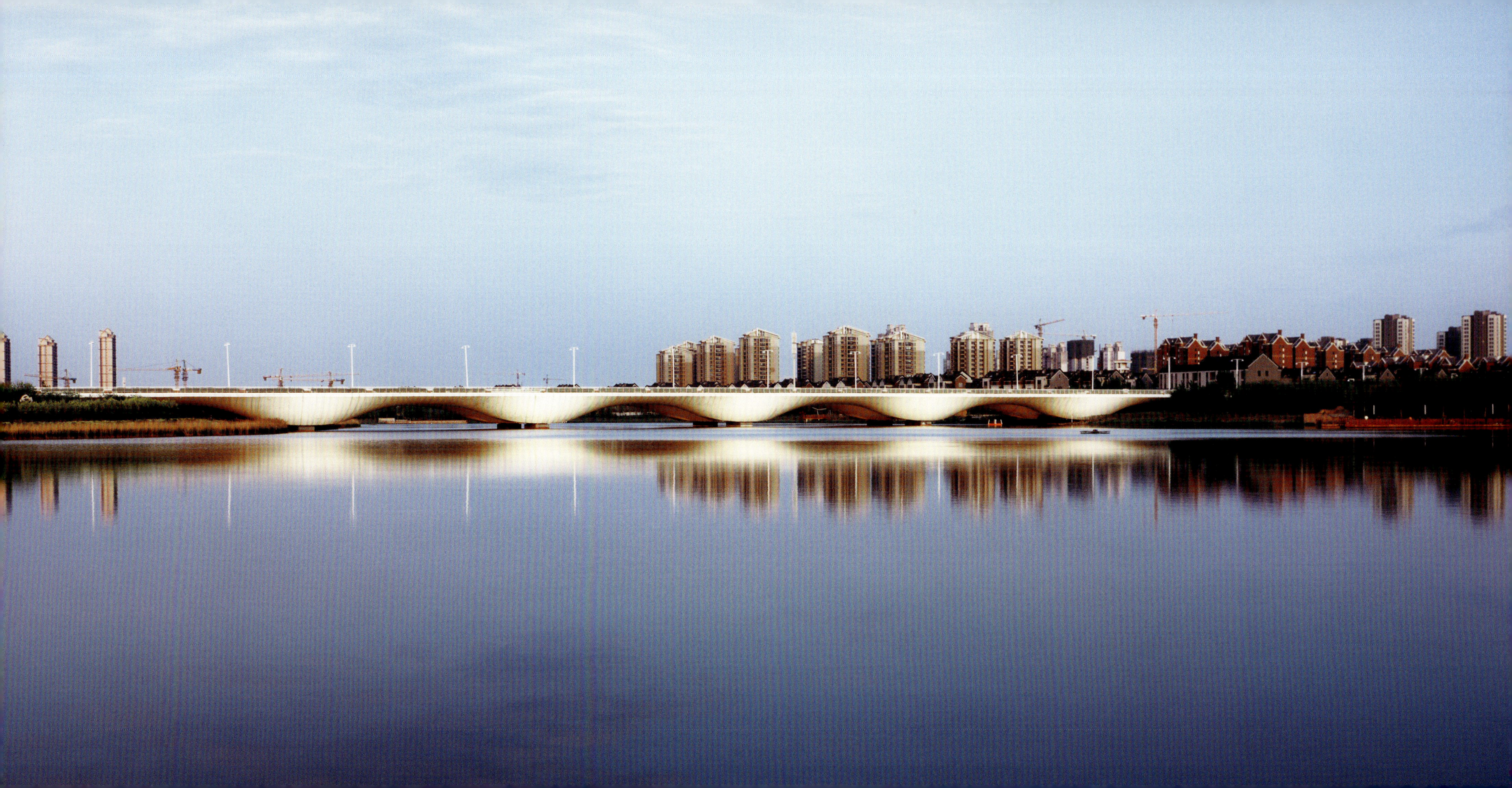

Phenomenal Precision:
Erieta Attali's Photography of Marc Mimram's Architecture

Ariel Genadt

Architecture in the second decade of the twenty-first century is more precisely documented in photographic clichés than it ever has been. Any hurried person's fingertips can eternalize buildings as static objects with unprecedented digital precision using a smartphone, and circulate the images around the globe instantaneously. This phenomenon has reaffirmed the increasing importance of artistic interpretation in professional architectural photography. As revealed in Michelangelo Antonioni's film *Blow-Up* (1966), the mechanical eye's precision, while enhancing the limits of retinal perception, also reiterates the pertinence of the photographer's gaze as an interpretive act. That idea is ever truer today, since technology has liberated art even further than in the age of its mechanical reproducibility. Within this context, photographer Erieta Attali's representations of Marc Mimram's architecture make us pause and contemplate its spatial-temporal limits. They add a dimension to the architecture through her painstakingly patient observation work and mastery of analog precision.

While Mimram has spoken of his architecture as a process of transformation of place and of materials, the transformation continues after the architect leaves the scene. In that light, Attali represents Mimram's structures as layered phenomena, responsive to human movements and the action of the sun, moon, and weather. Through long exposures of up to twenty minutes with an f/32 aperture, she uses her large-format ten by twelve-centimeter Linhof camera to overlay her subjects' changing phases. With the persistence of the long-distance runner that she is, Attali extracts and sediments those immeasurable qualities in the work that link them to a time of the day, the season, their longitude and latitude. Capturing the moment the sun strikes the surfaces and seeps through the structure's limbs, she aims to create a feeling of floatation, where one is being "rooted and uprooted at the same time," as she puts it. This motive is best demonstrated in the *chiaroscuro* effects she produces; for example, in the views of the Montpellier Train Station, with its undulating precast concrete shells and uneven array of perforations, or in the infinite fragmentation and reflections in the green houses that envelop the Roland Garros Stadium. Reminiscent of Cubist principles, the resulting superposition of light imprints seems less precise than a shot one can snap with the latest electronic gadget, but it is far closer to one's experience of architecture, as it depicts a dynamic relationship between inert structures, people, climate, and light.

Often Attali's interpretations continue the architect's idea that the building is a memory of geography and of local savoir faire involved in its construction. Her photos offer *précisions* (French for clarifications or focused observations) to his design, highlighting possible meanings by immersing the buildings in site-specific atmospheric conditions: Moroccan skies, Chinese waters, Mediterranean sun, or Paris twilight. To that end, she continues the process of transformation of matter, alluded to by Mimram, by capturing the buildings when they appear to be broken down by light or humidity, as aggregations of pieces, afloat. Attali's interest in representing buildings as fragmented arrays is likely rooted in her early photographic surveys of archaeological sites, and later, in her fascination with the work of Kengo Kuma. Now, that proclivity joins Mimram's sensibility to fabric, patterns, and assembling, which he has associated with his observation of his father's *métier* as a tailor. The ephemeral filigree in which he dresses his buildings is more evident in Attali's photos than in person, since the composed views reveal patterns that may elude a visitor's limited field of vision. Conveying these effects does not dematerialize the architecture, but rather makes it more concrete, in the original sense of the Latin *concrescere*, i.e., the pieces "grow together" into a whole. Attali further affirms that concreteness through her emphasis on the structures' relation to the ground datum. Her choice of a 2:1 aspect ratio for the panoramic view emphasizes the structures' earthliness, their entanglement with the ambient natural and human flows. It echoes Mimram's expressivity of frozen movement, most vivid in the undulating bridges at Sino Singapore, China.

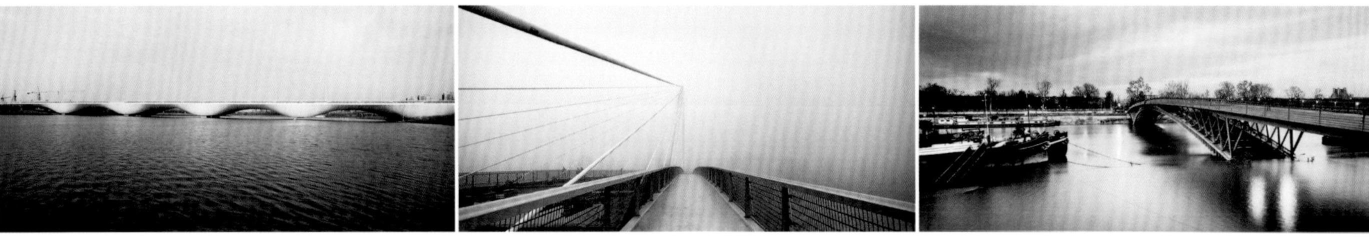

Attali's art can be further understood in light of Vittorio Gregotti's remarks on the changing role of precision in architecture at the end of the twentieth century. Gregotti maintained that while in the ancient world art was considered the activity that could produce precision, today art plays a different role, "attempting to exist outside measure-taking scientific and technological thought . . . the main task of art is precisely to produce things that defy measurement, or that raise . . . the need to find instruments of measure based not on the constancy of structures, but rather on the nature of the ever-changing constellation of relationships that connects them."[1] Similarly, rather than outlining the abstract logic that underlays Mimram's structures, Attali's lenses reproduce her perception of architecture as an interplay between artifice, humans, and nature, and between stasis and motion. For example, she pictures the elongated skeleton of the Solférino Pedestrian Bridge sharply delineated against the Seine's turbid waters and deep dark skies. Its intricate silhouette resonates with the lacy structure of a barren plane tree in the foreground, which, like the bridge, seems to emanate from a river of mercury.

Attali has pursued this kind of phenomenal representation of architecture over the last two decades, but the encounter between her approach and Mimram's work is particularly revelatory of both her art and his. *Ouvrages d'art*—large-scale engineering works, such as bridges, that transform the landscape through their structural expression—have most often been photographed in a way that emphasizes their static logic. *Ouvrages d'art* entered the canon of modern architecture when Sigfried Giedion, in *Bauen in Frankreich* (1928) praised their sublime aesthetic power as much as their engineering merit.[2] Attali, however, eschews diagrammatic depictions of Mimram's *ouvrages*, of the type that might have foregrounded the limpid rationale of stress and tension that holds them up in equilibrium. In a sense, she relieves them from the scientific precision that was necessary for their creation, shaking their obedience to the laws of physics by cropping, veiling or reflecting parts of the structures or their supports. Through this act of phenomenal precision she uplifts them into the realm of *oeuvre d'art*, and contributes to establishing Mimram's *ouvrages* in the lineage of modern masters as Eugène Freyssinet and Robert Maillart.

Though the photographer's and the architect-engineer's use of precision seem to point in opposite directions, they are in effect complementary: while he strives to thin out matter and space, citing Robert le Ricolais's "architecture is the art of placing holes," she uses light and time to thicken and amplify the architecture with climate and life. While he relates to the quantifiable *topos*, and aspires to overcome gravity, she fleshes out the nurturing matrix, the *khôra* that gives his creation its *raison d'être*. The phenomenal precision with which Attali represents Mimram's architecture demonstrates how photography can enhance, enliven, and even transform an architect's *oeuvre*, while anchoring it to place and giving it meaning against the boundless ocean of data streams that are also part of our environment.

1 Vittorio Gregotti, *Inside Architecture* (Chicago, 1996), pp. 45–46. Originally: *Dentro l'architettura* (Turin, 1991).
2 Sigfried Giedion, *Bauen in Frankreich, Eisen, Eisenbeton* (Leipzig, 1928). English edition: Sigfried Giedion, *Building in France, Building in Iron, Building in Ferroconcrete* (Santa Monica, CA, 1995). French edition: Sigfried Giedion, *Construire en France, en fer, en béton* (Paris, 2000).

On Marc Mimram
Zvi Hecker

Alexandre Gustave Eiffel erected the Eiffel Tower to welcome the twentieth century in the center of the world, Paris. He built it within a tight budget in a very limited time, avoiding usual fatalities and even making a small amount of money. His creation was saved from the hands and tongues of Parisian intellectuals by Marconi's invention of wireless that needed the highest possible antenna.

In a short time the Eiffel Tower, a naked structure, at first despised by the Parisian elite, became the seducing beauty of the avant-garde artists. The steel construction, undecorated and unashamed of its newly born strength, became the material and technology modern architecture embraced most dearly.

Marc Mimram was born into the new situation, in which the border between architecture and structure was greatly blurred. The ability of the steel prefabricated elements to reduce the dimensions of a structure brought about a new aesthetic awareness. The light and the transparent represented the new architecture. In the long historical process that has taken place in our civilization over the course of two millennia, architecture has undergone a dematerialization from the massive construction of pyramids to the Gothic skeleton construction of cathedrals, to the firmly established economy of material as an aesthetic factor. It was laconically summarized by Mies van der Rohe, who said "Less is more," and by Oscar Niemeyer who put the pyramid on its vertex.

Marc Mimram is aware of this process because he is its practitioner. As a young man, Marc visited my atelier in Tel Aviv at the beginning of the 1970s. At that time I was teaching at the Université Laval in Quebec, Canada, responsible for visiting lecturers in the school of architecture. In this capacity I invited Robert Le Ricolais for a series of three lectures. He spoke French. It was a great success.

Sensing Marc's desire to study architecture and engineering, I have encouraged him to look to Le Ricolais as an example of a creative engineer. It worked, and Marc wrote a beautiful book about Le Ricolais years later.

Marc follows his own path while also being aware of the French tradition of structural ingenuity as an aesthetic value.

Marc is also aware that the abundance of new technologies can easily result in technocratic architecture. One needs a non-conformist openness to explore new possibilities while preserving the common sense and the know-how of the past. That is exactly what Marc does, with perfection and inventiveness.

Biography Marc Mimram
Architect, Engineer

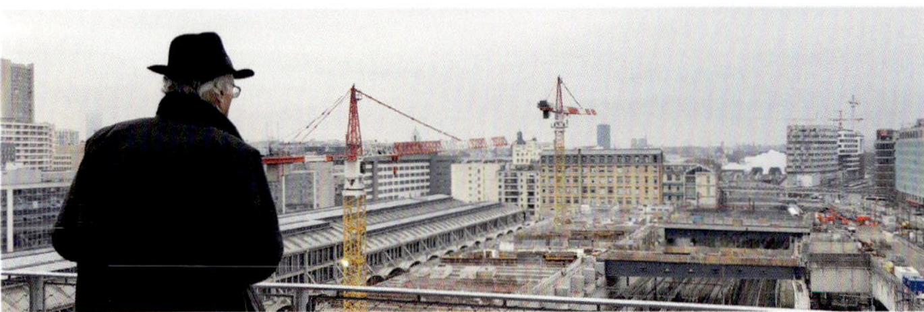

Marc Mimram (b. 1955, Paris) has a master's degree in mathematics from the Université Paris VII (1976), an engineering diploma from the École Nationale des Ponts et Chaussées (1978), a master's degree in civil engineering from the University of California, Berkeley (1979), an architecture diploma (DPLG) from the École Nationale Supérieure des Beaux Arts in Paris (1980), and a postgraduate degree in philosophy from the Université Paris I Panthéon-Sorbonne (1982). He founded his own consultancy and architecture and engineering firm in 1992.

He has been an architect-engineer since 1981, and has completed many civil engineering structures and architectural projects in France and abroad, including bridges in France (Solférino Footbridge, Paris), in Germany (Strasbourg—Kehl), in Morocco (Rabat—Salé), which won the Aga Khan Award, in China (Beijing, Tianjin, Yangzhou), large sport facilities (Roland-Garros Stadium, Paris), and infrastructure buildings (Airtime, Paris, and Montpellier Railway Station, France).

Mimram has taught at the École des Ponts et Chaussées in Paris, the École Polytechnique Fédérale in Lausanne, and Princeton University in the United States. He was appointed a Professor of Architectural Schools and currently teaches at the École d'Architecture de Marne-la-Vallée near Paris.

He has published several books, such as *Structure et Formes* (Paris, 1983); *Passerelle Solférino* (Basel, 2001); *Architettura Ibrida* (Milan, 2009); and *Marc Mimram: Architecture & Structure* (Munich, 2015). He has given numerous lectures all over the world, including lectures at Harvard University, Cornell University, Princeton, Tokyo University, as well as São Paulo, Venice, and Oslo.

In his work as an architect and an engineer, Marc Mimram has shown an interest in architecture that is intelligently built through the development of considered structures that relate to landscape, light, and materials. He feels that his work is about an attentive and generous transformation of the matter of which the world is made. In his hands architecture becomes an art of transformation, and materiality becomes the expression of culture.

Image: © Erieta Attali

Biography Erieta Attali
Landscape and Architecture Photographer

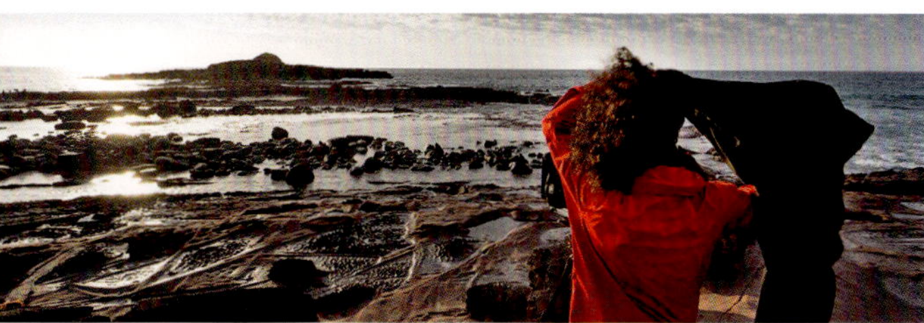

Erieta Attali was born in Tel Aviv and grew up in Istanbul and Athens. She currently resides between New York and Paris, photographing the work of contemporary architects from around the world. Attali began her photographic career in 1993 as a landscape and archaeology photographer with a specialty in underground burial sites. During the past twenty years she has been preoccupied primarily with architectural and landscape photography, with a body of work spanning from Europe to the Americas and from Asia to Australia, sponsored by national and academic institutions globally. Her work has been shown in several exhibitions and is the subject of many monographs. The National Gallery of Victoria (NGV) in Melbourne, Australia, has acquired her work for its permanent collection. After receiving her master's in photography from Goldsmiths, University of London, Attali continued her studies as visiting scholar at the Graduate School of Architecture, Planning and Preservation, Columbia University, in New York, with support of the Fulbright Foundation, and at Waseda University, Tokyo, with the support of the Japan Foundation. She holds a PhD from the School of Architecture and Design, RMIT University, Melbourne, Australia. Attali has taught architectural photography at GSAPP, Columbia University as an adjunct assistant professor between 2003 and 2018. She has been a visiting professor at the Technical University of Munich (TUM) Faculty of Architecture, The Catholic University of Chile, School of Architecture, the Royal Danish Academy of Arts in Copenhagen, Architectural Association in London, RMIT in Melbourne, University of Tokyo, Technion in Haifa, Israel, and the University of Sydney among others. Attali is currently a research fellow at the Académie d'architecture in Paris and an artist-in-residence at the Cité internationale des arts conducting a photographic survey on Paris and the Seine. She is the author and editor of numerous books such as *Glass | Wood: Erieta Attali on Kengo Kuma* and *Periphery | Archaeology of Light*, published by Hatje Cantz, Berlin, among others.

Image: © Rondo Wei

Contributor Biographies

Paul Chemetov

Paul Chemetov was born in Paris and graduated from the École nationale supérieure des beaux-arts in 1959, and was a member of the Architectes Urbanistes Associés (AUA) between 1961 and 1985. In 1980, he was awarded the Grand Prix national d'architecture. As Vice President of Plan Construction (1982–87), he jointly presided over the Grand Paris scientific committee (2009). He has taught at the École d'Architecture de Strasbourg (1968–72), the École Nationale des Ponts-et-Chaussées (1978–89), and the École polytechnique fédérale de Lausanne (1993–94).
Projects he has worked on include the underground developments in Les Halles and, with Borja Huidobro, the Finance Ministry and the renovation of the Great Gallery of the National Museum of Natural History. Winner of the international competition for the extension to the historic Paris Axis, he designed the Green Meridian (Méridienne verte) project in 2000.
Recent projects by the AUA PAUL CHEMETOV firm include: urban projects in Montpellier and Amiens, the development of the area around the Porte de Vincennes in Paris, the transformation of the Hôpital Boucicaut, the extension of the Lyon Sud School of Medicine, the Labège multimedia library, the Vendespace and many housing projects, the renovation of the Coursives in Pantin, and of the Science and Technology Campus in Bordeaux, France.
Paul Chemetov demonstrates his architectural and urban convictions not only through the constructions and developments for which he is responsible, but also in articles, books, and public statements.

Ariel Genadt

Ariel Genadt is an architect, a lecturer, and a scholar, based in New York. His research focuses on the design and construction of architectural envelopes and their capacity to express cultural and environmental aspects of various places. He also specializes in the history and theory of twentieth-century architecture in Japan. Genadt holds a PhD in Architecture from the University of Pennsylvania (2016), a Master of Arts in Histories and Theories from the Architectural Association School, London (2004), and a Bachelor of Architecture cum laude from the Technion, Israel (1997). Genadt has collaborated as an architect on a wide range of buildings, urban design and landscape projects, in France, Israel, Greece, Morocco, Japan, and China. He has taught at the University of Pennsylvania School of Design, Swarthmore College, and the Technion in Israel. In 2012 he was a Fellow Researcher of the Japan Society for the Promotion of Science at the Kengo Kuma Lab, Tokyo University, and in 2013, the first visiting scholar at the Fondazione Renzo Piano, Genoa. In 2018 he curated the exhibition *Critical Abstractions – Modern Architecture in Japan 1868-2018* at the Architectural Archives of the University of Pennsylvania. His scholarly articles have been published in *EAHN Architectural Histories, JSAH, Baumeister, Topos*, and *Architect's Newspaper*.

Zvi Hecker

Zvi Hecker (b. 1931, Krakow) spent his teen years in Samarkand, Uzbekistan. Back in Krakow after World War II, he enrolled into the School of Architecture at Tadeusz Kościuszko University of Technology, but immigrated soon after to Israel where, in 1954, he received his degree in engineering and architecture from the Technion – Israel Institute of Technology in Haifa.
He set up a private practice in 1959 in Tel Aviv with Eldar and Alfred Neumann. Together, they designed the Club Mediteranné in Arziv, the City Hall of Bat-Yam, and Dubiner Apartment House in Ramat Gan. In the 1970s Hecker worked on the design for Montreal City Centre, built the Military Academy in the Negev Desert, the Ramat HaSharon City Centre, and realized the Spiral Apartment House in Ramat Gan. Hecker would later move to Berlin to realize the winning design for the Jewish School in Berlin, the Jewish Cultural Centre in Duisburg, and the Memorial Site for the Lindenstrasse Synagogue in Berlin (with Micha Ullman and Eyal Weizmann). At the same time in Tel Aviv, together with Rafi Segal, he built the Palmach Museum of History. His recent projects include the design of the Jewish Museum in Warsaw and the Koningin Máximakazerne at the Schiphol Airport Amsterdam, among many others.
Zvi Hecker has been a visiting professor at universities in the US, Canada, and Austria. He has won a number of architectural competitions and prizes in Germany, Israel, the US, and Poland.

Le projet en appartenance | → p. 6

Marc Mimram

Représentation du projet

L'architecture est souvent représentée comme un produit, un objet désincarné. Cette représentation marchande, fréquemment magnifiée, met à distance et transforme l'habitant en spectateur d'une architecture dématérialisée, délocalisée, déshumanisée.
Il m'a paru important de présenter notre travail à travers les valeurs qu'il porte – valeurs sociales et matérielles, géographiques et culturelles – pour exploiter la raison des choses, des choix, de la démarche et de l'engagement qui le constituent.
Il fallait pour cela sortir des ciels éclatants, des angles panoptiques, des couleurs photoshopées, de la marchandisation du projet, pour exprimer une démarche disciplinaire, explicite, transmissible.
Le regard du photographe est d'importance. La rencontre avec Erieta Attali a permis de mettre en partage son « point de vue » et notre travail. Il ne s'agit pas ici de mettre la photographie au service d'une présentation publicitaire, mais de confronter des préoccupations sensibles et matérielles communes. Si la photographie est un art, elle n'en est pas moins technique et détermination.
La texture, le grain, le contraste résonnent avec la matérialité de notre architecture. Le cadrage, l'horizon, l'ancrage convoquent le paysage qui fonde le projet.
Le travail d'Erieta Attali se focalise sur les territoires extrêmes avec un regard ciselé, tendu, déterminé. Nous travaillons sur la frugalité, ou la massivité, sur l'expression des forces mécaniques dans l'univers technique, toujours avec une économie de moyens, une sobriété dont la photographie exprime le caractère ténu.
La valeur du paysage comme expression de toute condition initiale est pour la photographe comme pour nous une manière d'exprimer le caractère local, la nature située du projet.
C'est bien dans ce rapport entre local et global que notre intégration des conditions du lieu fonde la démarche de projet, que notre appartenance aux conditions d'exploitation de la planète fonde l'architecture en art de la transformation.

Ici et ailleurs

Ici, dans les racines d'une géologie fondatrice, dans la limite tendue entre sol et ciel que forme l'horizon gravitaire du lieu, dans la mesure du franchissement qui façonne le lien, dans l'orientation du soleil, dans les conditions géométriques des gabarits de circulation. Ici et nulle part ailleurs.
Ailleurs, car l'appartenance au lieu est concomitante de la dimension territoriale de l'infrastructure qui s'empare de l'unité géographique à grande échelle, pour fixer une unité globale tandis que le projet dialogue avec le lieu qu'il façonne.
Localité et globalité : telles sont les deux dimensions oxymoriques que le projet associe.
Voilà pourquoi il me paraissait important que la représentation de notre travail exprime cette vision géographique. La photographie y participe largement dans les temporalités des prises de vue, entre lumières et brouillard, en toutes saisons, sans emphase sous les nuages désignés et les cieux de festival.
Quelles que soient les saisons et les lumières, les projets résonnent, et cela accentue cette émotion qui m'est si chère, l'appartenance.

Le projet en résonance avec les conditions de son émergence

Il y a le site
La condition initiale. Le paysage est la raison fondatrice du projet, la matrice bouleversée, transformée radicalement, violemment par lui. Ni réceptacle, ni vide potentiel, mais condition géographique informée d'histoire. Ici se définit l'horizon gravitaire, la tension entre ciel et terre, les limites de la pièce dans laquelle se situe l'observateur, les forces telluriques de la topographie, les ancrages, la faille, la brèche, son ouverture, la portée réelle ou lue, les conditions géologiques fondatrices.
Le site est l'expression du temps, des saisons, des vents, de la lumière… des lumières.
Ici se définissent l'échelle du projet, ses échelles de lecture – unité ou assemblage, continuité formelle ou discontinuité des composants hiérarchisés, opacités ou transparences, unité matérielle ou diversité des ordres constructifs. C'est dans cette lecture du paysage que se fonde le projet, dans un dialogue avec l'horizon tendu jusqu'à la rupture, un équilibre stabilisé par une métamorphose radicale du monde, une morphogenèse raisonnée, à la fois intense et délicate.

Il y a le lien
Par-delà la simple raison fonctionnelle, souvent triviale, les hypothèses du paysage offrent des conditions d'usage plurielles que révèle le dispositif choisi – parcours multiples, vide habité, ancrages et limites, situations topographiques désignées. Entre les lignes de force se jouent les lignes de parcours, de déambulation, de résidence, dans la continuité ou l'altération du dispositif, dans les variations géométriques qu'autorisent les composants de la structure. Le lien devient alors un lieu. La vie prend place, expression du partage que désigne l'espace public, celui de tous, pour tous, et construction physique de la représentation démocratique.

Il y a la gravité
Les ouvrages ne sont pas de simples schémas statiques bâtis, mais l'interprétation d'une hypothèse gravitaire révélée. Ouvrage de sol ou de ciel, expression d'une massivité apparente ou d'une légèreté exacerbée. L'ouvrage s'ancre dans les puissances d'attractivité ou s'en libère, dentelle de matière ordonnée sous les lumières ou feuille plissée tendue continûment entre ses appuis, érection abstraite dans le ciel ou modelage tellurique.
Les expressions de la gravité sont plurielles, raisonnées, choisies délibérément. L'ouvrage est cette expression, la structure son interprétation.

Il y a la matérialité
Une mise en œuvre de la matière qui donne sens, tant par l'expression de l'art de la transformation – depuis son extraction planétaire jusqu'à la mise en œuvre d'un travail artisanal ou industriel, humain – que par la manière dont le projet en devient la mémoire offerte et lisible, comme une trace des savoirs accumulés.
Une matière à penser le projet pour inscrire sa genèse dans la transformation radicale du monde qu'il opère. Joindre la pensée et le faire, c'est intégrer le chantier dans un projet qui, sinon, serait coupé du réel pour se complaire dans une virtualité frustrée, hémiplégique ; c'est marquer son appartenance au monde pour s'opposer à une dématérialisation de l'esprit.

Il y a la structure
Expression sensible des contingences statiques et gravitaires, de la résistance des matériaux, de la résilience du site.
Le projet est la fabrique de ce choix raisonné, la structure de l'ouvrage est la mise en cohérence des conditions ici exprimées.
Il ne s'agit évidemment pas d'une solution idéale, parfaite, univoque, dont la rationalité du schéma statique serait la garante. Il n'y a pas de solution unique, mathématique qui valoriserait un catalogue abstrait et sublime de modèles référents. Le spécifique doit se substituer au générique : le lieu parle, le projet est de là et de nulle part ailleurs, il est sentiment et raison, délicate mise en forme des rapports savants entre statique et géométrie, entre plaisirs du paysage et conscience de la radicalité de la transformation engendrée, entre universalité des contraintes et spécificité de leur mise en œuvre.
Les logiques sont plurielles, mais toujours le projet manifeste une contemporanéité généreuse, attentive au monde. Sa forme exprime soudain une douce jubilation.
L'ouvrage d'art devient alors œuvre d'architecture.

Entre structure et infrastructure

Les projets que nous développons intègrent le plus souvent les conditions d'une infrastructure. C'est le cas des ponts ou des passerelles, bien sûr, mais également des équipements ou des bâtiments que nous projetons.
Je considère que notre travail est au service du bien commun et qu'il doit offrir, au-delà du programme que le projet réinterprète, des conditions généreuses pour une appropriation et une affectation plus large par ses usagers. Le projet doit dépasser cette condition initiale du programme pour permettre une habitabilité de tous, une représentation de chacun dans l'espace offert, mis à disposition.
En ce sens, le projet est une infrastructure, un réseau de conditions qui autorise le dépassement. Le pont n'est pas un lien, pas uniquement. Évidemment il permet de passer d'une rive à l'autre, mais le projet peut le muter en lieu. Le lieu est offert à tous en partage. Le lieu prend place dans le paysage qu'il veut habiter. L'espace ainsi créé légitime cette transformation radicale de la vallée escarpée, du réseau routier, du fleuve tumultueux ou ferroviaire, pour offrir davantage : une facilit un dispositif généreux et appropriable par tous, une émotion.

Le tablier se transforme en balcon sur le paysage, l'espace dilaté devient un espace public offert. La place prend place. Le passage se métamorphose en dispositif de rencontre, de contemplation, de compréhension du paysage, de la géographie, d'une nature transformée par l'homme, jamais vierge et toujours hostile, le plus souvent socialement révélateur. L'infrastructure est habituellement considérée comme un mal nécessaire. Transformons-la en un bien partagé. La route gêne, l'autoroute nuit plus encore. Le rail est utile et respecté s'il est mis à distance. Seul le fleuve semble offrir un agrément, sauf dans les tumultes de ses fluctuations rapides.

Notre travail est de franchir, de couvrir, de parcourir les infrastructures en les valorisant à travers la capacité qu'elles ont de définir d'autres horizons qu'elles-mêmes, de mettre en regard la géographie et l'organisation sociale du territoire, de créer des lieux où se croisent, se rencontrent, prennent place des manifestations d'aménité et de bienveillance entre les hommes. Alors, l'infrastructure que nous créons et celle que nous franchissons se joignent dans un projet commun, un bien commun.

L'espace public comme condition initiale

Lorsque la société se représentait à travers les bâtiments du pouvoir, de l'institution, de la religion, elle investissait l'architecture d'un rôle que la discipline traduisait en ordre, en composition. Son écriture, sa facture même en était l'expression. L'espace public joue ce rôle, prend le pouvoir pour l'offrir à tous et donner à chacun la possibilité de se l'approprier : c'est l'espace de la démocratie.

C'est dans cette hypothèse que notre travail trouve son sens. Elle qualifie une attitude face au projet et adresse celui-ci à une pratique collective, au quotidien et à l'exceptionnel. C'est une démarche pour tous face au pouvoir de certains lorsque l'institution se construit des monuments d'architecture.

La rue, la place, le lien que le franchissement opère, sont au centre de cette approche attentive à qualifier de manière généreuse et délicate l'espace public. L'infrastructure n'est pas un outil fonctionnel abandonné à la rationalité des contraintes, comme celle de la vitesse, qui isole du monde pour s'autocentrer sur le gain de temps en toute sécurité, qui segmente en espaces dédiés et différenciés selon les moyens de transport. Bien au contraire, il nous faut assembler, partager, mettre en commun le bien commun de l'espace public pour valoriser cette condition du vivre ensemble. L'infrastructure coupe, sépare, divise de part en part autant qu'elle relie deux points à l'échelle territoriale. Il nous faut inverser cette hypothèse insupportable.

Nous en faisons la condition du projet.

À Rabat, la sous-face du viaduc d'accès devient un toit qui abrite un long espace public appropriable, à l'instar du *Borough Market* de Londres.

Sur le Rhin, la place centrale permet par l'appréhension des conditions géographiques de souligner non pas une histoire qui oppose, mais l'appartenance à un paysage qui assemble.

Au stade Roland-Garros, les serres qui enceignent le court de tennis réunissent sport et jardin dans un projet positif, valorisant des programmes qui semblaient antagoniques.

À Paris, le bâtiment Airtime se transforme en bâtiment-pont et suspend la couverture des voies ferrées pour installer une continuité urbaine ouverte sur l'horizon de la ville.

Ces projets parmi d'autres montrent combien une approche positive de l'infrastructure peut créer de la valeur en installant l'espace public au centre des réflexions, en dépassant les conditions d'une programmation souvent restrictive pour faire du projet un outil d'appropriation démocratique.

Appartenance ou intégration

Il est souvent demandé au projet de s'intégrer dans son site d'accueil. Quelle posture !

Comment peut-on imaginer que les gorges de la Truyère laissent le viaduc de Garabit et toute la rougeur de sa structure de treillis riveté se fondre en elles ? Il ne s'agit pas plus ici qu'ailleurs d'une intégration dans le paysage. Cette terminologie laisse entendre une dissolution par symbiose, voire par camouflage. Or, il n'en est rien. Quelle que soit son échelle, aucune infrastructure, aucun ouvrage d'art ne peut disparaître, et c'est très bien ainsi. Notre travail se fonde davantage sur la lecture du paysage, cette géographie informée d'histoire, pour y prendre place en intelligence, en résonance.

Lire l'horizon et les variations topographiques ou construites qui l'habitent ; comprendre la place du ciel, son étendue, son installation, sa découpe ; saisir les mouvements du sol dans l'artifice de nature modelée par le travail de l'homme ; observer les étendues végétales dans le cycle des saisons ; comparer les traits et les lignes de niveau d'une topographie en mutation.

Les conditions initiales du projet sont préexistantes. La présence construite de l'ouvrage se révèlera dans cette situation toujours unique pour qualifier une appartenance visible, souvent forte, parfois brutale, déterminante dans la mutation opérée.

Le choix structurel est ici essentiel dans la manière dont il fixe le schéma gravitaire en se faisant l'expression d'un ancrage ou d'un soulèvement, d'un encastrement ou d'un effleurement. Faire flotter une massivité magnifiée comme pour le pont Zhong Sheng Da Dao, à Tianjin, ou bien faire jaillir une dentelle de béton de part et d'autre du Bouregreg à Rabat ?

Suivons Louis Harel de la Noë sur les chemins de fer bretons ou Gustave Eiffel à Saint-André-de-Cubzac ; suivons les variations d'échelle, les assemblages disruptifs de matières, les confrontations aux paysages.

Le schéma gravitaire est l'outil de cette transformation raisonnée de l'horizon dans lequel s'installe le projet. La structure peut être massive ou arachnéenne, façonnée dans un continuum de surfaces à résistance de forme ou dans un assemblage de membrures discontinues, texturée dans le grain de la matière ou réfléchissante sous les lumières, elle peut associer statiquement des composantes articulées ou globalement encastrées… Ces choix raisonnés induisent toujours une expression formelle,

mais la multitude des possibles révèle la détermination des choix. Quel plaisir que ce dialogue entre intuition et raison, entre la grande échelle du paysage et celle de l'assemblage, entre la force du tout et le choix des composants, du pas, de la portée !
Le calcul est libératoire par la révolution numérique qui rend possible ce qui, hier, était limité, réduit à un éventail de choix éprouvés. La résolution fastidieuse a laissé place à une liberté sous surveillance mathématique.
La matière construite s'exprime dans la dissidence des mises en œuvre, dans l'ordre de la structure en résolution spécifique.

Le dispositif structurel est ici au service de ce dialogue apaisé ou déterminé avec le paysage. Il est raisonné, mais jamais imposé par une prétendue solution structurelle idéale ou suggérée à travers un catalogue de solutions universelles.
Rien n'est plus terrible que de voir se répandre d'Helsinki à Shanghai ces voussoirs préfabriqués qui franchissent indifféremment les sites sous prétexte d'une rationalité indiscutable invitant souvent un idéal de pureté mathématique.
Tout cela n'est que détournement de fond. Convoquons l'impur pour retrouver les conditions de résonance avec le paysage, pour rétablir le dialogue avec le site, fût-il radical.

Et par-delà les solutions calculatoires prédéterminées, laissons le projet qualifier les choix raisonnés de son appartenance au site plutôt que de croire en une illusoire intégration.

L'ouvrage d'art n'est pas une œuvre d'art

Une autre confusion rend le projet inopérant, celle qui voudrait confondre ouvrage d'art et œuvre d'art.
La position sociale, culturelle, intellectuelle de l'artiste dans la société n'est pas celle de l'architecte. Notre travail se fonde sur la transformation de la matière en projet à partir d'une raison située. Le contenu théorique qui le porte convoque le savoir-faire de l'artisan et prend position dans le cadre de la discipline architecturale.
Il ne s'agit pas d'interroger la société à travers l'œuvre, de porter un regard critique, ni de mettre en perspective en offrant les outils d'un questionnement théorique, même si celui-ci peut néanmoins exister à partir d'une expérience physique, celle des sens.
Le projet de paysage n'est pas du *land art*. Le développement des structures n'est pas de la sculpture. Confondre ces approches relève d'une vision réductrice de l'œuvre d'art, souvent cantonnée dans son apparence matérielle ou onirique.
Si le travail sur la tôle d'acier et l'équilibre des installations de Richard Serra me guide dans le façonnage en continu de la feuille métallique, les passerelles de Toulouse ou de Yangzhou ne sont pas pour autant des sculptures. Si le travail sur le reflet et la matérialisation de la non-transparence du verre chez Dan Graham m'offrent l'expérience de l'espace difracté, rien ne laisse croire à la dématérialisation de l'architecture dans les projets que je développe.
Le dialogue entre art et architecture est fondateur d'une pensée critique de notre rapport au monde. Mais l'architecte n'est pas un artiste, pas plus que l'ouvrage d'art n'est une œuvre d'art.

L'architecture comme un art de la transformation

L'architecture serait ainsi bien plus à considérer comme un art de la transformation matérielle du réel.
Le « construit », nous le savons bien, se façonne à partir des ressources limitées de notre planète, cet unique fournisseur matériel de l'architecture. Notre appartenance au monde débute ici. Rien n'est exogène et le système ne s'alimente d'aucune production « extra-terrestre ».
Ainsi, il y a une responsabilité de l'architecture dans le processus consumériste, et ce paramètre devrait fonder notre approche. Car si la rupture moderniste du projet vernaculaire initie une abstraction au lieu, la consommation globalisée semble accélérer cette absence de conscience du lien entre matérialité et architecture.
Il nous faut donc renouer avec cette raison théorique de la mise en œuvre, cette acuité des sens qui distingue construction et architecture, mais fonde le projet sur une matérialité critique.
Dans le cycle long du bâti, depuis l'extraction des matériaux jusqu'à la démolition des bâtiments, en passant par l'énergie grise et la requalification, sans forfanterie verte ni préciosité d'apparat, nous devons développer une écologie constructive informée, raisonnée, qui accepte toujours l'hypothèse du progrès.
Sans flagellation, mais en conscience, l'architecture se place dans une démarche de responsabilité face à la transformation du monde qu'elle opère, de l'extraction des ressources jusqu'au chantier.
Alors, le savoir-faire et l'expression raffinée de cette attention au monde installent l'architecture dans les plaisirs du faire. Faire à penser. Faire à expérimenter. Faire à refuser les effets spécieux d'une formalisation outrancière au profit d'une science du touché, des assemblages innovants, d'une acceptation du vieillissement ou encore de l'impur.
N'oublions jamais que le sens étymologique de « poésie » trouve son origine dans le verbe *poiein* qui signifie : faire. Retrouvons ce lien indéfectible entre poésie et faire, cette poésie du faire.

Le projet de mémoire

Le projet construit peut alors être compris comme une mémoire accumulée de moments absents dont l'architecture serait le témoin.
Mémoire d'une situation bouleversée : celle de l'avant, de ce paysage sans la présence physique du projet. Et pourtant, cette rencontre avec le paysage est bien la condition originelle de sa création.
Mémoire d'une transformation du monde : celle des ressources accumulées planétairement et dont le projet se montre le dépositaire de manière révélée ou cachée, structurelle ou ornementale.
Mémoire du chantier : celle du travail, du labeur souvent, du raffinement aussi. De cette accumulation d'heures, de savoir-faire et de passions que le chantier diffuse en architecture, comme une condition pour penser le projet.

Les architectures de papier valorisées comme des fondements théoriques ont trop souvent situé le projet dans un ordre prévalent qui conçoit le chantier comme une simple phase d'exécution sans âme, sans appartenance au processus de conception. En réalité, il n'en rien. Le chantier permet de penser le projet. Il n'exécute pas, il fonde matériellement et théoriquement celui-ci. Ne laissons pas l'architecture en dehors du champ du progrès – progrès des conditions de travail autant que de la révolution numérique et robotique, progrès des caractéristiques physiques des matériaux comme des modes de mise en œuvre, progrès des géométries complexes et des structures frugales et sophistiquées.
En retrouvant le chemin de l'appartenance au monde qu'elle transforme, l'architecture se meut en mémoire et s'ouvre aux plaisirs du partage des savoirs : ceux oubliés d'hier, ceux proposés aujourd'hui, ceux des hommes au chantier, ceux des hommes qu'elle accueille. Elle devient ainsi cette architecture généreuse, sans idéologie ordonnatrice, qui autorise et suscite la sensibilité.

Préface | → p. 12
Paul Chemetov

Pendant quelques années, de 1978 à 1989, j'enseignais l'architecture à l'École nationale des ponts et chaussées (ENPC). L'école était alors rue des Saints-Pères, face à la faculté de médecine, voisine de l'École des beaux-arts, entre la Seine et Saint-Germain-des-Prés. Et s'il fallait poursuivre cet inventaire, les cafés, les boutiques de mode comme les musées étaient proches. L'école de la ville s'offrait à portée de curiosité.
L'enseignement que nous proposions, Bruno Fortier, Jean-Louis Cohen, Yves Lion, Christian Devillers et moi-même, servait aussi à déchiffrer la bibliothèque urbaine que Paris mettait en rayon. Marc Mimram – on le sait ou on ne le sait pas – fut l'un de nos premiers élèves.
Il est vrai que Marc apportait son ouverture d'esprit dans cet échange où nous ne prenions plus les ingénieurs pour des calculatrices, mais pour les inventeurs qu'ils sont et doivent être. Nous ne nous présentions pas en dessinateurs du bon goût, en arbitres des élégances, mais en architectes cultivés pétris d'histoire, de formes, d'usages, et attentifs aux modes de construire.
Bref, nous apprenions, élèves ou enseignants, à être polytechniques.
Au sortir de l'école, après avoir passé une année à l'université de Berkeley, Marc partit au Brésil pour y accomplir son service national, y rencontrant Oscar Niemeyer. Dès son retour en France, je lui demandai de travailler tout d'abord au Plan Construction puis, de façon plus professionnelle, pour nos projets des Halles, du ministère des Finances et du Muséum national d'histoire naturelle.
En 1983, il y a vingt-cinq ans, Marc Mimram publiait son premier livre, *Structures et Formes. Étude appliquée à l'œuvre de Robert Le Ricolais*. Il m'avait demandé de le préfacer. Pas un mot à retirer de ces deux pages qui situaient Marc dans ses filiations, jusqu'à celle de Camille Polonceau, inventeur de la sous-tension des pièces de charpente. En voici la conclusion : « Aux naïvetés des encyclopédistes ont succédé les certitudes des ordinateurs. Ce qu'ils permettent dans le calcul des réseaux – impossible manuellement – dans la simulation presque instantanée des conséquences d'une solution, s'accompagne aussi des routines de la prédétermination. S'ils n'ont mis fin au fastidieux, avec lui risque de disparaître cette interrogation indéfiniment répétée sur des contraintes à peine différentes, où nous discernons une des conditions de l'invention : cette évidence fulgurante d'un autre chemin alors que, depuis toujours, l'habituel paraissait le seul possible. Mais il faut cette répétition presque mécanique, cette tentation constante de ramener l'inconnu à des lois pour qu'une fois, avec force, il dicte la nouvelle loi ! ».
Le témoin que je lui tendais, il me le retourne, posant sur ma table un jeu de photographies d'un format inusité, une image large, dilatée et pourtant précise.
Photos de chantier, d'ossatures articulées comme des cages thoraciques, englobant de l'air mais surtout des volumes capables.
On pourrait feuilleter ces pages et les rebattre comme un jeu de cartes, pour initier un rapprochement entre les demi-jours filtrant sous les filets de protection du chantier de l'avenue de France et ceux des voûtes minces de la gare de Montpellier, pour comparer la série des ponts ou s'attarder sur la passerelle Solférino, le seul franchissement moderne de Paris qui, à mon avis, peut affronter formellement et constructivement la longue série de ponts parisiens du pont Neuf à celui de la Concorde – à l'origine dessiné par Jean-Rodolphe Perronet, fondateur de l'ENPC –, jusqu'aux ponts métalliques de Jean Résal ou aux viaducs de pierre et d'acier du métro parisien.
Trois ponts exotiques en Chine et au Maroc complètent cet inventaire. Le premier ricoche comme un galet sur l'eau devant le paysage consternant de la construction à tout va. Au premier plan, une silhouette penchée dans les roseaux redonne quelque espoir et provoque l'inquiétude, l'interrogation sur le monde comme il est, entre deux rives, entre deux vies.
Le travail sur le lien qui lie Rabat à Salé en franchissant le Bouregreg est assez surprenant puisqu'il reprend des thèmes d'Eugène Freyssinet, mais les rend plus tranchants – le célèbre effort qu'il faut aux ingénieurs vaincre – grâce à un usage du béton qui renoue avec les âmes et les ailes de la charpente métallique. Là aussi, des constructions inattentives boursoufflent la ligne d'horizon, une petite barque de pêche, forme utile elle aussi, remonte le courant, le pont se prolonge par un très beau viaduc d'approche, la partie la plus difficile de tout franchissement. On le voit à Tancarville comme au pont de Normandie, prouesses incontestables par ailleurs.
Mais on trouvera certainement d'autres photos : Roland-Garros ou le pont de Bordeaux, la passerelle des Batignolles et celle des deux rives à Strasbourg, où Marc a édifié l'École d'architecture.
Je voudrais m'attarder sur deux projets. Parce qu'ils sont les plus illustrés et qu'ils sont tous deux à Paris, à portée de main et d'examen.
Le chantier de l'avenue de France est maintenant terminé et les photographies nous montrent un état archéologique que nous ne verrons plus. On peut le regretter. Car tout se télescope dans notre imaginaire – et ces images, et nos références, et notre nostalgie.
C'est à la fois New York et les ouvriers avec leurs *lunch box*, assis sur des poutres de quelque gratte-ciel en construction, et le peintre perché de

la tour Eiffel, funambule et clown à la fois. C'est ce monde de carcasses, qu'on aimerait conserver comme une grotte verticale, ces volumes d'air capables, aussi beaux que les grues qui aident à les construire. Sur une photo, la façade de la Bibliothèque de France semble hésiter à quitter son ancrage pour traverser la rue et venir clore ce monde de l'acier victorieux.
J'avoue cependant ma tendresse pour la passerelle Solférino. Elle reprend et amplifie la pensée structurelle qui, du pont des Arts aux fermes sous-tendues, anticipait la précontrainte. Sur certaines photos, l'inondation qui fait surgir la passerelle de l'eau la rend encore plus tendue – et la voilà qui quitte la terre ferme pour s'affirmer comme pur franchissement, théorème matérialisé, comme les lames ondoyantes de cet autre pont en Chine.
Mais revenons à Paris, à la Seine, à nos amours, aux péniches ou aux bateaux-mouches figés par la crue. La lumière faiblit, la grande roue s'illumine, quelques promeneurs, quelques couples et leurs sacs de pique-nique, flâneurs des deux rives, modernes tritons et naïades contemporaines, sont là pour nous prouver l'évidence de ce projet. Ils le contemplent, nous aussi.
Même si « portée infinie, poids nul » n'est qu'une métaphore asymptomatique, les projets de Marc Mimram pèsent de toute leur invention attentive, nous transportant non seulement d'une rive à l'autre, d'une hypothèse construite à l'autre, de l'ombre à la lumière, mais aussi du passé au présent, de l'avant à l'après.

Parcourir les courbes | → p. 16
Erieta Attali

Je suis née à Tel Aviv mais j'ai grandi entre Istanbul et Athènes, toujours à proximité de mers entourées de terres. Je me souviendrai toujours d'avoir assisté, enfant, à la construction puis à l'achèvement du pont enjambant le Bosphore, à Istanbul, reliant ainsi l'Europe à l'Asie. Je devais avoir sept ans à l'époque. J'étais assez mature pour être intriguée par cette infrastructure impressionnante et je me suis alors plongée dans les livres de géographie à la recherche d'autres merveilles de ce genre. C'est ainsi que j'ai découvert le canal de Panama, cette voie navigable reliant l'Atlantique et le Pacifique, et le détroit de Gibraltar entre la Méditerranée et l'Atlantique. L'observation des infrastructures, des axes routiers, de la façon dont les océans et les mers sont connectés entre eux, des terres lointaines et extrêmes, devint mon passe-temps favori pour ne pas dire mon obsession.
À vingt ans je me voyais déjà courir aux quatre coins du monde pour photographier les océans, les territoires reculés, les ponts, les routes, les aéroports... Il y a maintenant trois décennies que je me consacre à cette activité, au point que ces lieux constituent mon véritable domicile. Entre 2014 et 2016, alors que je parcourais l'Australie et ses paysages extrêmes pour photographier des bâtiments contemporains, j'ai commencé à diriger mon regard sur les mégastructures et les villes en expansion. Ce tournant m'a menée à Paris où depuis 2003 je m'étais promis de revenir.

C'est environ à cette époque que dans un auditorium plein à craquer du Victoria & Albert Museum de Londres, j'ai assisté à une conférence de Marc Mimram. Cela a été comme une révélation. Avec ses ponts bardés de prix au Maroc, en Chine ou encore à Kehl, il s'était donné pour mission de relier des géographies, la mer avec la terre. Je voyais des courbes plonger dans l'eau, des fenêtres s'ouvrir sur le ciel, de nouveaux croisements se créer, se répondre, flotter. Quand j'observais ses ponts en Chine, j'avais l'impression de pénétrer dans *Le Courant de Humboldt*, la toile de Max Ernst, tandis que son bâtiment Airtime me rappelait l'œuvre de Lyonel Feininger.

Les toutes premières photographies que j'ai montrées à Marc représentaient des paysages reculés, ces lieux que j'aime appeler « les limites du monde ». Ils étaient presque dénués de toute structure, de toute trace humaine. Je ne cherchais absolument pas à attirer l'attention de Marc grâce à des images de papier glacé mais plutôt à le défier en lui proposant un nouveau langage commun à nos pratiques respectives.

À travers mon objectif, j'ai entrepris de suivre les lignes qu'il traçait, les courbes qui s'affaissaient lentement au sol pour rebondir à nouveau. J'ai voulu capter les espaces illusoires qui se reflétaient au sein des vides dans l'eau mais aussi les véritables espaces nourris par une conception profondément démocratique de la vie publique. Il est rare de découvrir une expression de la beauté aussi rationnelle, car le binôme émotion / logique vient souvent perturber les choses. Les créations de Marc n'ondulent pas seulement formellement ; elles ondulent aussi expressivement, dans un parcours allant du civique au poétique. Elles m'ont aussi invitée à entreprendre un voyage qui est loin d'être achevé, celui de la création d'un monde qui exige à la fois d'être vécu et capturé.

Passerelle Solférino,
aujourd'hui passerelle Léopold-Sédar-Senghor
Paris, France | → p. 20
Marc Mimram

J'entends encore résonner ce cri de joie. À 37 ans, je venais de gagner le concours pour la nouvelle passerelle Solférino à Paris, le trente-sixième franchissement de la Seine.
Quel incroyable moment ! Celui d'un engagement assumé, sans distance critique, sans crainte, presque insouciant devant le projet d'une construction en plein cœur de la ville historique, entre le jardin des Tuileries et le musée d'Orsay.

La typologie structurelle est classique – un arc de 105 mètres de portée –, mais le détournement d'usage est fondateur : il s'agit d'amplifier les parcours à l'intérieur de la structure, de multiplier les liens entre quais hauts, entre quais bas, de faire de l'ouvrage d'art un véritable espace public, tant par la multiplicité des cheminements possibles que par la générosité de la place qu'il offre, balcon ouvert sur le paysage du fleuve et de la ville.

La structure est parcourue. Le vide entre l'arc et le tablier, ce vide qui qualifie l'ouvrage, est habité, et je me souviens de l'émotion à parcourir le vide signifiant qui sépare les deux coques du dôme de Brunelleschi, à Florence. Ce vide qui donne sens et résistance à la structure.

Ici, le parcours des forces joint le parcours du promeneur. Entre le sol et le tablier s'ouvre une fenêtre sur le ciel.
La structure des arcs encastrés dans les culées varie de 55 centimètres à la clé à 105 centimètres en pied, et se développe selon des poutres Vierendeel. Ici, pas de diagonales caractéristiques de l'architecture metallique rivetée du XIXe siècle, mais des montants encastrés par soudure. Les tôles oxycoupées et façonnées sont de forte épaisseur (120 millimètres), et la soudure sur le chantier est rendue possible par le contrôle *in situ*.

La technologie est contemporaine, le vocabulaire constructif qu'elle autorise bénéficie de ces atouts.
Et pourtant, pas de rupture radicale. Les plaisirs du lieu, les plaisirs d'être là.
Un bon projet d'ouvrage d'art est un projet spécifique, indéplaçable, ancré dans son site d'accueil.
Pour beaucoup, la passerelle semble avoir toujours été là. Elle ne montre pas ses muscles, n'impose pas de rupture formelle triomphale. Ce pourrait être le paradigme d'une modernité sensible, d'une contemporanéité généreuse.
J'ai depuis lors construit bien d'autres ouvrages. Le vocabulaire constructif s'est adapté aux différents projets, aux savoirs spécifiques, aux caractéristiques des lieux, des pays. Mais les fondements étaient dans ce projet déjà présents : l'attention au faire, l'expression des capacités technologiques, l'ambition d'offrir davantage que la simple liaison pour transformer le lien en un lieu. Et la volonté, toujours, de se mettre en résonance avec le site.

J'aurais pu être pris d'un doute à occuper le « vide » entre le pont de la Concorde et le pont Royal, à tendre la structure dans le panorama des Tuileries, à installer les parcours au-dessus du fleuve nourricier. Mais c'est au contraire la raison déclinée en responsabilité que j'appris dans le développement de ce projet… et les plaisirs qu'elle autorise.

Pont Hassan II
Rabat — Salé, Maroc | → p. 28
Marc Mimram

S'inscrire dans l'horizon paysage

Tout ici est tendu, beau et fragile. L'esplanade du mausolée Mohamed V marque un plateau, la médina et la kasbah des Oudaïas forment au loin une fine texture entre le ciel et l'embouchure du fleuve préparant la découverte d'un autre horizon : la mer.
La citadelle de Salé s'installe dans cet ancrage au sol.
Le nouveau pont doit dialoguer avec cette horizontalité construite, préserver les vues, offrir des regards, laisser filtrer sans obérer, cadrer les ouvertures sans masquer et surtout laisser intact le ciel. Car de cette minéralité ciselée émerge seule à l'horizon la tour Hassan.

Le projet d'ouvrage d'art est un service public situé, projeté à partir du paysage qui l'accueille.

La fine dentelle de béton prend place sur le site pour construire un véritable équipement public, un toit urbain en dialogue avec le paysage – un paysage ici délicat et précieux, où le fleuve est la matrice du développement historique de la ville.

Une structure évolutive et orientée
Il ne s'agit pas ici de créer un viaduc solitaire mais de s'inscrire en continuité, en urbanité.
La structure toujours évolutive s'adapte aux conditions pour croître vers le Bouregreg. Les travées latérales sont composées de demi-portiques qui vont croissant vers le centre du fleuve, jusqu'à former la voûte centrale.
Cette évolution continue se fait au long d'une grande courbe virtuelle ouverte sur le ciel et centrée sur le fleuve.

Une dentelle minérale
Un motif unique croissant fonde les arcs évolutifs.
Le pont est composé de trois tabliers juxtaposés indépendants qui préservent entre les voûtes les lumières variant au gré des mouvements du soleil. À l'ouest, le spectacle de la médina et de la kasbah des Oudaïas est offert aux piétons et aux passagers du tramway.
Cette structure est délicate et sophistiquée. Sculptée dans le béton clair, elle varie continûment au long de ses membrures adaptées au schéma statique.
Sur 800 mètres de long, le tablier du viaduc d'accès parfaitement horizontal construit un toit au-dessus de la douce pente de la plaine alluviale vers le fleuve. La structure du tablier protège un espace public accueillant, une promenade. Il se transforme en toit protecteur, celui d'un marché ou de toute autre occupation publique éphémère.

Ce pont est projeté pour ce lieu et aucun autre, il est issu de cette attention portée aux conditions d'un paysage unique ciselé de blanc et d'ocre sur l'horizon. Cette ligne tendue entre Rabat et Salé dialogue avec le fleuve pour y puiser son rythme, sa géométrie, sa structure dans les lumières changeantes de l'oued.

Sur ce projet, c'est l'aventure humaine qui résonne. Celle des ouvriers, des hommes au travail, du labeur. Ces métiers sont durs mais ils rendent fiers. Le projet fait la part du travail de construction et de celui de conception. Ici se mêlent très haute technicité du calcul et de la mise en œuvre et savoir-faire artisanaux. Cette complémentarité est la marque du projet. Le paysage mais aussi cette mise en œuvre en font un projet situé.

L'ouvrage d'art construit un lien généreux autour de l'espace public qu'il façonne, et sa prouesse technique est au service d'une modernité attentive au délicat paysage du Bouregreg.

Passerelle Marcelle-Henry – ZAC Clichy-Batignolles
Paris, France | → p. 38
Marc Mimram

La passerelle Marcelle-Henry de la ZAC Clichy-Batignolles relie la rue Saussure pour ancrer le projet urbain du secteur Clichy-Batignolles dans le tissu parisien dense au-delà du faisceau ferré de la gare Saint-Lazare. L'enjeu est de taille puisqu'il s'adresse à la pratique locale de l'espace public ainsi qu'à l'ancrage territorial du nouveau développement urbain, mais aussi parce qu'il s'adresse au proche et au lointain, le proche de la pratique quotidienne et le lointain du paysage depuis les voies de chemin de fer, depuis le fleuve ferroviaire que la passerelle franchit et auquel elle se réfère.
Le projet s'inscrit dans la continuité sensible de l'espace public, dans cette continuité des sols, des espaces destinés à l'agrément, entre la placette qui fait lien avec la topographie de la rue Saussure et l'ancrage végétal vers le parc.

Créer un véritable lieu public au-dessus du réseau ferroviaire

La structure de franchissement est un ouvrage d'art qui dépend tout à la fois des contraintes statiques et des protections au-dessus des voies de chemin de fer que nous avons voulu intégrer à la structure de l'ouvrage. La structure composée de poutres courbes se déformant continûment d'une rive à l'autre accueille au sein de l'ouvrage des dispositifs de pose, de repos, de contemplation. Ici, espace public et structure sont intégrés dans la géométrie surfacique de l'ouvrage.
Le tracé du tablier est formé par des alcôves situées de part et d'autre et ouvrant de longues courbes qui dilatent la promenade.
Ces balcons accompagnent la variation d'inertie de la structure au droit des appuis pour créer une douce ligne continue à la rive de l'ouvrage tant en élévation qu'en plan, dans le faisceau des arcs courbes et cintrés qui rigidifient la rive en constituant des poutres Vierendeel à inertie variable. Ainsi, de part et d'autre, les lectures de l'ouvrage sont asymétriques et croisées, fines puis ouvertes, courbes puis élégies, pour mettre en cohérence l'attention apportée à l'espace public et le schéma statique de l'ouvrage.
Le lien devient un lieu.
Cette structure fine et légère s'ouvre sur le ciel et installe la transparence de sa maille périmétrale en auvent pour construire un filtre vers le ciel. Le jeu des lumières à l'intérieur de l'ouvrage varie selon l'orientation de cette passerelle à l'est et à l'ouest, dans la vision qu'elle offre depuis l'infrastructure.
L'économie de matière, la frugalité, sont ici la garantie d'une attention durable au développement de cette structure.

Le confort d'une structure légère et pérenne

D'une extrémité à l'autre de la passerelle, le projet met en cohérence les parcours et l'expression construite raisonnée de sa structure au service des piétons et de l'espace public.
La nouvelle passerelle appartient à l'espace public qu'elle façonne en créant une très grande fluidité, un repère urbain à différentes échelles, attentif aux piétons qui la parcourent, qui l'habitent et qui s'y tiennent, mais également aux regards lointains dans le paysage urbain qui ici se transforme.
Par sa silhouette continue et gracile, par son ancrage dans l'univers de la ville, la nouvelle passerelle constitue un lien généreux dans la douceur courbe de sa géométrie.

Pôle nautique de Mantes-la-Ville
Mantes-la-Ville, France | → p. 46
Marc Mimram

La nouvelle piscine de Mantes-la-Ville s'inscrit dans le développement urbain et paysager autour de la gare.
Le caractère urbain de la piscine est une condition importante de son développement architectural. Il s'agit ici d'offrir un équipement qui préserve le caractère nécessairement privé de la pratique aquatique, sans limiter les plaisirs des lumières associés aux plaisirs de l'eau.
L'ouverture de l'équipement sur le jardin est perceptible dès l'entrée de l'équipement par une transparence totale sur le parc. Le toit forme alors un dais léger, qui offre aux nageurs des lumières en toutes saisons, et aux bâtiments voisins une façade d'ondulations et de lumière.
La couverture est ici pensée comme «un outil de confort». Les larges verrières au long des poutres principales filtrent la lumière et orientent l'espace en faisant vibrer la halle des bassins au rythme des lumières, au rythme des saisons. La forme variable de cette couverture galbée permet d'assurer un doux confort acoustique de l'espace des bassins.
En s'ouvrant au sud, l'équipement offre une lumière généreuse. L'éclairement par la façade est complété grâce au dispositif de couverture. La toiture est transformée en un capteur adapté aux lumières chaudes et rougeoyantes de l'ouest, celles du soir qui rasent la couverture et l'animent dans ses courbures sans gêner les nageurs.
Nous avons considéré la toiture comme l'addition de grands volumes abrités sous les feuilles de larges palmes bombées qui marquent des espaces et permettent d'introduire de manière adaptée les lumières variables.
La structure s'estompe pour laisser apparaitre le galbe des surfaces à double courbure vêtues de bois qui se développent continûment entre façade et franchissement. Le volume du bâtiment semble décomposé dans la disjonction entre l'opacité des surfaces en bois et la transparence

du verre, dans la discontinuité entre structure et lumière. Ce dispositif valorise les plaisirs de l'eau sous le ciel largement offert, en associant les plaisirs du lieu, du paysage, de la ville qui se forme.

Gare de Montpellier
Montpellier, France | → p. 52
Marc Mimram

Parce qu'elles appartiennent au réseau territorial de l'infrastructure ferroviaire, les gares semblent devoir être délocalisées, détachées de leur site d'ancrage pour faire corps avec le réseau. Nous avons proposé ici une toute autre démarche : faire de la nouvelle gare située, spécifique, une gare de Montpellier, une gare méditerranéenne.

Le train, le rail sont par essence territorialisés, à grande échelle : il s'agit de gagner de la vitesse, de gagner du temps. Mais cette vitesse qui aménage de manière globale le territoire de l'infrastructure permet également de joindre la dimension locale, au départ et à l'arrivée.
La gare est alors ce lieu de rencontre entre l'absence de la distance parcourue et la présence du lieu, celui du départ et de l'arrivée.
Ici, le local rencontre le global. Une gare ancre le parcours dans le territoire, inscrit la grande échelle dans la géographie du lieu.

La gare méditerranéenne est une gare attentive à la variation des lumières et du climat.
Il ne s'agit pas ici de limiter l'espace par un voile de verre, mais bien au contraire de construire de l'ombre pour guider la lumière dense à travers un filtre opaque.
Le voyageur est protégé, et la structure de couverture est au service de ce jeu des lumières.

Le plissé de la couverture permet à la fois de réaliser la grande portée et de construire une entrée lisible de la gare au sud, sur le pôle multimodal et le jardin du parvis.
Cette feuille à double courbure est façonnée à partir d'une dentelle minérale qui lui donne son statut tant de structure que de filtre de lumière.
La grande structure de couverture prend son origine dans les plaisirs de la lumière filtrée, dans la raison du traitement climatique et dans l'ouverture sur le paysage, tout en s'inscrivant dans les caractéristiques éoliennes du lieu qui fondent le traitement bioclimatique de la halle des voyageurs.

En pénétrant dans la gare, le voyageur est happé par les variations d'ombres et de lumières, par le climat tranquille et apaisé de la grande toiture nervurée qui s'offre aux qualités des saisons et fabrique un abri protecteur.

Ce projet est une première. En effet, il lie en une pièce unique deux éléments toujours distincts : la structure et la couverture.
Les 115 palmes en béton fibré ultra-performant (BFUP) portent chacune sur 18,4 mètres avec une épaisseur moyenne de 4 centimètres.
De par la compacité du béton et sa faible porosité, aucune étanchéité n'est requise sur les coques. Les inclusions de verre sont rapportées sur la surface à double courbure des palmes de béton. Les grandes palmes de couverture bénéficient d'une forte inertie grâce à la résistance de forme assurée par courbure et pliage.
Cette couverture a nécessité une longue période de développement tant pour le calcul que pour les expérimentations en usine de préfabrication.
Elle a été rendue possible par le lien endogène que nous développons entre structure et architecture, mais plus encore par la capacité de ce lien à nous rapprocher de l'entreprise, du constructeur.
Caractéristiques intrinsèques du matériau et rhéologie rencontrent ici le calcul statique. La définition des moules de coffrage suit l'expérimentation liée à ces pièces très fines et très élancées. La géométrie des palmes s'adapte aux besoins de résistance autant qu'à ceux du transport et du levage. La forme de l'ouvrage prend naissance dans cette confrontation de contraintes de nature si différente, voire divergente.

L'architecture évoque tout à la fois la richesse des variations des lumières et la frugalité d'une structure efficiente. Le chantier s'est invité à la table du projet. Il met en avant et suscite un dialogue avec le grand paysage autant qu'avec les hommes de l'usine de préfabrication, avec la mécanique des structures autant qu'avec le jeu des difractions de la lumière, avec la géométrie différentielle des surfaces plissées autant qu'avec la rhéologie du béton fibré.
La réussite du projet tient dans cette convergence expérimentale. Nous avons voulu faire une gare des sens, de l'émotion, fondée sur l'attention à l'ombre et aux lumières, au climat de Montpellier. Une gare dédiée au plaisir du lieu, à l'émotion des voyageurs.
Aujourd'hui, voir les voyageurs parcourir ces éclats de soleil sous la couverture-structure me tend ce miroir de mémoire qu'est le projet autour des plaisirs partagés.

Pont Amédée Saint-Germain / Armagnac
Bordeaux, France | → p. 66
Marc Mimram

Le nouveau pont Amédée Saint-Germain / Armagnac est avant tout un dispositif urbain indispensable à la reconquête du quartier Saint-Jean Belcier, à Bordeaux.
Cette pièce centrale du désenclavement des quartiers est à considérer comme un outil du dialogue avec l'infrastructure – celle de la gare, celle des voies de chemin de fer – que nous voulons regarder positivement comme un service urbain en ville en considérant les voies de chemin de fer comme un fleuve ferroviaire.
L'enjeu est de taille puisqu'il s'adresse à la pratique locale de l'espace public ainsi qu'à l'ancrage territorial du nouveau développement urbain.

Le projet est avant tout une ode à l'espace public, réalisé à partir d'un très grand balcon destiné aux piétons et aux cycles, indépendant de la partie de la voirie réservée aux véhicules motorisés.
Tout ici doit se faire dans cette attention portée aux qualités de l'espace public. Nous voulons inscrire ce projet dans la continuité sensible de l'espace public, dans cette cohérence des sols, des espaces destinés à l'agrément, en lien avec la gare Saint-Jean.

Un projet unitaire inséré dans le tissu urbain

Nous avons centré le projet sur l'unité du traitement géométrique de l'ouvrage et particulièrement sur la qualité de la rive continue, les trottoirs destinés au public. En effet, l'ouvrage est asymétrique : il possède d'un côté un très grand trottoir, tandis que de l'autre côté, plutôt destiné à la circulation automobile, le trottoir est réduit à un simple trottoir de service. Nous avons accompagné l'asymétrie des parcours d'une asymétrie de la structure du tablier de l'ouvrage.
Si le projet s'applique à respecter ces contraintes, il met en cohérence le schéma statique avec le plaisir du lieu et le développement d'un espace public varié.

Une structure fine et légère

L'ouvrage exprime tout à la fois, transversalement, cette asymétrie fonctionnelle par la mise en évidence des circulations piétons et cycles autonomes et, longitudinalement, le cheminement des efforts dans la continuité du dispositif au-dessus des deux piles.
Il s'agit de créer au centre de l'ouvrage une place ouverte en ce lieu où les efforts sont les plus faibles. La distribution des moments étant maximale sur appuis, nous avons créé deux poutres en superstructure constituées à la fois par les membrures supérieures en forme d'arcs courbes et par le caisson en partie inférieure. Ces deux membrures sont reliées par une maille diagonale décomposée en barres comprimées et tendues.
Au-dessus du fleuve ferroviaire, ces deux yeux ouverts sur les voies de chemin de fer constituent une structure à inertie variable remarquable.

Dans la géométrie variable de ses courbes, la superstructure offre une élégance statique au pont, en contact direct et lisible depuis l'espace public, mais aussi en regard lointain depuis l'horizon ferroviaire.
L'économie de matière, la frugalité, sont ici la garantie d'une attention durable au développement de cette structure.
Le nouveau pont appartient à l'espace public qu'il façonne en créant une très grande fluidité, un repère urbain à différentes échelles ; il est attentif aux piétons qui le parcourent, qui l'habitent et qui s'y tiennent, mais également aux regards lointains dans le paysage urbain qui ici se transforme.
L'ouvrage est donné à lire de manière explicite, dans la géométrie de sa structure autant que dans sa pratique quotidienne.
Par sa silhouette continue et gracile, par son ancrage dans l'univers de la ville, le nouveau pont constitue un lien généreux qu'exprime aussi la douceur courbe de sa géométrie.

Bâtiment Airtime
Paris, France | → p. 72
Marc Mimram

Entre l'avenue de France et la halle Freyssinet coule le fleuve ferroviaire, avec ses variations de largeurs et de contraintes.
Ici, au droit du bâtiment Airtime, la portée possible sans appuis intermédiaires est de 58 mètres. Partout ailleurs, les bâtiments qui se développent au-dessus du réseau ferroviaire ont été implantés sur une dalle épaisse, une table de béton sur laquelle peut s'installer, de manière aléatoire et indéfinie préalablement, n'importe quel assemblage de bâtiments contenus dans les règles d'urbanisme. Les urbanistes ont abandonné la *tabula rasa* pour la *tabula nova* ; une dalle en attente d'urbanisation. Ce dispositif est irrationnel et peu économe.

Notre proposition inverse le processus : au lieu de s'installer sur une dalle en attente, nous avons proposé de suspendre la dalle de couverture des voies ferrées au bâtiment-pont. Cette hypothèse nouvelle modifie l'équation économique et permet d'intégrer le coût de la structure invisible de la dalle dans la superstructure du bâtiment et, par là même, de requalifier son architecture au regard de cette disposition géographique particulière.
Le bâtiment ainsi projeté devient un bâtiment-pont appuyé de part et d'autre du plateau ferroviaire à 58 mètres de distance, ses 16 000 tonnes étant suspendues au-dessus des trains. Ce dispositif structurel s'avère néanmoins libérateur et permet de transformer la contrainte gravitaire en une situation d'usage particulière. Puisque les contraintes sont concentrées dans les étages intégrant la structure de franchissement, les autres parties du bâtiment sont libres. Suspendues ou supportées par la structure principale, elles peuvent varier d'épaisseur et dégager des terrasses, des balcons, des loggias, des mezzanines – autant de prolongements de l'espace de travail qui qualifient celui-ci selon les orientations et les vues.
L'architecture devient alors plus cohérente, et la situation structurelle est évoquée sans ostension. Demain, la présence du plateau ferroviaire disparaîtra sous la couverture de l'ensemble du réseau, mais le dispositif adopté continuera d'évoquer cette situation extraordinaire. Les poutres du grand franchissement sont concentrées dans les étages aux façades percées selon une densité évoquant la poutre Vierendeel utilisée. Les étages portés et suspendus sont libres dans la variation des terrasses qu'ils accueillent.

Un équilibre stabilisé
Nous avons souhaité évoquer le chemin gravitaire dans ses capacités d'assemblages sophistiqués, avec des membrures soulevées du sol évoquant un « équilibre stabilisé ».
Nous avons choisi de mettre en suspension le bâtiment. La structure de franchissement n'est pas issue d'une simple contrainte de portée, c'est un élément libérateur qui fixe les directions des grandes poutres principales décollées pour offrir des vues et des assemblages multiples.
La structure est ici au service du dialogue entre urbanité et usage. C'est elle qui libère le panorama. C'est elle qui fait varier les usages.

La massivité en suspens de ces grands éléments structuraux permet d'interroger à nouveau l'expression des chemins gravitaires de manière plus sensible aux plaisirs du lieu, plus généreuse face aux plaisirs d'être là.
Les bureaux s'ouvrent sur de longues terrasses qui prolongent les espaces de travail dans toutes les directions du regard urbain, proche et lointain : bancs, plantations et prises électriques devraient rendre plus domestiques, plus empathiques, des bureaux trop souvent cloisonnés.
Ce bâtiment n'est pas standard, la vie au travail ne devrait pas l'être.
Dans les transparences de la cour intérieure, les espaces suspendus dialoguent en légèreté au-dessus de la cour plantée sous laquelle les trains ont disparu.

École d'architecture de Strasbourg
Strasbourg, France | → p. 82
Marc Mimram

Entre urbanité et pédagogie

La nouvelle école de Strasbourg est située en ville. Cette disposition somme toute assez vue pour une école d'architecture permet d'installer un dialogue particulier entre ville et enseignement de l'architecture. Ce projet signifie ce dialogue.
Le projet est composé de deux bâtiments : l'un ancien, un garage automobile des années 1930, réhabilité, l'autre neuf appelé bâtiment Moll. Le bâtiment Moll est façonné à partir d'une hypothèse d'ouverture. L'espace public y pénètre largement au rez-de-chaussée et se transforme en un grand hall vertical, sur quatre niveaux, à la fois circulatoire mais aussi pédagogique dans sa capacité à faire se croiser et se représenter les enseignements.
Pour ce faire, le bâtiment est soulevé, comme installé sur des talons aiguilles, afin de libérer les espaces de contraintes structurelles en les ouvrant généreusement sur la ville.

Le bâtiment dans sa volumétrie maximise les potentialités réglementaires. Il s'agit d'offrir le volume construit maximal dans les contraintes fixées par le règlement d'urbanisme ; respecter les alignements, maintenir les gabarits et respecter les attiques préconisés.
L'idée consiste à tirer parti de ces contraintes pour constituer trois corps de bâtiments superposés de deux étages chacun, dégageant le vide des activités communes ouvertes sur la ville.
Ces trois unités morcelées par les obligations réglementaires forment alors trois unités constructives structurellement superposées, comme dans un équilibre stabilisé, unifiées par une enveloppe commune variant au gré des orientations, du mouvement des lumières.
Cette enveloppe structurelle rigide et de forte inertie permet de libérer les salles d'enseignements de points porteurs en faisant ici apparaître le lien entre support et surface, en rendant habitable le vide de l'enveloppe structurelle.
Ce qui gère le rapport à l'extérieur, à la vue, à la ville, aux lumières, est alors essentiel. Depuis l'intérieur, chaque salle trouve son prolongement sur la ville par les vues qu'elle offre, par les regards qu'elle permet en fonction des usages et des spacieuses terrasses accessibles. Une fois cette ouverture sur la ville généreusement offerte, la structure porteuse se hiérarchise simplement autour des contraintes gravitaires, en exploitant les effets de ces grandes plaques percées dans l'ordre qu'elles impriment à la structure.
Alors l'enveloppe de métal et de lumière unifie l'ensemble sans occulter la réalité constructive de l'édifice. Les reprises de charges laissent libre le rez-de-chaussée dans sa transparence ouverte sur la ville. Il s'agit par l'attention portée à ce bâtiment non pas d'une leçon de chose destinée aux étudiants, mais d'une expression raisonnée des potentialités offertes par le jeu des matières et la raison structurelle.
La façade porteuse est composée d'une charpente hybride de treillis d'acier façonnée à la mesure des efforts qui transitent tout en ouvrant de larges baies sur la ville : une structure visible et pédagogique.

Sur la peau externe, un rideau de métal mobile filtre la lumière. La nuit, la lecture du dispositif s'inverse à l'instar d'un rideau de scène, laissant lire la structure variable porteuse.
Entre matérialité et structure, entre pédagogie et urbanité, les deux bâtiments unis par la fine passerelle se sont installés pour mettre en dialogue contemporanéité et ville historique.

En ville : pérennité / modernité

La nouvelle école d'architecture trouve sa cohérence dans le lien qu'elle opère entre ville, pédagogie et matérialité.
Il s'agit ici d'appartenance, de partage.
Les bâtiments appartiennent à la ville dont ils prolongent l'histoire dans la stratification construite des bâtiments mis en commun autour de l'outil pédagogique. Ils s'ouvrent sur la ville pour accueillir non seulement les étudiants, mais aussi les habitants autour de la question architecturale.

Roland-Garros, court Simonne-Mathieu, nouveau court des serres
Paris, France | → p. 86
Marc Mimram

Lorsque Michel Corajoud propose le projet d'aménagement du site de Roland-Garros pour le tournoi international de tennis, il souhaite le rendre plus perméable, plus ouvert sur la ville.
Cela supposait d'ouvrir un large espace public et de construire un nouveau court de 5 000 places dans le jardin adjacent où se trouvaient des serres de production de mauvaise facture, construites très récemment.
La marque particulière de ce jardin, ce ne sont pas ces serres horticoles, mais d'autres serres botaniques construites en 1898 par Jean Camille Formigé, constructions exemplaires auxquelles il n'a bien sur jamais été envisagé de porter atteinte.

C'est dans ce dialogue avec les serres historiques à l'architecture de fonte et de verre très caractéristique du XIXe siècle que naît le projet du nouveau court de tennis. Celui-ci sera semi-enterré dans un socle de gradins en béton, surmonté d'une structure en acier et enceint de serres botaniques de très hautes performances techniques.

Les nouvelles serres réalisent un écrin de verre accueillant des plantes de quatre continents. Il s'agissait de revenir à ce sujet de référence de l'architecture métallique que propose le gabarit des serres voisines, mais sans mimétisme, en dialogue avec ce qui, depuis le Crystal Palace de 1851 à Londres, constitue une référence absolue de légèreté, de frugalité, de relation délicate entre lumière et structure.
Les nouvelles serres nécessitaient cependant du double vitrage et des performances d'isolation très supérieures aux constructions précédentes. Aussi, pour ne pas aboutir à une bulle de verre collé, le projet reprend une décomposition en écailles de verre à bords décalés dans deux directions. Cela permet de façonner une peau qui varie sous les lumières dans un effet de diffraction, de vibrations soutenues par des reflets sur les plans biais décomposés. La structure en acier des serres ordonne le mouvement et fait écho à la charpente en équilibre des gradins qui libère une galerie périmétrale.

Entre ombres et transparences filtrées, les lumières jouent ici de la structure et prolongent les effets si caractéristiques de l'architecture du XIXe siècle en y intégrant des techniques contemporaines de fabrication par oxycoupage et soudure.

Comme le souhaitait Michel Corajoud, le dialogue entre jardin et sport, entre botanique et tennis, entre performances techniques et physiques, s'installe dans un espace partagé.
La présence de cette référence historique n'interdit aucunement une architecture contemporaine assumée, bien au contraire. Les pratiques se croisent dans le temps et le tournoi participe au développement du jardin botanique. Le nouveau court Simonne-Mathieu montre s'il en était besoin la perméabilité nécessaire des plaisirs urbains dans une mixité d'usages toujours plus grande.

Passerelle Strasbourg – Kehl
Strasbourg, France | → p. 94
Marc Mimram

Un projet ancré dans la géographie du fleuve

La nouvelle passerelle sur le Rhin s'inscrit totalement dans la logique géographique et géométrique du jardin des deux rives.
Le fleuve ne peut être vu comme une césure à franchir de manière abstraite, c'est la matrice de cette géographie qui fonde le lieu, lui donne vie, lui donne sens.
Le projet se veut être la rencontre de ces deux ancrages, sur les berges du fleuve, et au-delà, au-dessus de la digue, au long de la promenade circulaire. Ainsi, le pont est double et ce dédoublement multiplie les parcours, offre un point de rencontre, une place au centre du fleuve.
Ici, la géographie prend le pas sur l'histoire, et l'espace public offert au-dessus de l'ancienne frontière met en partage visuellement le territoire commun entre la Forêt-Noire et les Vosges. Le lieu créé à la rencontre des parcours flotte au-dessus du Rhin pour mettre en paix les regards sur le lointain, pour assurer la proximité du paysage unitaire.

Une structure ouverte sur le paysage

Le fleuve et le pont dialoguent grâce à cette légèreté apparente du franchissement et au jeu des courbes qu'il offre sur l'horizon.
L'ouvrage est haubané afin de détacher d'un ouvrage gravitaire les tabliers qui se croisent, celui de l'arc en plan, celui de l'arc en élévation. Les parcours semblent définir une bande de Möbius qui pourrait symboliser la relation franco-allemande.
La passerelle doit être dans ce paysage ouvert sur le ciel une intersection de fines lignes de structure offrant une multiplicité de promenades et de rencontres avec le Rhin.
Il ne s'agit pas ici d'obérer l'horizon ou de prendre avec force des ancrages dans le paysage, mais bien au contraire de marquer le lien de manière ténue et légère, comme le fil tendu entre les deux rives d'une géographie marquée par une histoire hier douloureuse, aujourd'hui pacifiée.
La passerelle unit dans la multiplicité des parcours possibles, dans la légèreté de sa structure arachnéenne, et inscrit de manière pérenne le franchissement dans la symbolique de cette réunion délicate, attentive au fleuve qui la fonde.

Trois ponts en Chine | → p. 102
Marc Mimram

Lorsque j'ai réalisé mon premier projet en Chine, il y a 15 ans, la mutation de la société chinoise débutait mais personne n'imaginait l'explosion urbaine qui l'accompagnerait. On roulait encore à vélo, et Pékin ne possédait que deux anneaux périphériques, contre six aujourd'hui.
Cette métamorphose des villes chinoises s'accompagne évidemment d'un développement incommensurable des infrastructures et, par là même, des ouvrages d'art.
Nous avons ouvert une agence à Tianjin où réside Liu Chengyin, sa directrice. Cette ville de 15 millions d'habitants participe de la mégalopole qui, de Pékin à Binhai, ouvre la capitale sur la mer. Nous y avons construit de nombreux ouvrages, sur le fleuve Hai He, à TEDA, la zone de développement économique et technologique, dans le district portuaire de Tanggu

et dans la ville nouvelle, l'éco-cité sino-singapourienne où se trouvent les projets de ponts Zhong Sheng Da Dao et Jin Liu Lu. Cette ville nouvelle se veut la vitrine du développement urbain durable, essentiellement fondé sur la technologie et l'infrastructure. En consacrant une place importante à l'eau, à son traitement, la ville se construit autour d'un lac que traversent les deux ponts.
Dans cette explosion urbaine, le pouvoir administratif chinois a souvent mis en avant la place symbolique que pouvaient prendre les ouvrages d'art. Il ne s'agit pas de les restreindre à leur place fonctionnelle mais d'en faire, dans la course au développement des villes, le signe d'une attention particulière aux ouvrages publics, l'attribut d'une modernité assumée. Si des débordements formalistes, maniérés ou historicistes résultent parfois de cette situation, cela ouvre aussi un champ d'expérimentation dont nous avons souvent tiré parti.

Deux ponts sur le lac artificiel

Le caractère durable affiché par l'éco-cité de Tianjin place le lac au centre du dispositif urbain. Il n'existe aucune contrainte de gabarit ni de portées. L'enjeu théorique ici est de dialoguer avec ce paysage artificiel, en évoquant le rapport à l'eau par analogie avec le pont flottant.

Le pont Zhong Sheng Da Dao
est composé de deux tabliers parallèles constitués de cinq coques en béton de 54 mètres de portée chacune. Ces volumes évidés, formés de surfaces à double courbure possèdent une très grande inertie grâce à l'efficacité de la résistance de forme.
La massivité apparente évoque comme un oxymore le caractère flottant de l'ouvrage. Le reflet des coques dans le plan d'eau le rend plus énigmatique encore. Le chemin gravitaire n'est pas ordonné ni hiérarchisé, mais le continuum du voile de béton assure le transfert des charges. Entre massivité et flottaison, entre opacité et soulèvement, s'installe un dialogue avec le plan d'eau se référant à l'horizon, ligne gravitaire entre ciel et terre.

La difficulté de réalisation résidait dans la décomposition de la surface complexe en éléments de coffrage réassemblables, manipulables, pouvant être réutilisés vingt fois par jeu de symétrie. Cette mécanique du coffrage a été réglée géométriquement et constructivement selon un modèle numérique partagé entre notre bureau et le constructeur, en installant le chantier et l'outil géométrique au cœur du projet.

L'attention portée par la ville nouvelle au développement durable me laisse penser que l'évocation de la louve romaine, associée à la mythique légende de Romulus et Remus, pouvait constituer un récit fondateur tant par le caractère formel de la louve nourricière que par l'idée d'une histoire urbaine en marche.

Le pont Jin Liu Lu
est pensé à partir du pont Zhong Sheng Da Dao. La démarche consiste ici à expérimenter une solution en dialogue avec la précédente, non plus dans la massivité opaque, mais au contraire à partir du vide creusé dans la surface. Le pas des coques est identique mais l'inertie est ici qualifiée par le vide, par la mise à distance entre le tablier et le ruban variable. Ce ruban est formé d'une surface en acier à double peau dont les ailes latérales varient dans la dimension, se soulèvent et se galbent pour reprendre le schéma statique et répondre au cheminement des forces gravitaires. Il ne s'agit plus ici d'une masse soulevée, d'un continuum de béton flottant sur l'horizon du plan d'eau, mais d'une feuille en acier associée aux vides qu'elle limite pour laisser filer le regard et offrir ses variations sous les lumières.
Le façonnage à double courbure de la tôle en acier convoque ici le savoir-faire de l'industrie navale, la chaudronnerie des coques évoquant un autre mode de flottaison.

La passerelle de Liu Shu à Yangzhou

Le caractère constructif de cette passerelle a été fondateur dans le principe développé pour le pont Jin Liu Lu. Il s'agissait ici de construire en moins de six mois, études comprises, un projet symbolisant l'anniversaire de la ville de Yangzhou. Cette ville portuaire possède l'une des plus importantes industries navales du pays. La maire, secrétaire du parti communiste, m'a permis d'intégrer ce savoir-faire dans un projet de faible ampleur par rapport au tonnage mis en place dans les immenses navires en construction. Et quel plaisir, quel bonheur que de transposer cette technologie savante dans la structure de cette légère passerelle ! La tôle chaudronnée, façonnée, cintrée selon une double courbure respecte très directement le schéma statique. À travers les variations d'inertie, l'ouvrage reflète ici formellement la distribution des moments de flexion d'un arc bi-encastré dans les culées de l'ouvrage. La découpe des tôles en acier par oxycoupage automatisé suit la géométrie des patrons formée à partir d'un modèle numérique complexe devant permettre l'assemblage des surfaces non développables.

Ce rapprochement entre l'industrie navale et la construction métallique de cette structure légère, permettant l'usage de surfaces continues en acier plutôt que de membrures de charpentes métalliques souvent développées à partir de treillis, montre à quel point le chantier informe le projet, le façonnage exprimé à partir du schéma statique pouvant ainsi assumer une mise en forme délicate à travers les douces courbes des surfaces gauches.

La passerelle tient son nom de la feuille de saule dont l'arbre borde les rives. Les habitants y trouvent une analogie formelle.

Cet ouvrage n'est pas sans évoquer la passerelle PSO que j'ai réalisée à Toulouse il y a près de 30 ans. Et le projet devient mémoire…

Précisions phénoménales :
quand Erieta Attali photographie
l'architecture de Marc Mimram | → p. 114
Ariel Genadt

En cette fin de deuxième décennie du XXIe siècle, l'architecture apparaît documentée avec plus de précisions qu'elle ne l'a jamais été auparavant en matière de clichés photographiques. Tout passant pressé peut immortaliser un bâtiment du bout de ses doigts et le transformer en objet statique avec une précision numérique inédite grâce à son smartphone, puis faire circuler ses images instantanément dans le monde entier. Ce phénomène vient renforcer l'importance que revêt l'interprétation artistique dans le domaine de la photographie professionnelle d'architecture. Comme l'a suggéré Michelangelo Antonioni dans son film *Blow-Up* (1966), la précision de l'œil mécanique étend les limites de la perception rétinienne, mais elle souligne en même temps la pertinence du regard du photographe en tant qu'interprète. Cette idée est d'autant plus d'actualité aujourd'hui que la technologie a libéré l'art bien d'avantage qu'à l'époque de sa reproduction mécanisée. Dans ce contexte, les représentations de l'architecture de Marc Mimram proposées par la photographe Erieta Attali nous invitent à marquer une pause et à contempler ses limites spatio-temporelles. Elles ajoutent une dimension à l'architecture par le biais d'un travail d'observation patient et rigoureux et d'une grande maîtrise de la précision argentique.

Mimram décrit de son architecture comme étant un processus de transformation du lieu et des matériaux, mais cette transformation se prolonge après que l'architecte a quitté la scène. À cet égard, Attali représente les structures de Mimram sous forme de phénomènes stratifiés, réactifs aux mouvements humains et à l'action du soleil, de la lune et du climat. Grâce à des durées d'exposition pouvant atteindre jusqu'à 20 minutes et une ouverture du diaphragme à f/32, elle utilise son appareil Linhof grand format 10 × 12 centimètres pour superposer les différentes phases par lesquelles passent ses sujets. Avec une persévérance qu'elle a développée dans sa pratique de la course de fond, Attali extrait et sédimente les qualités phénoménales des œuvres, qui les lient à une heure de la journée, à une saison, à une longitude et une latitude. En capturant le moment où le soleil frappe les surfaces et s'infiltre dans les limbes de la structure, elle cherche à créer une sensation de flottaison, où l'on est « à la fois enraciné et déraciné » selon ses propres termes. Cet objectif est des plus manifestes dans ses effets de clair-obscur, par exemple dans ses images de la gare de Montpellier, avec ses palmes ondulatoires en béton fibré et leurs perforations irrégulières, ou dans la fragmentation infinie et les reflets des serres qui enveloppent le stade de Roland-Garros. Rappelant les principes du cubisme, cette superposition d'empreintes lumineuses est certes moins précise qu'un cliché pris avec le dernier gadget électronique, mais elle est beaucoup plus fidèle à l'expérience que l'on peut avoir de l'architecture, puisqu'elle dépeint une relation dynamique entre les structures inertes, les gens, le climat et la lumière.

Souvent, les interprétations d'Attali perpétuent l'idée de l'architecte selon laquelle le bâtiment incarne la mémoire de la géographie et du savoir-faire local qui a permis sa construction. Ses photos offrent des précisions – dans le sens de clarifications ou observations attentives – sur sa création, soulignant des significations possibles, en immergeant les bâtiments dans des conditions atmosphériques propres au lieu : les ciels marocains, les eaux chinoises, le soleil méditerranéen ou encore le crépuscule parisien. Pour ce faire, elle prolonge le processus de transformation de la matière auquel faisait référence Mimram en saisissant les bâtiments au moment où ils semblent décomposés par la lumière ou l'humidité, telles des agrégations de particules, en flottaison. La raison pour laquelle Attali cherche à représenter les bâtiments comme des constellations fragmentées a certainement à voir avec ses premiers travaux photographiques sur les sites archéologiques, et plus tard avec sa fascination pour le travail de Kengo Kuma. Cette approche rejoint le goût de Mimram pour les tissus, les motifs et l'assemblage, qu'il explique lui-même par les heures passées à observer son père tailleur. Le filigrane éphémère dont il revêt ses bâtiments est plus manifeste dans les images d'Attali que de visu, car ses vues composées révèlent des motifs qui peuvent échapper au champ de vision limité du visiteur. Traduire ces effets ne dématérialise pas pour autant l'architecture mais la rend plutôt concrète, au premier sens du terme, dérivé du latin *concrescere* : les fragments « croissent ensemble » en un tout. Attali insiste encore plus sur cet aspect concret quand elle s'intéresse à la relation entre les structures et les données du terrain. En choisissant un ratio de 2 : 1 pour ses vues panoramiques, elle souligne l'aspect terrestre des structures, leur enchevêtrement avec les flux naturels et humains ambiants. Elle fait ainsi écho à la traduction du mouvement figé à laquelle s'adonne Mimram, en particulier dans ses ponts ondulants de l'éco-cité de Tianjin, en Chine.

On peut également analyser l'œuvre d'Attali à travers le prisme des écrits de Vittorio Gregotti sur l'évolution du rôle de la précision en architecture à la fin du XXe siècle. Gregotti affirmait que si dans l'Antiquité, l'art était considéré comme l'activité pouvant produire de la précision, il joue de nos jours un rôle différent « en tentant d'exister en dehors de la pensée scientifique-technique liée à la prise de mesures [...]. La tâche principale de l'art est précisément de produire des choses qui défient les mesures ou qui provoquent [...] le besoin de trouver des instruments de mesure fondés non sur la constance des structures mais plutôt sur la nature de la constitution évolutive des relations qui les relient entre elles ». De la même façon, plutôt que d'exposer la logique abstraite qui sous-tend les structures de Mimram, l'objectif d'Attali reproduit sa perception de l'architecture comme une interaction entre l'artifice, les humains et la nature, entre l'immobilité et le mouvement. Ainsi, elle montre le squelette élancé de la passerelle Solférino qui se détache des eaux troubles de la Seine et du ciel gris et profond. Sa silhouette délicate résonne avec la structure dentelée d'un arbre au premier plan, qui, comme la passerelle, semble émaner d'un fleuve de mercure.

Attali poursuit ce type de représentation phénoménale de l'architecture depuis deux décennies, mais la rencontre entre son approche et le travail de Mimram est particulièrement révélatrice de leurs arts respectifs. Les « ouvrages d'art » – ces œuvres d'ingénierie de grande échelle telles

que les ponts qui transforment le paysage par le biais de leur expression structurelle – sont plus souvent photographiés de façon à ce que leur logique statique soit mise en valeur. Les ouvrages d'art sont entrés dans les canons de l'architecture moderne quand Sigfried Giedion a loué leur valeur esthétique de l'ordre du sublime tout autant que leurs mérites techniques dans *Bauen in Frankreich* (1928, paru en France en 2000 sous le titre *Construire en France*). Attali évite néanmoins les représentations schématiques des ouvrages de Mimram, du type de celles qui mettent en avant la logique de tension et de compression leur permettant de rester en équilibre. En un sens, elle les soulage de la précision scientifique indispensable à leur création, ébranlant leur obédience aux lois de la physique en recadrant, voilant ou reflétant des parties des structures ou de leurs supports. Grâce à cet acte de précision phénoménale, elle les élève au rang d'œuvres d'art et contribue à inscrire les ouvrages de Mimram dans la lignée de ceux de maîtres modernes tels qu'Eugène Freyssinet ou Robert Maillart.
La photographe et l'architecte-ingénieur ont des approches de la précision qui semblent contradictoires mais qui sont en fait complémentaires : alors que Mimram cherche à diluer la matière et l'espace – citant la phrase de Robert le Ricolais : « L'art de construire devient paradoxalement celui de faire des trous » –, Attali utilise la lumière et la durée pour amplifier l'architecture, l'étoffer du climat et de la vie. Alors qu'il s'en remet au topos quantifiable et aspire à vaincre la pesanteur, elle puise dans la matrice féconde, la *khôra* qui donne aux créations de Mimram leur raison d'être. Les précisions phénoménales qu'apporte Attali sur l'architecture de Mimram démontrent combien la photographie peut nourrir, animer et même transformer l'œuvre d'un architecte, tout en l'ancrant dans un lieu. C'est ainsi qu'elle lui confère un sens face à l'océan infini de flux de données qui font aussi partie de notre environnement.

À propos de Marc Mimram | → p. 118
Zvi Hecker

En édifiant la tour Eiffel, Gustave Eiffel accueillait le XXe siècle au centre du monde qu'était alors Paris. Son budget était restreint et il termina la construction en un temps record ; on ne déplora exceptionnellement aucun mort sur le chantier et il réussit même à en tirer un modeste profit. Sa création échappa aux diatribes des intellectuels parisiens grâce à l'invention récente par Marconi de la télégraphie sans fil, qui nécessitait une antenne installée le plus haut possible.

En très peu de temps, la tour Eiffel, cette structure nue méprisée à ses débuts par l'élite parisienne, séduisit les artistes d'avant-garde par sa beauté. L'utilisation de l'acier, l'absence de décorations et cette façon d'assumer sans vergogne une force toute nouvelle furent adoptées sans retenue par l'architecture moderne.

Marc Mimram est né dans ce contexte nouveau où les frontières entre architecture et structure sont devenues extrêmement floues. La capacité des éléments préfabriqués en acier à réduire les dimensions d'une structure a débouché sur une nouvelle prise de conscience esthétique. La lumière et la transparence symbolisaient la nouvelle architecture. Durant le long processus historique que notre civilisation a connu au cours de deux millénaires, l'architecture a subi une dématérialisation qui a mené des pyramides massives aux silhouettes squelettiques des cathédrales gothiques, puis à une économie de matériaux considérée comme un facteur esthétique. Cette évolution a été résumée de façon laconique par Mies van der Rohe avec sa formule « less is more » et par Oscar Niemeyer avec sa pyramide renversée.

Marc Mimram est bien conscient de cette évolution qu'il met lui-même en œuvre. Au début des années 1970, le jeune homme qu'il était est venu me voir dans mon atelier de Tel Aviv. À l'époque, j'enseignais aussi à l'Université Laval au Québec et j'étais en charge de la sélection des professeurs invités à l'école d'architecture. C'est à ce titre que j'ai fait venir Robert Le Ricolais pour une série de trois conférences données en français. Cela a été un grand succès.

Devinant le désir que Marc avait d'étudier l'architecture et l'ingénierie, je l'ai encouragé à voir en Le Ricolais un modèle d'ingénieur créatif. Cela a fonctionné et Marc a écrit des années plus tard un très beau livre sur Le Ricolais.

Marc trace son propre sillon tout en s'inscrivant délibérément dans la tradition française d'ingéniosité structurelle érigée en valeur esthétique.

Marc est aussi conscient du fait que l'abondance des nouvelles technologies peut facilement aboutir à une architecture technocratique. Il faut savoir faire preuve d'une ouverture d'esprit non conformiste pour explorer les nouvelles possibilités tout en se faisant le gardien du bon sens et des savoir-faire du passé.
C'est exactement ce que fait Marc, avec perfection et inventivité.

Biographie de Marc Mimram
Architecte ingénieur | → p. 120

Né à Paris en 1955, Marc Mimram est titulaire d'une maîtrise en mathématiques de l'université Paris VII (1976), d'un diplôme d'ingénieur de l'École nationale des ponts et chaussées (1978), d'une maîtrise en génie civil de l'université de Californie à Berkeley (1979) et d'un diplôme d'architecture (DPLG) de l'École nationale supérieure des beaux-arts de Paris (1980).

Depuis 1992, il développe au sein d'une même structure une double activité d'architecte et d'ingénieur.
À partir de 1981, date à laquelle il débute comme architecte ingénieur, il réalise de nombreux ouvrages d'art et projets architecturaux en France et à l'étranger : des ponts en France (comme la passerelle Solférino à Paris), en Allemagne (avec la liaison Strasbourg – Kehl), en Chine (à Pékin, Tianjin et Yangzhou) ou encore au Maroc (entre Rabat et Salé), ce dernier projet ayant remporté le Prix Aga Khan, ainsi que des bâtiments tels que de grandes installations sportives (stade Roland-Garros, piscines, etc.) et des infrastructures (comme le bâtiment Airtime à Paris ou la gare de Montpellier).
Marc Mimram a enseigné à l'École des ponts et chaussées à Paris, à l'École polytechnique fédérale de Lausanne et à l'université de Princeton aux États-Unis. Il a été nommé professeur des écoles nationales supérieures d'architecture et enseigne actuellement à l'école d'architecture de Marne-la-Vallée, près de Paris.
Il a publié différents ouvrages de réflexion sur sa discipline et son travail. Citons par exemple *Structure et formes* (Paris, Dunod, 1983), *Marc Mimram, Passerelle Solférino* (Bâle, 2001), *Architettura Ibrida* (Milan, Electa Architettura, 2009), *Marc Mimram, Architecture et structure* (Munich, Prestel, 2015).
Dans le cadre de conférences, il intervient en outre dans le monde entier (Harvard, Cornell, Princeton, Tokyo, São Paulo, Venise, Oslo, etc.)
Dans son travail d'architecte et d'ingénieur, Marc Mimram démontre un intérêt pour une architecture intelligemment construite à travers le développement de structures réfléchies qui se rapportent au paysage, à la lumière et aux matériaux. Il conçoit son travail comme une transformation attentive et généreuse de la matière dont le monde est fait. Entre ses mains, l'architecture devient un art de la transformation, et la matérialité une expression sensible de la culture.

Biographie d'Erieta Attali
Photographe de paysage et d'architecture | → p. 121

Née à Tel Aviv, Erieta Attali a grandi à Istanbul, puis Athènes. Elle vit actuellement entre New York et Paris et photographie le travail d'architectes contemporains à travers le monde. Elle a commencé sa carrière en 1993 en tant que photographe de paysage et d'archéologie, s'intéressant plus particulièrement aux sites funéraires souterrains. Depuis vingt ans, elle se consacre avant tout à la photographie de paysage et d'architecture aussi bien en Europe que sur le continent américain, en Asie ou en Australie. Ses travaux commandités par des institutions publiques ou universitaires ont fait l'objet de plusieurs expositions et monographies. Son œuvre fait partie de la collection permanente de la National Gallery of Victoria (NGV) de Melbourne. Diplômée en photographie du Goldsmiths College de l'université de Londres, Erieta Attali a ensuite poursuivi ses études à la School of Architecture, Planning & Preservation (GSAPP) de l'université de Columbia à New York grâce au soutien de la Fulbright Foundation, ainsi qu'à l'université Waseda de Tokyo avec le concours de la Japan Foundation. Elle est également titulaire d'un doctorat de la School of Architecture & Design de la RMIT University de Melbourne. Entre 2003 et 2018, Erieta Attali a enseigné la photographie d'architecture à la GSAPP de Columbia. Elle a été professeur invitée à la faculté d'architecture de l'université technique de Munich (TUM), à l'école d'architecture de l'université catholique du Chili, à l'Académie royale des beaux-arts du Danemark à Copenhague, à l'Architectural Association à Londres, à la RMIT à Melbourne, à l'université de Tokyo, à Technion à Haïfa en Israël ou encore à l'université de Sydney. Erieta Attali effectue actuellement un travail de recherche au sein de l'Académie d'architecture à Paris. Elle est également artiste en résidence à la Cité internationale des arts où elle mène un projet photographique sur Paris et la Seine. Elle a écrit et édité de nombreux ouvrages parmi lesquels on compte *Glass | Wood*, *Erieta Attali on Kengo Kuma* et *Periphery | Archaeology of Light*, publiés par les éditions Hatje Cantz.

Biographie de Paul Chemetov | → p. 122

Paul Chemetov, né à Paris, diplômé de l'École nationale supérieure des beaux-arts (1959), rejoint l'Atelier d'urbanisme et d'architecture (AUA) entre 1961 et 1985. Il reçoit en 1980 le Grand Prix national d'architecture. Vice-président du Plan Construction (1982–1987), il co-préside le comité scientifique du Grand Paris (2009). Il enseigne à l'école d'architecture de Strasbourg (1968–1972), à l'École nationale des ponts et chaussées (1978–1989) et à l'école polytechnique fédérale de Lausanne (1993–1994). On compte parmi ses réalisations les équipements publics souterrains du quartier des Halles et, avec Borja Huidobro, le ministère de l'Économie et des Finances ainsi que la rénovation de la Grande Galerie du Muséum national d'histoire naturelle. Lauréat du concours international de la prolongation de l'axe historique de Paris, il conduit le projet de la Méridienne verte en l'an 2000.
Parmi les réalisations récentes du cabinet AUA PAUL CHEMETOV, citons les projets urbains de Montpellier et d'Amiens, à Paris le secteur de la porte de Vincennes et le plan d'aménagement de l'hôpital Boucicaut, l'extension de la faculté de médecine Lyon Sud, la médiathèque départementale de Labège, le Vendéspace et de nombreux logements, la réhabilitation des Coursives à Pantin, et celle du campus Sciences et Technologies de Bordeaux.
Paul Chemetov exprime ses convictions architecturales et urbaines dans les constructions ou les aménagements dont il a la charge, mais aussi à travers ses articles, ses livres et ses prises de position publiques.

Biographie d'Ariel Genadt | → p. 122

Ariel Genadt est architecte, enseignant et chercheur résidant à New York. Son domaine de recherche principal est la conception et la construction d'enveloppes architecturales et leurs capacités à exprimer des aspects culturels et environnementaux de milieux divers. Il se spécialise également en histoire et théorie de l'architecture du XXe siècle au Japon. Il est titulaire d'un doctorat en architecture (PhD) de l'Université de Pennsylvanie (2016), d'un Master of Arts en Histoires et Théories de l'Architectural Association School of Architecture de Londres (2004) et d'un Bachelor of Architecture cum laude du Technion, Israël (1997). Il a collaboré sur divers projets d'architecture, d'urbanisme et d'aménagement paysager, en France, en Israël, en Grèce, au Maroc, au Japon et en Chine. Il a enseigné à l'Université de Pennsylvanie, à Swarthmore College et au Technion. En 2012, il a bénéficié d'une bourse de recherche de la Japan Society for the Promotion of Science au Kengo Kuma Lab à l'Université de Tokyo, et en 2013, il a été le premier chercheur admis à la Fondazione Renzo Piano, Gênes. En 2018, il a été commissaire de l'exposition « Critical Abstractions – Modern Architecture in Japan 1868–2018 » à la galerie des Archives Architecturales de l'Université de Pennsylvanie. Ses articles ont été publiés dans les revues *EAHN Architectural Histories*, *JSAH*, *Baumeister*, *Topos* et *Architect's Newspaper*.

Biographie de Zvi Hecker | → p. 122

Né en 1931 à Cracovie, Svi Hecker a passé son adolescence à Samarcande. De retour à Cracovie après la Seconde Guerre mondiale, il s'est inscrit à l'école d'architecture de l'Institut polytechnique de la ville, puis a émigré peu de temps après en Israël où il a passé en 1954 un diplôme en ingénierie et architecture du Technion – Israel Institute of Technology à Haïfa. Il a fondé une agence en 1959 à Tel Aviv avec Eldar et Alfred Neumann. Ensemble, ils ont conçu le Club Méditerranée à Arziv, l'hôtel de ville de Bat-Yam et l'immeuble d'habitation Dubiner à Ramat Gan. Dans les années 1970, Zvi Hecker a participé à l'aménagement du centre-ville de Montréal ; il a construit une académie militaire dans le désert du Néguev, conçu le centre-ville de Ramat Hasharon et réalisé la Spiral Apartment House à Ramat Gan. Il s'est ensuite s'installé à Berlin où il a remporté les concours pour la conception de l'École juive de la ville, pour le Centre culturel juif de Duisburg et pour le mémorial de la synagogue de la Lindenstrasse à Berlin (avec Micha Ullman et Eyal Weizman). Au même moment, il a conçu à Tel Aviv, en collaboration avec Rafi Segal, le Palmach Museum. Parmi ses projets les plus récents, citons le Musée juif de Varsovie et la Koningin Máximakazerne à l'aéroport Schiphol d'Amsterdam.
Zvi Hecker a été professeur invité dans plusieurs universités aux États-Unis, au Canada et à Vienne. Il a remporté de nombreux concours et prix architecturaux en Allemagne, Israël et Pologne.

Remerciements de Marc Mimram | → p. 142

Ce livre est le fruit d'une rencontre entre le regard sensible et exigeant d'Erieta Attali et nos convictions construites ; je la remercie pour cette attention, cette détermination sans limite.

L'architecture se représente le plus souvent dans ses atours resplendissants, sous des cieux tropicaux quelle que soit leur situation, parés du maquillage informatisé de transformismes éclatants.
Difficile de créer une émotion, de refléter une atmosphère, d'exprimer une matérialité tant les codes de la représentation photoshopée abandonnent le réel pour plonger dans une virtualité virtuose mais délétère, mortifère, alors que notre engagement porte générosité et sensibilité au monde.
La rencontre avec la photographe Erieta Attali a permis de sortir de cette course à la « fake representation » qui, comme la « fake news », ne serait pas un mensonge mais une interprétation du réel.
Erieta Attali a depuis trois ans mis ses pas dans ceux de nos chantiers, glissant son regard dans l'objectif de son appareil. L'objectif est subjectif, le travail d'interprétation est toujours présent, et pourtant la photographe construit ici une mixité qui n'est pas stylistique, mais s'inscrit dans une figuration de l'architecture sensible et émotionnelle. Les reflets matérialisés des lumières, les textures et le grain de la peau ou la massivité prolongent un travail disciplinaire tant sur l'architecture que sur la facture de celle-ci. Entre l'éphémère du chantier et la permanence apparente des enjeux construits, Erieta Attali aura porté son regard sur les chantiers en cours, les projets construits d'ouvrages d'art ou de bâtiments, pour montrer qu'au-delà d'un style affirmé et délocalisé, il s'agit bien d'une démarche cohérente, engagée.

J'apprécie sans réserve sa disponibilité et ses qualités d'abnégation. Cette quête est rare, je souhaitais ici la souligner.

L'architecture n'est pas un projet solitaire, il est partagé tant dans le processus de conception que de construction.
Les maîtres d'ouvrages m'ont fait confiance en développant des projets dont les références structurelles, constructives, économiques étaient rares, voire inexistantes. C'est grâce à leur clairvoyance que ces projets ont pu voir le jour.
Je remercie particulièrement Emmanuelle Baboulin, Pierre Lejeune, Joseph Giordano, Gilles Jourdan, Hakim Essakl, Saïd Zarrou, monsieur Dou, Jean-Claude Dumont.

Ces projets ont fait l'objet de développements attentifs, aussi bien par les architectes que par les ingénieurs qui y ont collaboré. Les équipes de projets ont été nombreuses tant au sein de Marc Mimram Architecture & Associés que Marc Mimram Ingénierie. Je les remercie pour leur engagement, et particulièrement Guillaume André, Martin Fougeras Lavergnolle, Razvan Ionica, Liu Chengyin et Anne-Marie De Matos.

Ces projets sont la mémoire du travail de tous ceux qui ont donné courage et intelligence, souvent dans l'anonymat. Qu'ils soient ici remerciés, car leur participation au projet est une matière à penser l'architecture. Les bâtiments, les ouvrages d'art réalisés forment la mémoire construite de notre travail partagé. Ouvriers ou ingénieurs, ils entreprennent au sens noble du mot, et le projet met ses espoirs en leur savoir.

KOMA AMOK, nos graphistes, ont montré une finesse dans l'interprétation graphique des photographies en résonance avec l'architecture des projets. Aris Kafantaris a été un indispensable ordonnateur.

Je dois une reconnaissance particulière à Paul Chemetov et Zvi Hecker pour leurs textes remarquables, délicats et amicaux.

Remerciements d'Erieta Attali | → p. 79

Le 14 juillet 2016, j'ai eu la chance d'être invitée par Farrokh Derakshani, directeur du prix Aga Khan d'architecture, à « Beyond The Bridge », une conférence au Victoria & Albert Museum de Londres. Parmi les intervenants, j'ai remarqué le nom d'un homme, Marc Mimram. Je ne le connaissais pas mais sa courte biographie m'a donné envie de l'écouter parler de ses ponts. Avant la fin même de son intervention, j'ai su quel serait mon prochain projet : explorer ses infrastructures à travers la France et au-delà, ses ponts, ses gares et ses piscines.
Avant la conférence de Marc, j'avais déjà photographié des monuments, historiques ou contemporains, à travers le monde. Je venais juste de finir mes études doctorales en Australie et j'allais publier quelques monographies. Le timing était donc parfait : je pourrais mettre ma vision et mes désirs au service de cette nouvelle entreprise – un périple de trois ans à travers les réalisations et les créations sculpturales de Marc Mimram.

Je remercie Marc pour sa confiance. Il ne me l'a pas donnée d'emblée ; j'ai dû la gagner étape par étape et nous avons fini par atteindre une sorte d'apogée : l'achèvement d'une série d'études décodant le paysage par le biais de constructions infrastructurelles se déployant à travers les paysages, reliant et créant de nouvelles réalités pour le quotidien de tous. Pour moi, cela a aussi été un voyage au sens littéral du terme : des régions les plus reculées du monde où j'avais passé plus de deux décennies vers le cœur de Paris. Et puis je n'ai pas fait que capturer le monde de Marc ; j'ai eu la grande chance qu'il partage avec moi ses visions et ses rêves.

Merci Marc.

Je suis reconnaissante à tous les membres de l'agence Marc Mimram et en particulier à :
Anne-Marie De Matos, Marine Farouault, Cynthia Jupin,
Ignacio Olalquiaga Varela, et Liu Chengyin, Chine.

Je remercie les personnes suivantes qui m'ont aidée à différentes étapes de ce projet :

Chez Hatje Cantz :
Son ancien directeur, Holger Liebs, ainsi que Claire Cichy et toute l'équipe pour avoir cru en mon art et m'avoir soutenue tout au long de ce projet.
Tous les traducteurs et relecteurs :
Aaron Bogart, Caroline Higgit, Anne Levine, Isabelle Liber.

Mise en page :
Merci à KOMA AMOK, l'agence de graphisme de Stuttgart, pour son soutien inconditionnel et l'intensité exceptionnelle avec laquelle son équipe s'est plongée dans cette monographie complexe en trois volumes, traduisant ainsi mon regard photographique et la façon dont j'ai capturé l'ingénierie et l'architecture de Marc ; je les remercie pour leur conviction et leur amitié.

Le responsable éditorial des textes :
Merci à Aris Kafantaris, architecte et responsable éditorial basé à Tokyo, pour son soutien à toutes les étapes de la création de cette monographie, de la naissance de l'idée de ce livre à son impression.

Les auteurs des textes :
Jean Attali, Paul Chemetov, Sir Peter Cook, Ariel Genadt, Zvi Hecker.

Services photographiques et assistance :
DIGID'A Lab à Rome, Davide Di Gianni et Fabio Barilo,
pour la qualité exceptionnelle de leurs services.
Assistants photographes :
Philipp Valente et Lukas Walcher, TUM University, Architecture ;
Daniel Raphael Zuvia, Graduate School of Architecture,
Planning & Preservation, Columbia University, NYC.
Assistance technique pour le volume III sur Roland-Garros :
Michel Ellert et Gilles Cargueray, Leica, France ;
Charles Plumey, Paris.

Et enfin, et surtout :
Mon respect éternel à Kleio & Kazim.

Acknowledgments of Marc Mimram

This book is the result of an encounter between the sensitive and demanding eye of Erieta Attali and our architectural beliefs; I thank her for this attention, this limitless determination.

Architecture is generally depicted in all its dazzling splendor beneath impossibly blue skies, dramatically transformed by digital manipulation. The rules of such Photoshopped creations depart so far from the truth in their search for virtuosic virtual reality that it is hard to create a mood, reflect an atmosphere, or express materiality. They damage and deaden where our collaboration seeks to bring generosity and sensitivity to the world.

Our meeting with the photographer Erieta Attali made it possible to turn away from the race to “fake representation” which, like “fake news,” is not so much a lie as an interpretation of reality.
Erieta Attali has spent three years following our building projects, observing them through her photographic lens. The lens is subjective and interpretation is always present, but here the photographer has constructed an architecture through the senses and emotions. The materialized reflections of light, the textures of flesh or the sensation of mass can all be found in her work whether dealing with architecture or the creation of architecture. The photographer has depicted both building sites and completed projects, demonstrating a committed and coherent approach.

I am grateful for her generosity with her time and her selflessness. I cannot stress enough how rare these qualities are.

Architecture is not a solitary pursuit. It involves cooperation from conception to construction.
Clients have trusted me to develop projects where structural, constructive, and economic references were rare or even nonexistent. It is thanks to their farsightedness that these projects have seen the light of day.
My thanks go particularly to Emmanuelle Baboulin, Pierre Lejeune, Joseph Giordano, Gilles Jourdan, Hakim Essakl, Saïd Zarrou, Monsieur Dou, and Jean-Claude Dumont.

These projects are the object of attentive development from both the collaborating architects and engineers. Many people have been involved in the project teams, Marc Mimram Architecture & Associés and Marc Mimram Ingénierie. My thanks go to them for their contributions, and particularly to Guillaume André, Martin Fougeras Lavergnolle, Razvan Ionica, Liu Chengyin, and Anne-Marie De Matos.

These projects represent a record of the work of all those who have encouraged and advised us. Though their names remain anonymous, I am greatly indebted to them; their involvement in the project is part of how we see architecture. Buildings and civil engineering projects stand as a concrete memory of our shared labors. Workers or engineers, these people are ready to meet the challenge; the project rests its hopes on their knowledge.

KOMA AMOK, our graphic designers, demonstrated a subtle finesse in their reproduction of the photographs illustrating the architecture of the projects. Aris Kafantaris has been invaluable in overseeing this publication.

I owe a particular debt to Paul Chemetov and Zvi Hecker for their admirable texts, full of delicacy and friendship.

Acknowledgments of Erieta Attali

On July 14, 2016, I was fortunate to be invited by Farrokh Derakhshani, Director, Aga Khan Award for Architecture, to a conference at the Victoria and Albert Museum in London called Beyond the Bridge. In the list of speakers I saw the biography of a man named Marc Mimram. I didn't know him at the time, but I was curious to listen to him speaking about his bridges. Already before the end of his lecture, I realized that this had to be my next exploration in the world: I had to explore his infrastructure-scale works across France and beyond the borders of his country, his bridges, train stations, and swimming pools.
Up until Marc's lecture, I had already photographed monuments, both contemporary and historic, across the world. I had just completed my doctoral studies in Australia, with monographs on their way to being published. The timing felt right, then, for my visions and desires to be channeled to this new direction: a three-year journey over the works and sculptural creations of Marc Mimram.

I am thankful to Marc's trust, which was not to be taken for granted; instead, it was gained step by step, which gratefully led us to a moment of a great accomplishment: the completion of a circle of studies, decoding the landscape through infrastructure works spanning across landscapes, connecting and creating new realities for the life of all people.
It has also been a literal journey for me: coming from the most isolated edges of the world, where I spent over two decades, into the heart of Paris. And then, not only capturing Marc's works, but having the great opportunity to be sharing with him his visions and dreams.

Thank you Marc.

I am grateful to all the members of Marc Mimram Architecture et Ingénierie and especially to:
Anne-Marie De Matos, Marine Farouault, Cynthia Jupin,
Ignacio Olalquiaga Varela, and Liu Chengyin, China.

I am thankful to the following people for supporting several stages of this work:
Hatje Cantz, and specifically former managing director Holger Liebs, as well as Claire Cichy and all the Hatje Cantz staff, for having sincerely embraced my art and showing support throughout.
To all the translators and copy editors:
Aaron Bogart, Caroline Higgit, Anne Levine, Isabelle Liber.

Graphic design:
KOMA AMOK, Stuttgart-based graphic designers for their long-lasting devotion and the exceptional artistic intensity with which they dived into the complexity of this three-volume monograph, translating my photographic gaze and the ways with which I capture Marc's engineering and architecture, for their true faith and friendship.
Managing editor:
Aris Kafantaris, Tokyo-based architect, for his intellectual support throughout the process of this three-volume monograph on Marc Mimram; following every stage of the work from the birth of idea of this book to its completion.

Text contributors for the three monographs:
Jean Attali, Paul Chemetov, Sir Peter Cook, Ariel Genadt, and Zvi Hecker.

Photography services, and general assistance:
DIGID'A Lab in Rome. Davide Di Gianni and Fabio Barile,
with special thanks for the exceptional, high quality of their services.
Photography assistants:
Philipp Valente and Lukas Walcher, TUM University, Architecture;
Daniel Raphael Zuvia, Graduate School of Architecture,
Planning & Preservation, Columbia University, NYC.
Technical assistance for Roland-Garros Volume III:
Michel Ellert and Gilles Cargueray, Leica, France;
Charles Plumey, Paris.

And last but not least:
Lifelong respect to Kleio and Kazim.

Marc Mimram
Structure | Light · Landscapes of Gravity · Selected Works
Through the Lens of Erieta Attali

Editor: Erieta Attali

Managing editor: Aris Kafantaris
Project management: Claire Cichy, Hatje Cantz
English copyediting: Aaron Bogart
French copyediting: Isabelle Liber
Translations: Anne Levine (French), Caroline Higgit (English)
Graphic design and concept:
Joerg Ewald Meißner, Gerd Sebastian Jakob,
KOMA AMOK, Kunstbüro für Gestaltung, Stuttgart
www.komaamok.com
Typeface: GT America (Noël Leu, with Seb McLauchlan)
Production: Heidrun Zimmermann, Hatje Cantz
Reproductions:
DIGID'A, Davide di Gianni, Fabio Barile, Rome, Italy
Jan Scheffler & Kerstin Wenzel GbR, Berlin
Paper: Condat matt Périgord, 170 g/m^2
Binding: Buchbinderei Terbeck GmbH, Coesfeld
Printing: Offsetdruckerei Karl Grammlich GmbH, Pliezhausen

© 2019 Hatje Cantz Verlag, Berlin and authors
© 2019 for the reproduced works by Erieta Attali: the photographer
© Photography copyrights: Erieta Attali, NYC

Erieta Attali, the artist, asserts her right to all image royalties

Published by
Hatje Cantz Verlag GmbH
Mommsenstraße 27
10629 Berlin
www.hatjecantz.de
A Ganske Publishing Group Company

ISBN 978-3-7757-4403-4

Printed in Germany

Developers:

1. Solférino Footbridge:
   Etablissement public du Grand Louvre
2. Hassan II Bridge, Rabat—Salé:
   Agence pour l'Aménagement de la Vallée du Bouregreg
3. Marcelle-Henry Footbridge:
   Direction de la Voirie-Ville de Paris
4. Pôle Nautique de Mantes-la-Ville:
   Communauté d'Agglomération de Mantes en Yvelines
5. Montpellier Railway Station:
   Réseau Ferré de France
6. Amédée Saint-Germain Bridge:
   Bordeaux Euratlantique
7. Airtime Building:
   ICADE / Investisseur: AG2R La Mondiale Matmut
8. Strasbourg School of Architecture:
   OPPIC-Ministère de la Culture
9. Roland-Garros, The Simonne-Mathieu Court:
   Fédération Française de Tennis
10. Strasbourg—Kehl Footbridge:
    Kehl City
11. Liu Shu Footbridge:
    Yangzhou City
12. Zhong Sheng Da Dao Bridge:
    Investment Company of Sino Singapore City, Tianjin
13. Jin Liu Liu Bridge:
    Investment Company of Sino Singapore City, Tianjin

MARC
MIMRAM
ARCHITECTURE
INGÉNIERIE